Wh38

Cycling and Cinema

Cycling and Cinema

Bruce Bennett

Goldsmiths
Press

© 2019 Goldsmiths Press
Published in 2019 by Goldsmiths Press
Goldsmiths, University of London, New Cross

London SE14 6NW
Printed and bound by TJ International, UK
Distribution by the MIT Press

Cambridge, Massachusetts, and London, England

A CIP record for this book is available from the British Library

ISBN 978-1-906897-99-4 (hbk)
ISBN 978-1-912685-05-9 (ebk)

www.gold.ac.uk/goldsmiths-press

Contents

Acknowledgements

Writing a book is a little like completing a stage race. This is not to say that it is a heroic endeavour, but that it is an exercise in patient endurance. Constructing an argument involves making connections from one conceptual point to the next in the same way that a rider might trace a route across the landscape, sometimes sprinting, sometimes coasting easily, with a tailwind carrying them along, and at other times labouring in despair or 'going backwards', as TV commentators say of riders who struggle on the mountain stages.

And, of course, there are the ever-present risks of losing your way or crashing.

Like competing in a major bicycle race, writing a book is also an undertaking that can be completed only with the assistance of fellow riders and a support team of soigneurs, technicians, cooks, drivers and team sponsors. I am very grateful to the following people, all of whom have made contributions that have fed into the book in different ways: Sean Arnold, Simon Bayly, Gavin Bennett, Richard Bennett, Iain Borden, Peter Cox, Suman Ghosh, Tony Hill, Nick Hodgin, Joanne Hollows, Marc Jancovich, Kat Jungnickel, Bob Kemp, Brian Kennedy, Caroline Kennedy, Jenna Loyd, Feargal McKay, Kasia Marciniak, Derek Paget, Lynne Pearce, Bernadette Salem, Mimi Sheller, Jan Steffen, Paul Sutton, Rachel Thomson, Marie Ullrich.

I am also grateful to the Leverhulme Trust, which awarded me a 12-month research fellowship, making this book possible.

Most of all, I want to thank my lead-out train, Imogen Tyler and Brian Baker, who have provided invaluable support and encouragement throughout.

1

Cycling and Cinema: Revolutionary Technologies

Figure 1.1
The first cinematic cyclists ride through the factory gates in the first film, *La Sortie de l'Usine Lumière à Lyon* [*Leaving the Lumière Factory in Lyon*] (third version) (Lumière, 1895) (© Universal History Archive/ UIG via Getty images/REX/Shutterstock)

Cinema and the bicycle came into view, in tandem, at the end of the nineteenth century. Popular enthusiasm for these novel technologies coincided with the height of the second industrial revolution in Europe and the United States, which was marked by the development of the steel industry, chemical manufacturing, electrification, the refinement of mass production techniques and the expansion of the railway system. Cycling and cinema were products of this interval of intensive technical innovation and rapid, disorienting change, made possible by new developments in engineering. They were particularly visible signs of the economic, social and cultural transformations that swept violently across the globe during this period, altering the ways that people interacted with one another and experienced their own bodies, and the ways in which they understood and represented their place in the world.

This book examines the historical interplay between cinema and cycling as technologies, and as fields of activity that are normally regarded as separate from one another. Placing them within the same frame, this study aims to use cinema as a way of thinking about the expressive, affective, political and culturally rich dimensions of cycling. At the same time, it uses the bicycle to navigate a different route through the history of the cinema, one that makes connections between an apparently disparate body of films and audio-visual material. Media theorist (and cyclist)[1] Marshall McLuhan has observed that the habits of academic specialization have meant that '[s]cholars tend to work on the archaeological assumption that things need to be studied in isolation', thereby overlooking the complex interrelatedness of different fields of study, such as 'the interplay between wheel, bicycle and airplane'.[2] Studying cinema and cycling in tandem allows us to see them both differently. While it can sometimes seem that contemporary cycling activism, bicycle design and transport policy are dominated by the interests of white, able-bodied, middle-class men, examining the wide variety of on-screen bicycles allows us to see that it is an inclusive technology with a richer and far more culturally diverse history than is typically imagined. Indeed, in reflecting on the ways in which the meaning of the bicycle has been the object of continual symbolic struggle, *Cycling and Cinema* opens up new ways of thinking about what cycling is, and for whom. Similarly, in exploring the cinematic history of the bicycle, this book brings a variety of fascinating, unfamiliar or largely forgotten films into focus alongside some more well-known titles.

Cinema Begins with the Bicycle

For many cinema historians, the screening held by Auguste and Louis Lumière in the Salon Indien of the Grand Café in Paris on 28 December 1895 marks the birth of cinema. Cinema emerged in multiple locations at different times and in different formats, such as Edison's first Kinetoscope parlour in New York in April 1894, or the screening of large-format Bioscop films by Max and Emil Skladanowsky in Berlin in November 1895. However, it was the Lumière screenings, and the practicality of their lightweight, all-in-one camera/film-developer/projector, the Cinématographe, that secured the medium's success. The admission charge was a franc for a programme of ten single-shot films, each lasting less than 50 seconds, and 'within weeks the Lumières were offering twenty shows a day, with long lines of spectators waiting to get in.'[3] Thus, the entry of this new medium into global culture coincided with the cycling boom of 1895, and this coincidence is marked emphatically by the first film in the programme.

The first screenings opened with the film *La Sortie de l'Usine Lumière à Lyon*, which shows workers leaving the Lumières' photographic factory, passing through the factory gates and heading off in different directions along the road outside the factory. There are three existing versions of the film, the first of which – the first film they shot – was filmed on 19 March 1895. The subject is bodies in motion, but, more specifically, we see scores of industrial labourers, the vast majority women, spilling out of the factory at the end of a shift. The film, which is itself an artefact of new industrial technology, presents us with a symbolic image of industrial modernity as a crowd of workers stream through the gates towards the camera. Tom Gunning has observed:

The twentieth century might be considered the century of the masses, introducing mass production, mass communication, mass culture. We could redescribe this transformation as the entrance of the working class (putatively the driving force of any age, but often eclipsed in the realm of official representation) onto a new stage of visibility.[4]

The cinema is a crucial component of this 'stage', and it is appropriate that the film shows us a *photographic* factory, a crucial infrastructural component of the emergent mass culture. The other nine films include shots of a baby being fed, trick horse riding, a practical joke, a street scene and blacksmiths at work, but it is the factory-gate film that condenses the accelerating social changes into a single moving image. One rarely noted detail is that, as well as pedestrians, dogs and horse-drawn carts, all three versions of the film feature cyclists pushing through the crowd.

The composition of the image is roughly the same in all three versions, the camera placed at head height across the street from the factory gates. In the first film, among the workers on foot, a man wheels his bicycle through a doorway to the left of the gates, and begins to mount it, while a horse and cart emerge from the gates, followed by another cyclist pedalling behind it. In the second version, a younger cyclist in a flat cap squeezes through the crowd and cycles quickly off to the left, followed shortly afterwards by another man in a straw boater who is trying to ride through a group of women; he is forced to dismount, though, and pushes his bicycle out of the frame on the right-hand side, talking to one of the women behind him. A third cyclist, again sporting a straw boater, then emerges from the gates in front of a horse-drawn cart, and cycles across the frame from right to left, smiling at the camera as he passes in front of it. In the third film, a man in a straw boater runs out of the crowd, steering a bicycle on which an identically dressed young boy is mounted precariously.[5] Shortly afterwards another man wheels a bicycle through the doorway on the left, this time with a colleague perched on it. While they wheel cautiously along the pavement and out of the frame, a man in a flat cap cycles confidently off to the left on a bike with drop handlebars, and another cyclist peels off to the right. Just before the end of the film a fifth cyclist comes through the gates and is slapped vigorously on the back by one of his workmates, causing him to wobble unsteadily, and, as he moves out of the frame, the factory gates begin to close behind him.

Film historian Richard deCordova has argued that early cinema constituted a radical, disorienting distortion of familiar representational conventions, 'a violent decomposition of the perspectival system that had been dominant since the 16th century in painting (the system upon which photography had been modelled)'.[6] What was disorienting for audiences about these first film sequences was not simply the illusion of movement but that figures moved *towards* the camera: 'The workers do not just move: they move *in perspective*'.[7] For deCordova, this is shown most clearly by the way that the cyclists in *La Sortie de l'Usine Lumière à Lyon* are initially hidden but then emerge from behind members of the crowd: 'Such an appearance had been impossible in both painting and photography'.[8] However, in pushing their way past their co-workers and riding out of a photographic factory, the cyclists introduced nineteenth-century viewers to three-dimensional cinematic space, showing them the new ways of seeing the world offered by the cinema. Cycling is not an incidental element here; rather, the presence of moving bicycles in this film demonstrated the unique formal properties of this revolutionary medium: it is cycling that makes this film a film. In short, the first film, *La Sortie de l'Usine Lumière à Lyon*, is a cycling film.

It is unlikely that viewers of *La Sortie de l'Usine Lumière à Lyon* realised they were witnessing a new order of pictorial space and the beginnings of a cultural revolution. However, there are enough anecdotal accounts of audiences' confusion and anxiety at the uncanny spectacle of moving images to suggest that viewers *felt* intensely that they were seeing something more than just a diverting novelty, something radically new.[9] By contrast with a static painting or still photograph, the film image undergoes continuous transformation. As deCordova observes, 'the elements are in constant flux – in a mechanical movement', but, in retrospect, it is clear not just that this film is an early example of the visual spectacle of mechanical movement, but that it is also a document of a society undergoing radical transformation through mechanical movement – a high-tech, industrialised, globalised society in constant flux.[10] The bicycle is an ideal subject for the first film since, in western Europe in 1895, it was an increasingly ubiquitous, visible and thrilling example of mechanical movement, as well as a harbinger of the ways in which modern life would become progressively dominated by mechanical motion.

The historical coincidence of the film camera and the safety bicycle is explained partly by their status as precision-engineered machines that are dependent upon developments in industrial production. They have similar mechanisms, both relying upon systems of cranks, sprockets and axles, chains and gears, powered by rotary motion (and hands and feet). Indeed, an early film projector looks almost exactly like an upturned bicycle, the two wheels replaced with reels of film. This visual similarity reveals an operational similarity: watching moving images and riding a bicycle both involve making wheels turn. Writing about the development in the nineteenth century of proto-cinematic devices such as the phenakistiscope, Jonathan Crary observes of the functioning of these machines that 'it is a question of a body aligned with and operating an assemblage of turning and regularly moving wheeled parts'.[11] Jennifer Barker's description of such contraptions makes the similarity with bicycles clearer still:

The situation presented by early cinema viewing machines, in which the spectator seeks entertainment through a medium that cannot operate without his or her continuous participation, and in which, in the case of the mutoscope, the speed of the spectators' bodily movements determines the speed of the images, demonstrates the remarkable extent to which the human body is figured as an intimate and integral component of the cinema.[12]

Indeed, for Marshall McLuhan, the film camera is a development from the wheel:

[O]ne of the most advanced and complicated uses of the wheel occurs in the movie camera and in the movie projector.... The movie camera and the projector were evolved from the idea of reconstructing mechanically the movement of feet. The wheel that began as extended feet... took a great evolutionary step into the movie theater.[13]

As products of industrial technology, the historical coincidence of the bicycle and the film camera is more than mere contingency, and one of the central questions this book will explore is how examining the historical parallels between these two technologies can help us understand their social and cultural significance more fully.

Forerunners and Technical Histories

In the introduction to *The Modern Bicycle*, his 1877 instruction manual and consumer guide for novice cyclists, Charles Spencer writes,

There is no necessity for me to go into a detailed account of the various stages of improvement which the bicycle has gone through, or to give an elaborate description of the first 'hobby-horses', 'tricycles', &c., &c., or a long and tedious narrative telling who enlarged the fore wheel and diminished the hind one, or to whom we are indebted for steel spider-wheels and india-rubber tyres.[14]

A long and tedious account of the technical development of the bicycle is similarly undesirable here; however, an outline of the circumstances in which the bicycle was developed is helpful for understanding the meanings associated with this machine over the last two centuries, its relation to industrial modernity and its intersections with the development of cinema.

The earliest reliable record of a precursor of the bicycle appears to be that published by French mathematician Jacques Ozanam in 1696 within a study of 50 'useful and entertaining' problems.[15] In *Recréations Mathématiques et Physiques*, he describes a number of 'self-moving' vehicles being used in Paris, including one in which a 'servant, riding on the back, drives it by pressing alternately with each leg on two pieces of wood which are connected to two little wheels hidden in the back set between two driving wheels'.[16] Elie Richard's four-wheeled carriage, with humans providing the motive power in place of horses, was the basis for a number of early eighteenth-century vehicles, and it is significant that, even in this provisional state, this proto-bicycle was a technology structured by visibly unequal social relations, the servant reduced to the subhuman status of an animal or mechanical component. From the beginning, the history of the bicycle is both a history of the intimate integration of humans with machines and a history of shifting, often antagonistic class relations.

The first clear forerunner of the modern bicycle seems to have been the Laufmaschine ['running machine'], patented in 1818 by German polymath Karl von Drais, which he described as a 'facilitator' that could assist those who found walking difficult, or an 'accelerator' that allowed the rider to move more quickly than walking pace, and whose military value he attempted to demonstrate by staging races with stagecoaches. The draisine, or velocipede, had a wooden frame suspended between two small cart wheels, and riders sat astride the frame, steering the front wheel with a wooden handlebar, and pushing the vehicle along with their feet. The velocipede could easily outpace the coach and exemplifies the principle of increasing speed – what Benjamin Noys terms 'accelerationism' – that became central to the development of the bicycle and to capitalist modernity as well.[17]

The machine was developed further by British cartwright Denis Johnson, who introduced elegant iron components and decorative details, and manufactured separate versions for men and women, demonstrating that the bicycle's history offers a case study in the gender politics of technological development, as gender difference is supposedly engineered into the form of the machine. Johnson established a riding school in Soho, London, renting out his velocipedes to those unprepared to buy them, and his machine became known dismissively as the 'hobby horse', after the children's toy, and the 'dandy horse', due to its popularity with the aristocratic young men with the leisure and public confidence to enjoy this expensive accessory. Velocipedes briefly became internationally popular, encouraging amateur engineers to work on improving the design. A variant called the 'swift walker' prompted 'the first American cycling craze',[18] as recalled in the comedy film *Our Hospitality* (Blystone, Keaton, 1923), which shows an urbane Buster Keaton riding one of these unstable machines through the countryside around New York in 1830. In the same year the Paris Bureau de Poste issued postmen with three- and four-wheeled velocipedes to speed up delivery, thereby securing the association between the *facteur* and the *vélo* later celebrated in Jacques Tati's films.[19]

Cycling Culture and Velocipedomania

For the next three or four decades the manufacturing process became increasingly professionalised. The development of the bicycle maps very closely onto the development of industrial capitalism and specialised, mechanised manufacturing processes, as building velocipedes became 'more of a business in its own right rather than an appendage of the blacksmith's forge'.[20] However, the two-, three- and four-wheeled velocipede remained a machine with restricted appeal until Pierre Michaux and his son Ernest began mass-producing velocipedes in Paris with curved iron frames, suspension and, most importantly, pedals attached to the front wheel.[21] A *New York Times* headline of 1867 declared Michaux's machine a 'Revolution in Locomotion', and the Michauline (or, in Britain, the 'boneshaker', due to the discomfort of riding over rough or cobbled roads) was a phenomenal success in Europe and the United States, establishing bicycles as more than an eccentric affectation, or a curious, technological novelty.[22] In that sense,

[c]ycling began in the late eighteen-sixties. Then, they talked about 'velocipedes' and 'velocipeding', and only during the last two years of the decade did the words 'bicycle' and 'bicycling' come into circulation. 'Bicycle' was used to distinguish a two-wheeled velocipede from all the other kinds.[23]

It was at this point that the concept of the bicycle began to enter into circulation. The emergence of bicycling as a distinct practice or mode of travel and the recognition of the bicycle as a distinct form of transport marked the insertion of the bicycle into the scenography of modern life. The popularity of the machine was termed 'velocipedomania' by satirists, and saw the emergence of a newly visible hybrid figure, a fantastic fusion of human and machine; a writer in 1869 relates, 'The veloceman, as he styles himself, is to be seen in all his glory careering at full speed through the shady avenues of the Bois du Boulogne or skimming like some gigantic dragonfly over the level surfaces of the roads intersecting the Champs-Élysées.'[24] A contemporaneous article in *The Scientific American* proposes, 'The art of walking is obsolete. It is true that a few still cling to that mode of locomotion, are still admired as fossil specimens of an extinct race of pedestrians, but for the majority of civilized humanity, walking is on its last legs.'[25] Beneath the sarcasm, there was already a clear sense of the bicycle's potential to catalyse a reorganisation of society, an idea that still underpins twenty-first-century cycling advocacy: 'The question is getting to be an interesting one, as to how extensively the social system is to be revolutionized.'[26]

The 'mania' for cycling was partly a result of its affordability to people across a broader social spectrum as the class structure of European society changed, with industrialisation and urbanisation driving the growth of middle-class and skilled working-class populations in the 1860s.[27] With the international enthusiasm for the velocipede, a rich, complex cycling culture began to take shape on a broader scale. This new culture extended from sport and social cycling to print media, with the production of specialised publications, such as the first buyer's guide, Favre's 1868 *Le Vélocipède: Sa Structure, ses Accessoires Indispensables*; the fortnightly *Le Vélocipède Illustré* (1869–1872); or the periodical *Ixion: A Journal of Velocipeding, Athletics and Aerostatics*, launched in 1875. Indeed, media commentary was a feature of cycling culture from very early on, as, some 50 years earlier, 'the media (i.e., broadsheets) played a key role both in bringing the draisine to the public's attention and in helping it to fade away by ceasing to report on the subject.'[28] Moreover, given that cycling is a form of public performance or display, fashion quickly became an integral dimension of the new cycling culture as specialised cycling outfits were adopted; Tom Ambrose says: 'Over the early years of cycling a form of casual uniform had emerged that featured a straw boater or billycock hat. After 1870 the style had changed and a polo cap or pillbox hat became de rigueur for the fashionable gentleman rider.'[29] Cycling culture was shaped from the outset by commerce.

The velocipede also fuelled the growth of tourism, making it relatively easy to escape from towns and cities into the surrounding countryside during a period of accelerating industrialisation and accompanying urbanisation. This enhanced mobility offered riders a new perspective on their surroundings, both literally and conceptually, making them more readily visible to the cyclist. In turn, cycle tourism reinforced a sense of what Benedict Anderson terms 'imagined community', which was firmly rooted in tradition, and guaranteed by picturesque, 'natural' landscapes and 'timeless' rural villages seemingly untouched by industrial progress and urban expansion.[30] In this sense the bicycle was a time machine, a futuristic technology that conveyed the rider from polluted, overcrowded cities to a pre-industrial rural world.

Bicycles allowed more people the opportunity to travel, and to travel farther and faster, so that

[h]ome tours could for the first time be completed in a few days at speeds in excess of 12 miles an hour.... Getting out to see the country had helped to assert a sense of national belonging in pedestrian tours of the 18th century, and now, in the 19th century, the bicycle allowed that process to be extended nationwide.[31]

Even today, as Jon Day writes,

getting on a bike can feel like a form of time travel. The needs of the cyclist – gentle inclines, quiet roads, protection from the wind – have more in common with those of cattle drivers or pilgrims than they do with most contemporary travellers. We seek the same routes.[32]

The Bicycle and Industrial Production

Through experiments with new materials and production techniques, manufacturers began to make bicycles with progressively larger front drive wheels, up to a diameter of over 150 cm, to improve speed and efficiency. A key development was the production by James Starley and William Hillman of the bicycle that they named the Ariel. Incidentally, Hillman later formed Hillman Motor Car Company, demonstrating a pattern in which the bicycle industry provided automobile manufacturers with capital, production techniques, marketing techniques, a technical support infrastructure for the maintenance and repair of vehicles, and a global population eager to travel independently. As Luis Vivanco observes, 'perhaps most important, the bicycle laid the foundation for a new concept of personal mobility that is taken for granted today.'[33]

Patented in 1870, with a large front wheel, small rear wheel and rolled steel rims and wire spokes, the Ariel was considerably lighter than a velocipede. For Donald Ritchie, '[i]n its perfected form, reached in about 1880, the [high-wheeled] Ordinary bicycle was the most efficient machine ever devised for the harnessing of human muscle power. It was one of the high points of communications technology in the nineteenth century.'[34] The high-wheeled bicycle was both a product and a symbol of new industrial processes, and this phase of modernity was exemplified by the Boston-based Pope Manufacturing Company, which began manufacturing the successful Columbia bicycle in the late 1870s before moving on to making motorcycles and cars. Albert Pope's company employed a systematic approach to reducing costs, observing the utilitarian maxim that 'the perfection of the machine lessened the number of the employees':[35]

Pope progressively modernized the labour process by extending the division of labour in his factories and, wherever possible, mechanizing each of the simplified steps. By 1894 there were 840 parts in a Columbia men's bicycle and nearly 1,000 parts in a woman's bicycle, and over 500 inspections were made during their assembly.[36]

The bicycle occupies a crucial role in the development of industrial manufacturing. In a striking early intersection of cinema and cycling, Pope employed Thomas Edison, the designer of the early film camera the Kinetograph and the future filmmaking mogul, to build 'the first electrified continuous-production assembly line, which was visited and admired by Henry Ford.'[37] Electrification allowed Pope to introduce night shifts, accelerating further the pace of production. This took place alongside the vertical integration of the business, including the production of the component elements such as tyres and steel tubing. The market for bicycles was stimulated through conventional advertising and promotion, and Pope also invested in the *Wheelmen* magazine and lobbied for cyclists' rights to greater mobility and better roads. He backed the Good Roads movement, giving financial support in legal cases involving the prosecution of cyclists.[38]

One measure of the high-wheeler's success was the rapid formation of cycling clubs in the 1870s, providing welcome support for cyclists, who were often regarded with hostility or contempt by other road users. A significant factor in the uptake of bicycles (and tricycles and quadricycles) was their affordability across a broader social range. While cycling might have been regarded as vulgar by the elite, '[m]ost of the people who took up bicycling in the early days were more or less middle-class people, tradesmen, shopkeepers, manufacturers, clerks, the occasional Civil Servant, doctor or teacher.'[39] Although an ultra-light racing machine might cost up to £25, by 1884 Wolverhampton firm J. Dewey and Company was selling 'The Working Man's Friend' at £4 10 shillings. Hire purchase schemes and a second-hand market (and the economies of scale achieved by industrial production) meant that high-wheel bicycles became widely affordable in the 1880s, leading Ritchie to conclude:

Bicycling was, in general, a leveller of classes. The new city suburbs were being redefined in terms of money and social status. It was the new urban proletarian and white-collar worker above all who felt himself to be in need of the intense exercise and pleasure which the bicycle could give and he was the kind of man who seized the new opportunity with relish.[40]

'Ordinary' Cycling

The high-wheel bicycle – later known as the 'ordinary' to distinguish it from the 'safety' bicycles that superseded it, or, much later in Britain, the 'penny-farthing', since its wheels resembled those differently sized coins – extended the rider's capacity to move quickly and cover ever-increasing distances. This was demonstrated in the attempts to set speed and distance records, including round-the world rides, while a 1928 Pathé newsreel film of a penny-farthing race at London's Herne Hill velodrome gives a good sense of the vehicles' size and speed; as the camera pans around following the frantically pedalling racers, the crowd and surroundings are reduced to a blur. However, although it was comparatively light and efficient, the high-wheeler was virtually unrideable for women, since it was impossible to mount and ride the machine in the heavy, layered, ankle-length skirts that were the only clothing that was publicly acceptable.[41] In fact, Starley produced an ungainly version of the Ariel for women in 1872, with the rear wheel out of line with the front wheel, allowing women to ride it side-saddle, rather than straddling the wheel. But the macho cult of speed – embodied by the supposedly reckless 'cycling cads' and 'scorchers' tearing up and down crowded streets and pavements, startling horses and colliding with pedestrians, along with the martial ethos of cycling clubs, complete with uniforms, ranks, buglers and echelon formation riding – ensured that the ordinary bicycle remained a young man's machine.

The fact that the rider sat directly on top of the front wheel meant that high-wheelers were very unstable. Braking sharply or hitting a pothole or loose stone (or dog) would tip the rider head first over the handlebars. These precarious machines were technically difficult to ride, and 'taking a header' was a potentially fatal but extremely common event, as satirised gently by Mark Twain in the unpublished essay 'Taming the Bicycle' (1884). In one of the earliest literary accounts of cycling, he recounts his catastrophic attempts, over eight daily lessons, to learn to ride a high-wheel bicycle. When it comes to dismounting, he writes: 'Try as you may, you don't get down as you would from a horse, you get down as you would from a house afire. You make a spectacle of yourself every time.' Having completed his 'apprenticeship', he set out to refine his skills, riding up and down a quiet back street, where he crashed repeatedly and unerringly into dogs, stepping stones and a farmer's wagon. 'Get a bicycle,' Twain advises in conclusion. 'You will not regret it, if you live.'

Addressing the high-wheeler's impracticalities and exploiting new engineering processes and materials, manufacturers produced alternative configurations, placing the large wheel at the rear, using treadles or cranks and chains, and shrinking the front wheel. The consequence was the development of the safety bicycle, with smaller, similarly sized wheels, a chain and cranks driving the rear wheel, a saddle situated between the two wheels, and a sturdy, diamond-shaped tubular steel frame. The Rover[42] safety bicycle, first produced in 1885 by James Starley's nephew, John Kemp Starley, with his partner, William Sutton, was a particularly successful iteration, and 'with the second model, produced a few months later, the distant prospect of the bicycle as we know it snaps suddenly into focus'.[43] The safety bicycle, which could be ridden with minimal effort and humiliation by women (especially on models without a crossbar) and less athletic riders, quickly displaced the ordinary bicycle, and was the basis for another 'boom' in cycling on a much grander scale than previous waves of enthusiasm. However, it was the pneumatic tyre that ensured the bicycle became a common sight in towns and cities around the world.

Consisting of a rubber inner tube, canvas bag and rubber tread on the outside, the pneumatic tyre was initially developed by John Dunlop, a Scottish vet living in Ireland, for his son's tricycle. On 23 July 23 1888 he applied for a patent for the device and began producing them in Dublin. Although not the first functional pneumatic tyre, Dunlop's version established its viability, and, with it, the success of the safety bicycle. Consequently, '[b]y the end of 1892 there were still a few solid-tyred bicycles to be found on the makers' lists, but the second-hand market was over-flowing with them for a few pounds each. The revolution was complete and Dunlop already a millionaire.'[44] Dunlop's tyre ensured that, whereas '[b]efore 1890 cycling had been the pastime of a small minority; after 1895 it was open to almost everyone' – including the factory workers riding their safety bicycles through the gates of the Lumière factory.[45]

An 1898 article from a cycling journal gives an indication of the scale and explosive speed of this shift: 'It would hardly be too much to say that in April of 1895, one was considered eccentric for riding a bicycle, whilst by the end of June, eccentricity rested with those who did not ride.'[46] As Robert Penn observes, 'One third of all patents registered at the US Patent Office in the 1890s were bicycle-related. In fact, the bicycle had its own dedicated patent building in Washington DC.'[47] He goes on, 'In 1896, the peak year for production, 300 firms in the USA made 1.2 million bicycles, making it one of the largest industries in the country. The biggest firm, Columbia, with 2,000 employees at the Hartford works in Connecticut, boasted of making a bicycle a minute.'[48]

Technological Progress and the 'Evolution' of the Bicycle

The history of the bicycle's technological development is often told as a story of progressive improvement, with the machine reaching a point of perfection in the mid-1890s with the development of the safety bicycle. This account often deploys metaphors of 'birth', 'inception' and 'evolution', which imply that this industrial technology is *natural*. This mystifying vocabulary works to erase the labour and exploitation that went into the development and manufacture of these machines. For instance, the rubber used to make vulcanised bicycle tyres in Europe and the United States was harvested by slaves in the Belgian Congo. So the bicycle boom, with its apparently emancipatory effects, was dependent upon punishing labour and the denial of freedom to a colonised people.[49] As late as 1938, *From Acorn to Oak* (Tully), a promotional short film commissioned by the Dunlop Pneumatic Tyre Company to celebrate the 50th anniversary of the invention of the pneumatic tyre and the global reach of the bicycle industry, includes shots of children harvesting rubber on a Malayan plantation. The symbolism of that film's title insists that the form of the bicycle and the growth of the industry were equally natural and inevitable, uninfluenced by social function or ideology. So, for example, the ordinary bicycle, which 'was a marvellous machine for athletic and bohemian young men, but...discriminated terribly against older people, staider people, people afraid of falling, and most of all against women', is nevertheless often understood by male historians as a *progression* from velocipedes and tricycles.[50] 'As the bicycle evolved,' observes Patricia Marks, 'it became more and more unsuitable for women.'[51] However, this was not a *natural* development, of course, but the result of socially dominant assumptions about the different capacities of men and women.[52]

The problem with the evolutionary metaphor so ubiquitous in descriptions of social, economic and technical change is the implication that technology is continually, inevitably improving and will eventually solve any and all social problems. On the one hand, this implies a comparatively uncritical understanding of industrialisation and industrial technology, and, on the other, it implies that earlier technological developments are intrinsically inferior. Consequently, 'when framed through this dominant historical narrative, it can be tempting to portray the bicycle as fundamentally anachronistic in today's society, as superseded or out-evolved by motorcycles and motor cars.'[53] Similarly, if the safety bicycle is regarded as the acme of the machine's technical and aesthetic development, this also suggests that 'any move away from the "ideal type" intrinsically results in inferiority.'[54] The wide range of bicycle-related vehicles, such as folding bikes, tricycles, women's bikes without crossbars (or top tubes), children's bikes, recumbent cycles, cargo bikes, cycle rickshaws, 'velomobiles', 'cyclecars', electric bikes, baby walkers, aircraft and 'hydrocycles', hand-cycles and various forms of wheelchair and mobility aid, and, by extension, their operators, are all 'inferior'. Thus, although bicycles belong to an increasingly broad spectrum of mobility aids, disabled or impaired cyclists remain relatively invisible in cycling films. The German film *Phantomschmerz* [*Phantom Pain*] (Emcke, 2009), based on the biography of Canadian Stephen Sumner, about a passionate, macho cyclist struggling to rebuild his life when his leg is amputated after he is hit by a car driver, is a rare, uplifting exception, along with the documentary *Benda Bilili!* [*Beyond Appearances!*] (Barret, de La Tullaye, 2010). This is a film about the improbable global success of Staff Benda Bilili, a group of homeless paraplegic musicians from Kinshasa. One of its most striking features is the extraordinary range of custom-built hand-cycles the band members ride. Of course, as Marja Evelyn Mojk observes, while disabled bodies might appear to be absent from the screen, in a fundamental sense 'disability remains at the heart of how we tell stories in Hollywood and Bollywood and in our homes, how we construct difference and how we understand ourselves.'[55] In particular, since cycling films are so concerned with the fragility and limits of 'normal' bodies, and trouble the idea of the 'natural' body, they are directly engaged with questions of bodily difference, ability and disability.

Although there may now be a broad recognition that these grand narratives of progress are merely that – *stories* – they remain seductive nevertheless. Accounts of the technological development of the bicycle are frequently offered as stories of emancipation in which this industrial technology can transport us into a healthy, pollution-free, egalitarian future. This is not to refute the emancipatory potential of cycling, which is crucial to the symbolism of the bicycle and is evident in film after film discussed in this book. Instead, it is to recognise the cultural significance of the bicycle as an example of industrial (and post-industrial) technology. Examining the history of the bicycle requires us to reflect upon broader issues concerned with the history of modernity, and the social function of technology, recognising, for example, that technology does not drive social change by itself. On the contrary, as Gilles Deleuze and Claire Parnet observe, the 'social machine' determines the way in which the technical machine is developed rather than the reverse: 'Tools always presuppose a machine, and the machine is always social before being technical.'[56] The same is true for the bicycle.

The success of the velocipede, the 'ordinary' and the 'safety' can be fully understood only as both a response to demands for greater mobility and a means of generating those demands. In this respect, the bicycle existed as a concept long before it took material form as a machine. Similarly, the development of cycling technology did not stop with the development of the safety bicycle because it was technically perfect but, rather, as Luis Vivanco observes, because of limited social interest in seeing it develop further or differently:

[A]s manufacturers and investors made important financial outlays in certain kinds of machinery and standardized production processes; as laborers began to organize into industrial worker unions in bicycle factories; as upper and middle-class people latched onto the bicycle as a way to show their social distinction and progressive modern attitudes; as women began appropriating the bicycle and influential suffrage leaders connected it to their claims for political and social rights; as a network of repair shops became established; as legal institutions began getting involved in regulating bicycle use; and so on, bicycle technology began to stabilize and close around the design and componentry of the safety bicycle.[57]

For Peter Cox and Frederick Van De Walle, a consequence of the 'artefactual' emphasis of histories of cycling is the exclusion of reflections upon 'the very *concept* of the cycle as a mode of transport: what exactly is it; what is it understood to be for;

and what is it understood to do? When is a cycle a cycle, and what makes it so? When does it cease being a cycle?'[58]

To answer the question of what exactly a bicycle is, we might examine the changing meaning of the bicycle in different historical contexts. In this respect, we can understand the bicycle as a signifying machine, a symbolic or representational system that generates new concepts and has a potentially transformative effect upon its socio-cultural context. As Vivanco suggests, '[o]ne of the most striking features of the bicycle's rise is that it involves an upheaval in the meanings surrounding the object itself.'[59] Paul Fournel, meanwhile, in conversation with Jon Day, describes the bicycle as a 'literary vehicle, a good place to think', and the double meaning of the term 'vehicle' invites us to think of the bicycle as a thinking machine.[60] Hollywood star and bicycle collector Robin Williams has described cycling in similar terms: 'I love to ride my bike, which is great aerobics, but also just a great time for me to think, so it's like this terrific double bill.'[61]

As well as literally conveying (thoughtful) passengers and cargo (and, sometimes, weapons), it also conveys meanings.[62] In a study of the historical relationship between railways and film, Lynne Kirby suggests that the steam train 'is a metaphor in the Greek sense of the word: movement, the conveyance of meaning', and precisely the same is true of the bicycle.[63] In this respect, what is most interesting about the bicycle is that it allows us to think about a variety of things. If we are concerned with the meaning of this machine, the cinematic bicycle is an ideal place to start. Placing the bicycle within the film frame transforms it from an object into an image, a symbolic representation that invites interpretation.

Revolutionary Images

The development of cinema runs parallel with the development of cycling technology. To paraphrase Charles Spencer, there is no need for a long and tedious account of the various stages of development the cinema went through during the nineteenth century, from the first extant camera photograph taken by Nicéphore Niépce in 1826, which took eight hours to expose, through the development of various optical toys and scientific apparatuses, such as the phenakistiscope or the zoetrope, and on to the 1870s, when photographs could be exposed in a fraction of a second, and inventors began to devise devices for shooting photographs in rapid succession. However, it is notable that one of the crucial technical challenges faced by inventors of the first motion picture cameras was to design a mechanism that would stop the unexposed film spooling through the camera intermittently allowing a photograph to be taken before the film is moved forwards to take another photograph, and so on. Film projectors employ the same mechanism, stopping the film print for a fraction of a second to project a still image onto the screen before advancing the film to the next image. 'Fortunately,' as film theorists Bordwell and Thompson observe, 'other inventions of the century also needed intermittent mechanisms to stop their movement many times a second. For example, the sewing machine (invented in 1846) held cloth still several times per second while a needle pierced it.'[64] As it happens, sewing machine manufacturers also played an important role in early bicycle production, since they possessed the skills and equipment necessary for the precision engineering and large-scale production of metal components such as wire spokes. For instance, the Coventry Machinists' Company, where Starley and Hillman, designers of the Ariel bicycle, were employed, and which began manufacturing velocipedes in 1868, was originally the Coventry Sewing Machine Company.[65] The link with the sewing machine is a further sign that the film camera and the bicycle emerged from the same industrial and technological matrix.

Two transitional figures played a key role in demonstrating photography's potential to capture and reproduce movement, although neither went on to produce motion pictures. The first, Eadweard Muybridge, was a British photographer who established himself in the United States as a technically expert landscape photographer. Muybridge was commissioned by former governor of California and racehorse breeder Leland Stanford to devise a way of photographing a galloping horse. In response, he designed an electronically controlled camera with a shutter speed of less than a thousandth of a second, and very sensitive film stock. A series of these cameras were placed alongside a racetrack and rigged with tripwires to operate the shutters, so that, as it galloped past, the horse triggered a photograph every half a second. In 1878 Muybridge showed the press his 'series photograph' showing Stanford's racehorse Occident in twelve successive positions, with three frames unexpectedly showing all four feet in the air. Muybridge went on to produce thousands of series photographs of 'human and animal locomotion', publishing books and touring the United States and Europe giving illustrated lectures with a proto-cinematic projector he called the zoopraxiscope. This hand-cranked device held spinning glass discs, on which were images traced from his series photographs, producing animated images on the screen.

The second transitional figure, French physiologist Étienne-Jules Marey, was primarily interested in the problem of analysing moving bodies, controversially defending 'motion' as a viable focus for medical research. Marey proposed that humans were ill-equipped to perceive movement, and felt that recording instruments should be developed and regarded as 'new senses of astonishing precision'.[66] Marey designed various devices for recording and analysing movement, including a portable sphyg-mograph to measure blood pressure (by measuring the movement of pulsing arter-ies), which 'transformed the subjective character of pulse feeling into an objective, visual, graphic representation that was a permanent record of the transient event'.[67] Marey was interested in Muybridge's work, but dissatisfied by its imprecision. Muybridge's series photographs, in which people and animals are positioned against grids and numbered lines, implied scientific objectivity but contained no information about the time intervals between successive images, the clear order of images, the dis-tance between cameras or the distance between camera and subject. Moreover, as a number of commentators have argued, Muybridge's photographic studies of clothed and unclothed bodies expressed highly conventional attitudes towards gender: men are frequently represented in muscular activities, such as sword fighting, wrestling, sprinting, pole-vaulting or sawing wood, while women are typically shown in more feminine activities, such as carrying pails of water, washing, skipping, dancing, tend-ing to children or making beds, and, when not naked, are dressed in diaphanous clas-sical gowns. However, from observing Muybridge's photographs, Marey developed a single camera, the *fusil photographique*, that could expose 12 successive photographs on a rotating glass plate, and which he used to 'shoot' birds in flight. In 1888, he then developed a camera that used paper roll film, shooting at up to 120 frames per second to produce *chronophotographes*, multiple-exposure photographs in which several stages of a particular movement (such as a naked man mounting and dismounting a safety bicycle, or a man riding a tricycle) are superimposed in a single image.

With these *chronophotographes*, Marey was concerned not with producing the illusion of movement so much as with freezing movement and slicing time into dis-crete moments, fixing the figure like a specimen under a microscope. Nevertheless, his innovations influenced other inventors who were trying to animate images. For instance, after unsuccessful attempts to make a cylinder-based motion picture cam-era and projector, Thomas Edison saw Marey's camera in Paris in 1889, and, as a result, by 1891 his assistant William Dickson had produced a working Kinetograph camera and Kinetoscope viewing apparatus.[68]

However, it seems that one of the earliest successful motion pictures was pro-duced in England in 1888, by French inventor Louis Le Prince. On 14 October, using Eastman Kodak film with a camera/projector he had designed, Le Prince shot two films of members of his family in a Leeds garden. The first is lost, but copies of the second, possibly just a fragment, remain. The earliest surviving film, then, was produced less than two months before John Dunlop received the patent for the pneumatic tyre, the innovation that triggered the bicycle boom of the 1890s. In this respect, cinema and the bicycle come into existence almost simultaneously. Le Prince's film is revolutionary in several senses: historically, it represents the emergence of a new medium that will have a transformative effect on global culture; technically, it depends on hand-cranked revolving sprockets to move the film strip through the camera mechanism; and, literally, it shows Le Prince's family dancing in a circle in front of the camera. It is notable that the other surviving film fragment, shot by Le Prince shortly afterwards, is a high-angled shot of pedestrians and carts crossing Leeds Bridge. The subject of the first motion pictures is bodily mobility.

Movement and Modernity

The bicycle and the film camera are technologies of mobility. In this respect, they exemplify the cultural transformations that characterised modernity as industrial capitalism remodelled the social and physical landscape. As Jonathan Crary writes,

Modernization is a process by which capitalism uproots and makes mobile that which is grounded, clears away or obliterates that which impedes circulation and makes exchangeable what is singular. This applies as much to bodies, signs, images, languages, kinship relations, religious practices, and nationalities as it does to commodities, wealth and labour power.[69]

The late nineteenth century was a period of dynamic social and cultural change in which bodies and *things* were in motion as communications and transport networks altered people's relationship with the rest of the world. New technologies contributed to 'a ceaseless and self-perpetuating creation of new needs, new production, and new consumption'.[70] Modernity is a condition of perpetual motion, then, and cycling and the cinema can be understood as expressions of a new world-view, which was epitomised by the figure of Charles Baudelaire's *flâneur* strolling through the city. 'In the nineteenth century, a wide variety of apparatuses turned the pleasures of flânerie into a commodity form, negotiated new illusions of spatial and temporal mobility,' writes Anne Friedberg in a study of the cultural history of cinema, and the film camera and the bicycle are key examples of this commodification of movement.[71] They both offer experiences of greater physical mobility, literally with the bicycle, and virtually with film. This experience was an important attraction from early cinema onwards with the proliferation of travel films and entertainments such as the Hale's Tours and Scenes of the World screening venues, which simulated a ride in a train carriage, the windows giving onto projection screens. As Walter Benjamin observes, an apparently emancipatory effect of cinema was to make the world available to the spectator:

Our taverns and our metropolitan streets, our offices and furnished rooms, our railroad stations and our factories appeared to have us locked up hopelessly. Then came the film and burst this prison-world asunder by the dynamite of the tenth of a second, so that now, in the midst of its far-flung ruins and debris, we calmly and adventurously go travelling.[72]

Similarly, for McLuhan, transport is the principal function of film: 'The business of the writer or the film-maker is to transfer the reader or viewer from one world, his *own*, to another, the world created by typography and film.'[73] Indeed, it is easy to overstate the distinction between physical and virtual mobility. As Tim Cresswell comments, in an observation that is axiomatic for this book, 'Often how we experience mobility and the ways we move are intimately connected to meanings given to mobility through representation. Similarly, representations of mobility are based on ways in which mobility is practised and embodied.'[74]

While cinema can produce such a powerfully visceral sense of physical motion that viewers of some films experience motion sickness, the experience of cycling can also approximate cinematic motion, the road spooling underneath the wheels like film through a projector, the animated landscape flashing across the cyclist's gaze. By contrast with the 'stop/start stress of the car', Jon Day writes, '[c]ycling flows, converting static and isolated glimpses of the city into a moving zoetropic flicker of life.'[75] The movement of the cyclist transforms an inert landscape into a mobile, cinematic spectacle. 'Cycling,' as J. D. Taylor puts it, 'one sees the landscape as a rolling movie, at times dramatic, comic, tragic, and plain mysterious.'[76]

In similar ways cycling and cinema offer the pleasure of *escape* from the mundane routines and environments of everyday life, an idea often exploited in bicycle adverts promising free movement, with images of '[e]ffortless movement and liberty convey[ing] an idealistic vision of modernity divorced from the social realities of industrial labour and the stress of urban life.'[77] A 1938 UK cinema advert for Rudge bicycles epitomises this with an animation of a cyclist pedalling uphill while a giant disembodied hand pushes him from behind, beneath the punning caption 'You've got to Hand it to Rudge'. Indeed, promotional culture played a crucial role in extending the popularity of cycling, while the bicycle was the focus for the development of a range of modern marketing practices.[78] Celebrity endorsements, the annual trade show and planned obsolescence (with manufacturers rolling out new styles every year) were all marketing techniques devised by bicycle manufacturers and later adopted by manufacturers in other areas.

Social Mobility, Cycling and Cinema

Bicycles are technologies of social as well as physical or spatial mobility, facilitating social movement in potentially radical ways. The increasing affordability of the bicycle from the 1880s onwards ensured that a broader range of people could take advantage of its capacity to extend individual mobility. This gave individuals access to much wider social circles, with geneticist Steve Jones going so far as to claim that 'there is little doubt that the most important event in [recent] human evolution was the invention of the bicycle', since it was responsible for greater genetic diversity by allowing cyclists to meet and reproduce with people outside their immediate locale.[79] The machine would 'give women and men unprecedented opportunities to extend their horizons socially and geographically, to transcend domestic confines and (to a limited extent) to move beyond the class and gender circumstances of their birth'.[80]

The bicycle allowed people from different social classes to travel in the same manner through the same spaces, rather than segregating them within different modes of transport, although, by producing a range of differently priced models, bicycle manufacturers ensured from the 1850s onwards that bicycles remained a clearly visible signifier of wealth and social class. Paul Smethurst recounts:

The safety bicycle's rise was inaugurated by the fashionable upper classes of Europe in the 1890s as they flaunted their expensive bicycles, riding hesitatingly and under tuition in the parks of London and Paris. Society women were especially drawn to the display and no expense was spared on their exclusive custom-built machines.[81]

An important dimension of the social mobility afforded by the bicycle was the independence offered to women, who were enabled to travel unaccompanied. They were thus able to attain some of the freedom of movement previously restricted to men. However, this was not uncontentious, as the public spectacle of women cycling and making incursions into masculine space was frequently met with disapproval, ridicule or anxiety, as is discussed later in this book and by Kat Jungnickel in *Bikes and Bloomers*.[82] In *The Wheels of Chance*, H. G. Wells' 1896 comic novel about cycle touring – possibly the first novel about cycling – when the protagonist, Hoopdriver, comes upon a female cyclist, Jessie Milton, who is wearing practical 'athletic bloomers', or 'rationals', rather than a skirt, he is overcome with alarm: 'Suddenly an impulse to bolt

from the situation became clamorous. Mr Hoopdriver pedalled compulsively, intend-
ing to pass her.'[83] The transgressive threat posed by 'New women' dressed in masculine clothing is captured in the comments of a barmaid fascinated by the ambiguous
figure of Milton (who is 'resolved to be Unconventional – ...to struggle, to take my
place in the world..., to shape my own career'); 'There'll be no knowing which is which
in a year or two,' the barmaid predicts.[84]

Moving through public spaces at speed is a means of occupation, of 'reclaiming
the streets' (as UK anti-capitalist activists put it in campaigns against building new
roads in the 1990s) or 'taking the lane' (the title of a US feminist cycling 'zine), asserting
ownership or a right of access. Smethurst proposes that cycling generates a sense of
'the mastery of space', of literally and symbolically 'gaining ground' as a result of physical labour, which is unavailable through motorised modes of transport, which 'enclose
the subject in a detached but moving space, in a perceptual envelope.'[85] The experience
of struggling to gain social and political ground – of cycling as a form of political representation – remains a feature of everyday cycling in various contexts: with regard to
gender, for example, with men two or three times as likely to cycle to work as women
in the United Kingdom; or with regard to the dominance of motor vehicles on the road,
epitomised by the title of the activist documentary *Bikes vs Cars* (Gertten, 2015).[86]

From early on the cinema too was a means of social mobility in several respects.
An affordable form of entertainment that coincided with the expansion of leisure
time for industrial workers in the late nineteenth century (after campaigns in different countries by trade unions and groups, such as the 'eight-hour day' or 'short-time'
movement in Britain), the cinema played a role in the emergence of working-class culture. As Tom Gunning observes, despite film historians' preoccupation with bourgeois
inventors and cosmopolitan urban audiences, 'the history of the cinema will always
reveal an important relation to the working class both as an audience, and as a subject
of representation.'[87] Film screenings often took place in socially unsegregated spaces,
and a great deal of the anxiety about early cinema's effects in Europe and the United
States was prompted by the supposed dangers of social mixing as much as by the
potential influence of the films being screened. With the 'nickel boom' of 1905, which
saw nickelodeons – the first permanent film theatres – spread across the United States
with astonishing speed, the single-price, 5-cent ticket and the absence of regulation or
a certification or censorship system meant that film screenings were widely accessible
even to low-paid manual labourers and children. The fact that early films were more
or less entirely dialogue-free also meant that they were accessible to illiterate viewers
and non-anglophone immigrants. Consequently, the broad social inclusiveness of the

new medium, as well as the sometimes sensational content of the films, meant that '[m]oving pictures were…rife with anxieties for the genteel representatives of American culture, including the issues of a working class audience and the sexual awareness of children'.[88] The emerging industry responded by trying to attract bourgeois viewers by raising ticket prices, building splendid 'picture palaces' resembling theatres or opera houses, introducing self-censorship systems (in the United States), producing literary adaptations and developing more complex storytelling systems. In retrospect, as Charles Musser suggests (echoing claims about the bicycle's social impact), '[t]he nickelodeons offered not only a kind of economic democracy but greater sexual egalitarianism, as women were encouraged to attend and did so in large numbers'.[89]

Both technologies also foreground the *experience* of social mobility, in so far as watching a film and taking a trip on a bicycle allows the subject to identify with other social classes. The film viewer and the cyclist are invited to fantasise, albeit transiently, that they belong to another class. Cycling through the English countryside in *The Wheels of Chance* (and the 1922 film adaptation by American director Harold M. Shaw), department store clerk Hoopdriver imagines himself to be a 'knight errant', gallantly rescuing Jessie Milton from her pursuers, as 'his machine becomes the vehicle and the "passport" that allows him to explore the leafy suburbs and country towns where he might rub handlebars with the better classes'; and, of course, identification is the mechanism by which films are comprehensible to the spectator.[90] Our intellectual and affective response to a film depends upon our capacity to identify with characters, situations, environments and visual perspectives.

Bicycles, Cameras and Cyborgs

These industrial technologies of mobility might therefore be understood in similar terms as examples of communications media. For McLuhan, a communications medium is not just a neutral vehicle for conveying information; instead, it alters the information it conveys – from the way that news media select, reframe and narrativise current events, through to the ways that digital audio recording and reproduction alter the sound quality of music – and can also have a transformative effect upon the social context within which it is located. Discussing the historical development of ever faster communications systems, McLuhan writes,

Each form of transport not only carries, but translates and transforms, the sender, the receiver, and the message. The use of any kind of medium or extension of man alters the patterns of interdependence among people, as it alters the ratios among our senses.[91]

It is a central premise for McLuhan that the effects of media technologies cannot be accounted for by attending to their content – the messages they convey; rather, to understand the social transformations effected by media technologies we must recognise the significance of the technology itself. The social impact of the internet cannot be understood by focusing on 'content' – the material that circulates through digital networks – but must be understood primarily in relation to the ways that business, education, crime, leisure and entertainment, consumption, government and political activism, warfare and terrorism, sex and sociality have all been reconfigured by this technology. Similarly, the revolutionary impact of cinema was attributable to the spectacular new technology on display to audiences, rather than the anodyne visual and narrative content of the films (for McLuhan, films were 'a supreme expression of mechanism'), and the same is true for cycling.[92] It was not just another form of transport that evolved seamlessly from the horse and cart but also a disruptive new technology that altered both social relations, 'the patterns of interdependence among people', as well as the cyclist herself, altering 'the ratios among our senses'.[93]

Another premise of McLuhan's conceptualisation of communications technologies is that '[a]ll media are extensions of some human faculty – psychic or physical', and are not simply 'used' by us, but also 'work us over completely'. Media

are so pervasive in their personal, political, economic, aesthetic, psychological, moral, ethical, and social consequences that they leave no part of us untouched, unaffected, unaltered. The medium is the massage [sic]. Any understanding of social and cultural change is impossible without a knowledge of the way media work as environments.[94]

As prosthetic extensions of the body, the bicycle and cinema function in similar ways, making cyborgs of us all. The cinema enhances our capacity to see and hear, but the bicycle does the same, bringing new sounds and images to us, as well as new scents and physical sensations. If, as Walter Benjamin suggests, '[t]he camera introduces us to unconscious optics', revealing 'hidden details of familiar objects', so the bicycle *re*introduces us to the space around us, which has become invisible through habitual routine. It invites us to navigate it by different routes and to move through it with a different consciousness of our body's physical presence in the world – an unconscious optics that is founded on – as is the case with cinema – an unconscious haptics. 'Cycling makes you *feel* a landscape rather than merely seeing it,' writes Day. 'By bike, your environment writes itself onto your body.... A bicycle unrolls a 360-degree panorama of the land, allows the rider to register gradual changes in gear ratios and muscle tension, and makes it hard to miss a single inch of it.'[95] Similarly, cycling extends other senses, drawing the rider's attention to her aural as well as visual environment: 'As an urban cyclist you quickly learnt to attend to the soundscape of the city.'[96]

Cycling and cinema also exemplify the intimate incorporation of technology into our lives. The histories of cinema and cycling depict the rapid change in status of these technologies from spectacular novelties, representing the most advanced industrial innovation, to ubiquitous and unremarkable textural components of everyday experience. The marvellous science fiction figure of the cyborg whose body is interpenetrated with electronic circuitry and metal and plastic components is realised both in the cinema spectator, for whom the cinematic apparatus is an extension of the perceptual apparatus of her body, and also in the cyclist, her body augmented by the mobile mechanism of the bicycle. This cybernetic fusion is illustrated directly in many instances, from cycle-powered cinemas through to the exercise bikes linked to screens discussed in the final chapter.[97]

Cycling and cinema extend the body's physical capacity, allowing us to move much faster and farther than would previously have been possible. More than just transportation systems that move individuals from one place to another, both media function as environments, altering, enhancing and introducing dynamic complexity into the visual and sensorial contexts through which the spectator/cyclist moves. Examining cycling and cinema in tandem invites us to see how both technologies function as narrative systems. Although it is conceivable that a film might consist of pure, arbitrary movement and a cycle journey might follow an entirely random route, in most cases film spectatorship and cycling typically involve travel along specific vectors, following a route towards a fixed end point (even if it is not always reached successfully), which is punctuated or interrupted by encounters and obstacles. As narrative systems, both involve the compression and dilation of time and space. In film, time is compressed through undercranking or elliptical editing – the excision of passages of time – and extended through slow motion and repetition. Cinematic space is similarly plastic, as vast distances can be folded into the instantaneous transition from one shot to the next, while large spaces can be constructed through judicious camera angles, editing and digital image manipulation. The subjective experience of cycling is also marked by a flexibility of time and space that is directly linked to physical effort, fitness and fatigue and the gradient of the terrain. The harder one works, the more slowly time appears to move (Bradley Wiggins observes, recalling his thoughts during the last few laps of his attempt to break the hour record in 2015, 'How can each minute take so long to pass?')[98] while distances can seem much greater when riding uphill, and are condensed when the rider coasts downhill.

Reflecting on the narrative parallels between writing and cycling, and the inherently literary, 'self-directed' quality of riding a bicycle, former cycle courier Jon Day observes:

Cycling, like writing, forces you to think not just in terms of individual steps, but in terms of conjunctions, routes and structures: how am I to get from here to there? How exactly will I navigate this particular snarl of metal and rubber and steel and chromium? How will I get to the end?[99]

This describes equally well the experience of film viewing in which we identify with a protagonist or several characters struggling to make their way towards some sort of resolution, attempting to anticipate, as the film progresses, how the story will develop. Cycling and film viewing are both narrative experiences. In his autobiography, *The Bicycle Rider in Beverly Hills,* the author (and one-time bicycle telegram messenger) William Saroyan reflects on the direct relationship between cycling and writing in similar terms, proposing that riding a bike taught him about style and imagination. The cyclist discovers 'that there are many excellent ways in which to ride a bike effectively, and this acquaintanceship with the ways and the comparing of them gives him an awareness of a parallel potential in all other actions. Out of the imagination comes also music and memory.'[100] Riding bikes since his childhood, Saroyan explains, shaped his career as a writer:

I was not yet sixteen when I understood a great deal, from having ridden bicycles for so long, about style, speed, grace, purpose, value, form, integrity, health, humor, music, breathing, and finally and perhaps best of all the relationship between the beginning and the end.[101]

Understood in this sense, cycling has a representational function. As Allan Stoekl suggests, '[c]ycling is not simply a series of techniques but rather a descriptive universe – colourful, lyrical, peopled with gods and demons – a coherent universe in which one lives, or wants to live, and from which, on occasion, one senses a bitter exile.'[102] As this implies, cycling always involves a degree of cinematic fantasy, desire and identification, so that when we ride a bike we periodically cross over into a parallel reality slightly out of phase with our own, imagining as we ride that we are gallant knights, suffragettes, professional racers, young girls, Edwardian clerks, fearless bike messengers or wide-eyed American children carried aloft by a mysterious alien force.[103]

Overview

Cycling and Cinema involved several years of deeply enjoyable research in the film archives. While it is difficult to comprehensively categorise the hundreds of films about bicycles and cycling I have had the pleasure to watch, a series of recurring themes emerged – comedy, work, sport, gender, childhood and technology – and it is around these dominant themes that I have organised this book.

In Chapter 2, 'Mischief Machines: Stunts and Slapstick Comedy', I explore the idea of cycling as a mode of public performance, a notion that is central to films of spectacular trick cycling from the late nineteenth century onwards, and to slapstick comedy films, in which riders are perpetually falling off, crashing and destroying their bicycles. The chapter concludes with a consideration of the comic films of Jacques Tati, some of the most refined depictions of the human/bicycle relationship in cinema.

In Chapter 3, 'The Hard Labour of Cycling', I consider the idea of cycling as work, the shifting significance of the bicycle as a badge of social class and the importance of the bicycle to various forms of labour. This is explored through a selection of films from around the world that feature bicycle workers – or cyclists searching for work – many of which allude to one of the most famous bicycle-related films in cinema, *Ladri di Biciclette* [*The Bicycle Thieves*] (De Sica, 1948). The chapter finishes with a discussion of the subgenre of films dealing with the figure of the bicycle messenger, a crucial component of the financial infrastructure and communication networks of the modern city.

The fourth chapter, 'Sport and Performance Machines', discusses films that focus upon the sport of cycling, a particularly specialised form of bicycle labour. Analysing a variety of fiction films and documentaries on individual cyclists and cycle races, I examine the interdependence of sport with news and entertainment media, and the way in which cycle racing functions to articulate and affirm a set of values around masculinity and the body, nationhood and the relationship between individual and community. This chapter ends by considering several films about the Texan cyclist Lance Armstrong, a figure who has been at the centre of an ideological and institutional crisis over the values and the symbolic integrity of professional cycling.

In the fifth chapter, 'Riding like a Girl', I discuss films that depict women and girls on bikes. Beginning with a consideration of the emancipatory potential the bicycle held for women in the late nineteenth century and early twentieth, this chapter looks at a selection of documentaries and dramas featuring women athletes, workers and cycle tourists. Although women cyclists appear in many of the films discussed in the book, this chapter considers films in which gender and women's social status are central themes. In their concern with the social and physical challenges faced by women cyclists in different contexts, these films are more consciously political than many of those discussed in *Cycling and Cinema*. Films about women and girls on bicycles are often centrally concerned with the capacity of this machine to mobilise the rider, giving her greater agency. Among the titles discussed in this chapter, the Iranian film *The Day I Became a Woman* (Meshkini, 2000) and the Saudi Arabian film *Wadjda* (al-Mansour, 2012) both use the bicycle as a powerful metaphor for independence.

Chapter 6, 'Kids with Bikes', concentrates upon films that deal with children and bicycles, and related questions of individual independence. A central theme in these films is the way that the bicycle enables the symbolic separation of children from their parents, whether they are young children or teenagers on the edge of adulthood and desperate to leave home. I discuss a variety of films for and about children, and a key case study here is one of the most widely viewed films about childhood of all, the blockbuster *E.T.: The Extra-Terrestrial* (Spielberg, 1982).

In the final chapter, 'The Digital Bicycle Boom', I discuss the way that representations of cycling circulate in contemporary 'post-cinematic' screen cultures. As well as discussing depictions of cycling on TV and the internet, I also consider the ways in which cycling increasingly involves studying screens, whether on an exercise bike in the gym or using a GPS device to follow a route. I go on to discuss the emergence of the cyclist-film-maker, documenting her commute or her leisure rides with a lightweight digital camera and then editing and uploading these videos onto the web. With this figure the story told by the book of the tandem revolutionary technologies, cinema and the bicycle, comes full circle, although, as I discuss in the conclusion, it is questionable how far we have travelled towards realising the emancipatory promise of the bicycle, or of industrial modernity.

While some of the titles discussed in *Cycling and Cinema* may be familiar, the range of films and audio-visual material covered in the book is broad and encompasses adverts, public information films, newsreel films, propaganda documentaries, children's films, student films, TV drama and made-for-TV movies, art cinema and experimental video art, mainstream commercial cinema and low-budget exploitation films. One of the fascinating and surprising consequences of tracking the bicycle through the history of cinema is that it reveals to us a radically different, non-canonical history of world cinema. Viewed through the frame of the bicycle, film history is not a succession of 'great' films by 'great' directors but a far more heterogeneous, messy spectrum of material, ranging from the disposable to the timeless.

Not all the films discussed are equally interested in bicycles. Some are concerned with documenting and dramatising cycling cultures or capturing the experience of riding a bike, but, for others, bikes are passing details, props or minor elements in the background of the image. Track racing is the central focus of the slapstick comedy *6-day Bike Rider* (Bacon, 1934), but in *Open All Night* (Bern, 1924) the six-day race at Paris's Velodrome d'Hiver is the sweaty setting for the rekindling of a bourgeois couple's stale marriage, the principal concern of this racy silent drama. Meanwhile, cycle racing is a convenient plot device in the bittersweet road movie *Kikujirô no natsu* [*Kikujiro*] (Kitano, 1999), as the irritable protagonist Kikujiro is reduced to hitch-hiking across Japan after losing all his money betting on 'Keirin' track racing (one of four sports in which gambling is legal). Cinematic bicycles are often convenient narrative instruments rather than objects of fascination in themselves. Bicycle brands and models are seldom named, and films that pay attention to the style, design, materials or componentry of bicycles are rare. Exceptions include promotional or educational films, such as Raleigh's *How a Bicycle Is Made* (Lee, 1945) and *The Moulton Bicycle* (1972); independent shorts such as *Izhar Cardboard Bicycle Project* (Kariv, 2016) and *Tall Bike Tour* (Zenga Brothers, 2016), focusing on unconventional bicycle design; and children's films *Pee-wee's Big Adventure* (Burton, 1985) and *The Sky Bike* (Frend, 1967), which feature marvellous machines. In *La Course en Tête* (Santoni, 1974) we see technically obsessive Eddy Merckx assembling a road bike in his garage, while for the Graham Obree biopic *The Flying Scotsman* (MacKinnon, 2006) and the documentary *Battle Mountain: Graham Obree's Story* (Street, 2015) the cyclist's innovative self-built racing machines are crucial to his story. *Klunkerz: A Film about Mountain Bikes* (Savage, 2013) documents the DIY development of this globally popular style of bike by Californian cyclists in the 1970s, but, more generally, cinematic bicycles are vehicles through which film-makers explore questions of identity. In *Dope* (Famuyiwa, 2015) the geeky schoolboy protagonist's retro obsession with '80s pop culture is symbolised by the BMX (bicycle motocross) bike he rides to school, while in the frothy 'swinging London' musical *Les Bicyclettes de Belsize* (Hickox, 1968) the Raleigh RSW commuter bike ridden by the romantic hero is a sign of his lightness of being and his difference from the 'poor things' queuing glumly at bus stops to travel to work. For many films about cycling – echoing the title of Lance Armstrong's autobiography – *It's Not about the Bike*; it's about labour, class and aspiration, technology, industry and progress, urbanisation and the environment, gender, sexuality and the body, maturity, empowerment, politics and ethics, inequalities of movement and access to public space, family, community, ethnicity and nationhood, pleasure and pain. Which is to say, cycling is a means through which film-makers have explored the full spectrum of human experience from the very beginnings of cinema.

2

Mischief Machines: Stunts and Slapstick Comedy

Figure 2.1
Village postman François (Jacques Tati) forces an impatient driver to wait as he wheels his bicycle slowly across the road in *Jour de Fête* (Tati, 1949) (© Francinex/Kobal/REX/Shutterstock)

The Spectacle of the Cyclist

Whenever we ride a bicycle we make a spectacle of ourselves. Whether we are hesitant, unstable novices or skilful, experienced riders, we risk drawing attention to ourselves when we venture out on a bike. This can be intentional, as a means of self-protection – since fluorescent, reflective clothing, colourful helmets and bright lights promise to make cyclists safer by making them more visible – but all too often the public visibility of the cyclist is a catalyst for ridicule, abuse, sexual harassment and aggression.

Thinking about the interrelation of cycling and cinema requires us to reflect upon the performative dimension of cycling. Placing the cyclist within the film frame invites us to see cycling as a mode of public performance. Whether we are watching a Super 8 home movie of a toddler's first unsteady attempts to ride without stabilisers, an uploaded digital video of cyclists negotiating city streets or an action scene featuring professional stunt riders in feature films such as Jackie Chan's Hong Kong comedy *Project A* (Chan, 1983), Shahrukh Khan's Bollywood thriller *Main Hoon Na* (Khan, 2004) or the American crime drama *Premium Rush* (Koepp, 2012), when viewed on the screen these actions become acts of signification, performances available for scrutiny and interpretation, more or less self-conscious displays that convey a variety of complex meanings.

For example, Bruce Banner, the protagonist of the blockbuster comic book adaptation *Hulk* (Lee, 2003), is first seen cycling to his lab at the 'Berkeley Nuclear Biotechnology Institute'. In the context of an American film, this is more than a simple depiction of a commuter travelling to work; in a culture that fetishises automobility, the fact that Banner cycles codes him as an eccentric, an environmentally aware Californian liberal who is unconventionally masculine in a context in which owning and driving a car is a sign of maturity. The bicycle is the semiotic equivalent of a pair of spectacles within American cinema's iconography of social inadequacy, and this is reinforced by his cycle helmet and shoulder bag. 'You look like a massive nerd, even around other scientists,' one of his colleagues comments. 'Can I just ask: were you wearing the helmet when she dumped you?'

Similarly, in *21 Jump Street* (Lord, Miller, 2012) the bicycle is a comically embarrassing prop because of its incongruity within the macho context of a crime narrative. A comedy adaptation of a US TV crime series from the late 1980s and early 1990s, the film tells the story of two recently graduated cops working undercover as high school students to expose a drug ring. However, at the film's beginning they are frustrated to find themselves in their first posting patrolling a public park on bicycles, dressed in shorts and skewed cycle helmets, retrieving frisbees and trying to stop children feeding the ducks. 'I really thought this job would have more car chases and explosions,' one of them reflects glumly. When they eventually spot motorcycle gang members sharing a joint, the action-film aesthetic of low camera angles, quick cutting and dramatic music underlines the bathos as they pedal across the grass on their squeaking bicycles, lights flashing, and sirens wailing – like children playing cops and robbers – while people in the background relax on park benches. Whereas the gang's tattoos, costumes and customised motorbikes are a hackneyed badge of machismo, in the context of mainstream American cinema the two bicycles are a sign of compromised masculinity.

What is funny about these scenes is the incongruity between the object and the context in which it appears. Bicycles are not intrinsically funny machines, although Pee-wee Herman's customised Schwinn bicycle is absurd and the broken track bike with off-centre hubs that Joe E. Brown finds himself riding in *6 Day Bike Rider* (Bacon, 1934) is laughable, as is the postman's bicycle that operates independently of its owner in *Jour de Fête*. What makes bicycles funny is the way that people operate and interact with them. Cinema regularly finds humour in the spectacle of awkward human–machine interaction. This spectrum of awkwardness ranges from sequences of people anxiously learning to ride, such as the pompous patriarch whose first attempt lands him in the river in the gentle comedy about the Edwardian cycling boom, *Isn't Life Wonderful* (French, 1954), through to the sequence in the silent comedy *Long Pants* (Capra, 1927), in which the child-like Harry Langdon seduces a vamp by cycling in circles around her open-topped limousine, effortlessly performing virtuoso tricks as a courtship display until she succumbs and they embrace. The comedy lies in the contrast between his childishness and eternally innocent expression and the improbably impressive tricks he pulls off – sometimes shot from an overhead camera – as he spins the handlebars, rides backwards and balances on the saddle.

Some cyclists ride with grace, moving with machinic regularity, casually performing impossible stunts or climbing mountains with apparent ease. Paul Fournel observes of Jacques Anquetil, the French cycling champion with film-star looks, that '[e]ven when he was scraping bottom he seemed on parade, in cahoots with the wind, feline and unreadable. For that's really the lie of class: you can read it only as harmony; effort leaves no trace.'[1] By contrast, there is amusement to be found in the undignified spectacle of the cyclist's sweating, labouring body, red-faced, backside protruding in the air, and in the mismatch between body and bicycle. Films find predictable humour in the images of fat people balanced precariously on little bicycles, for example, too many people balanced on a bicycle made for one, or even the relatively unusual sight of a tandem, which is glimpsed in the sweet Keystone comedy *Fatty and Mabel Adrift* (Arbuckle, 1916), as Mabel's elderly parents pedal furiously in their nightshirts to rescue her from drowning. One also appears in *Going! Going! Gone!!* (Pratt, 1919), a comedy starring Harold Lloyd and Snub Pollard in which the two characters share a tandem, Lloyd eating his lunch and reading a newspaper under a parasol at the rear while an oblivious Pollard struggles at the front.

Trick Cycling and Early Cinema

Perhaps the purest example of the cinematic spectacle of cycling is found in films of trick cyclists. The earliest of these is *Bicycliste* (1897), a well-composed single-shot *actualité* produced by the Lumière brothers, which shows a young man in a bow tie performing tricks in the middle of a wide, wintry street. In front of a few onlookers, the cyclist rides into the frame on a fixed-wheel bicycle and then comes to a halt, before riding backwards in a circle. He dismounts, spinning the bike around on its back wheel, and then hops back on and circles again, balancing with one foot on the saddle, his other leg out behind him. He rides towards the camera and out of the frame before reappearing riding in a circle, with one of his legs threaded awkwardly through the frame. His tricks may be unremarkable, and it's unclear to what extent the onlookers in the background are interested in the spectacle of cycling tricks rather than the novel spectacle of film-making itself, but as a depiction of a body in circular motion the non-narrative film is a clear example of what Tom Gunning and André Gaudreault term the 'cinema of attractions'.

Arguing that cinema before 1906 was not predominantly concerned with storytelling, Gunning suggests instead that early films were preoccupied with 'the harnessing of visibility, this act of showing and exhibition'.[2] For the first film-makers, cinema was 'a way of presenting a series of views to an audience, fascinating because of their illusory power…and exoticism'.[3] Rather than functioning as a self-contained narrative, *Bicycliste* would have been shown within a varied, thematically unrelated programme of films intended to solicit 'spectator attention, inciting visual curiosity, and supplying pleasure through an exciting spectacle'.[4] Cycling, especially stunt cycling, exemplified this spectacular cinematic attraction very well.

Moreover, early film screenings were often presented in close proximity to a diverse range of attractions in the context of fairgrounds, amusement parks or variety theatre bills. Before the establishment of permanent film theatres, the variety theatre or music hall was a principal venue for film viewing: 'Film appeared as one attraction on the vaudeville programme, surrounded by a mass of unrelated acts in a non-narrative and even nearly illogical succession of performances.'[5] While there may have been little thematic connection between the films and other attractions on the bill, popular theatre nevertheless provided early cinema with performers and acts, and the trick cycling film is a sign of the way that cinema drew on the virtuoso performance styles, genres and iconography of popular theatre, incorporating a commercial 'vaudeville aesthetic' to satisfy as broad an audience as possible.

The comedian Al St. John, who became famous co-starring with his uncle, Roscoe 'Fatty' Arbuckle, and Buster Keaton, was trained as a trick cyclist and was hired at Keystone studios after studio owner Mack Sennett saw a display of his cycling skills.[6] Cycling tricks were a distinctive component in the armoury of acrobatic technical skills possessed by the silent screen comedian and were put to use in a number of St. John's slapstick films. In the Keystone film *Bombs!* (Griffin, 1916) he plays an insolent bicycle messenger who cycles up the steps of a building and into the newly elected mayor's office, stealing a clerk's cigar and unwittingly delivering a parcel bomb, while in the comedy *Out of Place* (1922) he uses his bicycle to deliver a huge crate containing a horse, which he balances on his back. In the gag-strewn film *The Paper Hanger* (Raymaker, 1920) St. John plays a decorator's assistant, who is introduced riding to work with his hands off the handlebars, absent-mindedly lighting a match on the face of a car driver alongside him and eating his breakfast from the counter of a moving, horse-drawn food cart. Arriving at work he crashes through the front door and flies over the handlebars into the shop, knocking his boss into a barrel of wallpaper paste. When he cycles out to another job later, St. John carries his boss on his back, as well as a ladder, all the rolls of paper and several buckets. Inevitably, the ladder gets caught between two cars, leaving the two men hanging, and St. John summons his bicycle back to collect them (as if it were an animal). The bizarre film ends with St. John cycling away with a woman on his handlebars and his boss on the back of his bike, reading aloud from a book of sermons. The boss is thrown off the bike when they ride through a puddle, and St. John and the woman career down a hill and into a lake, the final destination of many comic cyclists.

Trick Cycling and the Digital Cinema of Attractions

Although titles such as the Edison films *Bicycle Tricks* (1899) and *The Trick Cyclist* (1901) exemplify early cinema's incorporation of vaudeville theatre and circus ring attractions, this aesthetic of visual spectacle did not disappear with the development of sophisticated storytelling techniques by film-makers in the early 1900s; stunts and special effects remained a draw for film-goers. One curious sign of this continuity is the revival of the trick cycling film exemplifying the emergence of a digital 'cinema of attractions' in the early twenty-first century.

This is best demonstrated by the breathtaking short films of Danny MacAskill. MacAskill is a professional Scottish trials rider, a form of competitive cycling derived from motorcycle trials in which riders must negotiate obstacle courses without putting their feet down, but he has become famous for a series of short promotional videos, sponsored by manufacturers of bicycles, soft drinks and camera equipment. These videos have been posted online and are also distributed on disc and screened at specialist film festivals dedicated to cycling or 'extreme sports', such as the annual Filmed by Bike Festival in Portland, Oregon, or the Banff Mountain Film festival. Films shown at these festivals have a number of conventions, most of which are shared by MacAskill's: an emphasis on picturesque 'natural' scenery, dynamic and varied camera movements including slow-motion shots and point-of-view shots that emphasise the kinetic spectacle of the athletes' stunts, product placement shots identifying the sponsors' logos and brand names of clothing, equipment, food and drink, and an audio-visual aesthetic that emulates the polish of tourism adverts. Narratives typically revolve around travel or a passage through unpopulated environments, in which the challenging physical journey stands as both metaphor and trigger for the athlete's emotional 'journey' and personal growth, discussed in voice-over commentary or talking head shots in which they reflect on their experience.

MacAskill's films show him performing skilful, dangerous and potentially fatal stunts on his trials bike, a low-framed variant of the mountain bike. The first, the five-minute *Inspired Bicycles* (Sowerby, 2009), has been viewed over 38 million times since it was posted online, and shows MacAskill performing a series of virtuoso stunts as he rides around the centre of Edinburgh. At the beginning he makes a couple of failed attempts to ride along the narrow top of an iron railing fence, damaging his bike in the process. He succeeds on the third attempt and then performs a series of increasingly impressive stunts, riding up vertical tree trunks, bunny-hopping, 'flairing' and leaping over bollards, railings and fences, balancing on narrow ledges and bars and, finally, leaping off overpasses and down steep flights of concrete steps. The use of slow-motion, repetition, a fish-eye lens, mobile camera and low-angle shots emphasise the difficulty and the stylish grace of his manoeuvres.

Subsequent films are progressively more spectacular, both in terms of the locations, film style and technical complexity of the shots and the difficulty of the stunts themselves. *Way Back Home* (Sowerby, 2010) introduces a narrative frame, blending the trick cycling film with travelogue as MacAskill travels from Edinburgh to his home town on the Isle of Skye, performing stunts in various locations along the way, using abandoned concrete bunkers, coastal defence structures and farm buildings as ramps and launch pads. *MacAskill's Imaginate* (Thomson, 2013), meanwhile, opens with a young Danny playing with toys in his bedroom. The film then takes us into the child's imagination as MacAskill performs a series of stunts in a Brobdingnagian version of young Danny's bedroom, as if cycling enables the 28-year-old athlete to return to his childhood.

More recent films introduce further variation by placing MacAskill in more visually dramatic or exotic locations, including the abandoned Argentinian town of Epecuén, the cascading seaside village of Las Palmas on Gran Canaria and the Playboy mansion.[7] That embarrassing film aside, Clara S. Lewis suggests that MacAskill's films challenge the hypermasculinity of extreme sports culture. Describing him as a 'gifted performance artist', she observes that 'he demonstrates a different attitude to what is possible on a bike both physically and conceptually'.[8] In their emphasis on play, rather than on danger, fear and adrenaline, they reject the earnest, narcissistic hypermasculinity of extreme sports culture in which whooping, high-fiving athletes are continually confronting their own limits through waterskiing, sky-diving, rock-climbing or various other expensive leisure activities. Lewis suggests that 'the popularity of MacAskill's unconventional videos hints at a willingness, or even longing, to see sport unbound from gendered clichés'.[9]

Following on MacAskill's wheel, some other cyclists have achieved celebrity through trick cycling films, including trials riders Fabio Wibmer, Martyn Ashton and Vittorio Brumotti, each attempting to top the stunts performed by the other riders, or perform them with more flair. Videos such as Ashton's *Road Bike Party* (Kitchin, 2012) and Brumotti's *Road Bike Freestyle* (2014) introduce the novel variation of performing similarly virtuosic stunts on delicate carbon-fibre-framed road bikes rather than the specially designed trials bikes. Some of these tricks are undoubtedly perilous; 'making-of' documentaries and out-takes shown during the credits emphasise the physical danger of the stunts by showing them falling repeatedly. Indeed, MacAskill underwent spinal surgery during the preparation of *Imaginate*, while Ashton was paralysed after breaking his back during a public riding display in 2013, although he has gone on to make a series of joyful, inspiring films, beginning with

Martyn Ashton – Back on Track (Kitchin, 2015), in which he rides an adapted mountain bike on downhill trails. However, for all the emphasis on authenticity and the
performers' physical prowess, the stunts we see in these films are nevertheless cinematic constructions, the illusion of continuous movement through coherent space
produced through the seamless assemblage of multiple takes from a variety of camera angles.[10]

MacAskill's films dramatise some of the most powerful attractions of cycling: the
sense of enhanced physical freedom and mobility, the opportunity for escape and
travel, the nostalgic association of cycling with childhood and the masculine (sometimes misogynistic) character of cycling culture. They also demonstrate the capacity
of the bicycle to transform our experience of space, with obstacle-ridden urban and
natural landscapes reconfigured creatively as spaces through which we can flow. For
MacAskill, blockages to movement such as walls, fences, boulders, barriers and bollards become an aid to movement, springboards that propel him forwards and backwards, vertically and horizontally.

MacAskill's films demonstrate how cycling reveals the topographic structures of
both built-up and rural spaces, and, as well as reframing our view of our physical landscape, his films also alter our view of the mundane action of cycling, something most
of us would regard as easy. These are case studies in human–machine interaction in
which MacAskill's virtuosity means that the metal, rubber and plastic apparatus of
the bike is a liberating extension of the limbs, freeing the body rather than pulling it
back down to earth. Cycling is depicted here as a technically complex, marvellously
skilful act of staying upright. In the most thrilling sequences MacAskill rides carelessly
above precipitous drops, landing safely after launching himself from bone-breaking
heights. As he jumps and bunny-hops with no apparent effort over various obstacles,
MacAskill rides in miraculous defiance of gravity.

What makes these films viscerally exciting is that MacAskill seems continually on
the verge of falling. The films propose that, at its core, cycling is the art of *not* falling.
More precisely, cycling is a matter of controlled falling, of catching ourselves before
we fall and converting that momentum into forward movement – of falling with style.
This is captured most succinctly in a 19-second silent film by Dutch performance
artist Bas Jan Ader, *Fall 2 Amsterdam 1970*: in the distance a cyclist can be seen riding along the road beside a canal, and as he moves closer he veers around a tree and
plunges into the water. The film is one of a small series of works by Ader that explore
the theme of falling. The 24-second *Fall 1 Los Angeles 1970* shows the artist rolling off
the pitched roof of his house in slow motion, for instance, and *Broken Fall (Organic)*

(1971) shows Ader hanging from a tree branch before dropping several metres into the stream beneath.

Unlike MacAskill, in *Fall 2* (and his other films and photographs) Ader succumbs to gravity. In the absence of any narrative exposition, the title invites us to understand the short film as an allegory of the human condition. It represents life as an absurdly brief moment of activity followed, inevitably, by a loss of bodily control and an undignified death.[11] It can also be interpreted as an allegorical account of humanity's moral corruption, as symbolised by the movement of falling, and his work's emphasis on the material weight of the body and the relentless downward force pulling it back towards the earth. As Alan Dale writes,

in Christian theology, falling has the worst possible connotations, of course. The Christian fear of falling, with the pit of hell always imagined down below, indicates a ceaseless resistance to physical existence, with our enslavement to gravity a symbol for all the animal lapses to which we're given.[12]

If *Fall 2* is an allegory for this fear of eternal damnation, and belongs to a lapsarian tradition of European art, it also recasts this as slapstick comedy. This silent black and white film appropriates one of the essential components of slapstick film comedy, the image of somebody falling over, and restages it without the narrative frame, characters and genre cues that might have made it straightforwardly funny. As Dale observes, slapstick comedy can be reduced to two physical actions, the fall and the blow: 'In their iconic form, the fall is caused by a banana peel and the blow is translated into a pie in the face. Thus, the essence of a slapstick gag is a physical assault on, or collapse of, the hero's dignity.'[13] Consequently, broad physical comedy always has a potentially ambiguous register. 'Because slapstick plays on our fears of physical and social maladjustment, many of the typical gags slide into nightmare territory.'[14]

Intransigent Objects: Bodies and/as Machines

If cycling is a matter of keeping one's balance – of not falling – then, of course, the spectacle of men and women struggling and sometimes failing to stay upright lends itself perfectly to film comedy; but there is an additional principle of film comedy on display here, in which humour is derived from the hapless protagonist's unsuccessful encounter with machines. These range from simple mechanisms such as roller skates, window sashes or revolving doors through to escalators, cars, locomotives and the factory machinery that swallows Charlie Chaplin in *Modern Times* (1936), or the huge sets of Buster Keaton's and Jacques Tati's films, where the environment operates as a vast machine. Whereas MacAskill's films present us with the spectacle of total mastery of machines, slapstick comedy offers the comic image of characters repeatedly defeated by 'what Frank Capra, a graduate of Mack Sennett two-reelers and Harry Langdon's feature production team, called the "intransigence of objects".[15] For screen comedians, the bicycle is a particularly intransigent object that rarely goes where the rider wants and is also liable to disintegrate, as Laurel and Hardy discover when fleeing from forest rangers on a stolen bicycle in *Duck Soup* (Guiol, 1927). As Ollie pedals strenuously, with Stan perched on the handlebars, the chain snaps and the brakes fail as they race out of control down a steep hill. 'The carburetor is shot!' Stan shouts unhelpfully, and the bicycle collapses underneath them when they reach the bottom.

In *Laughter*, his reflection upon the social and psychological function of humour, philosopher Henri Bergson suggests that falling is funny is because it is a sign of absent-mindedness, a body moving in one direction while our attention is directed elsewhere. However, one of Bergson's 'laws' of comedy is also that people are funny when they behave in a mechanical, automatic fashion: 'The attitudes, gestures and movements of the human body are laughable in exact proportion as that body reminds us of a mere machine.'[16] Conversely, objects and non-human animals are funny when they take on the qualities of humans, such as a bicycle with a mind of its own. This is exemplified by the sequence in Tati's *Jour de Fête,* when the village postman François races after his bicycle after it is accidentally towed away by a passing car, and then heads off by itself down the road with François in pursuit.

Bergson's proposition that a key source of comedy comes from 'something mechanical encrusted upon the living'[17] is helpful in understanding the comedy of cycling. As he suggests, bodies can be funny when they behave like automata or puppets, undertaking repetitive movements, imitating other bodies, becoming 'rigid' and losing their natural 'gracefulness and suppleness'. The spectacle of the frantically pedalling cyclist produces the impression of a mechanical body in a particularly direct, comic fashion.

Always Crashing on the Same Bicycle

One of the earliest instance of a comic film featuring cycling (as opposed to comic displays of trick cycling), *L'Arrivée d'un Train en Gare* (Pathé, 1906) employs the staple device of the bicycle crash.[18] This single-shot film parodies the most famous early film of all, *L'Arrivée d'un Train en Gare de La Ciotat* (Lumière, 1895); it has an identical composition and, like the Lumière film, shows a steam train pulling up to a station platform and passengers disembarking. However, whereas the Lumière *actualité* stops there, the Pathé film extends this into a short narrative, which concludes with an act of ideological resolution, re-establishing social order. As the passengers crowd onto the platform a male cyclist rides into the frame and collides with a woman and a waiter who are in conversation, knocking them to the ground. The waiter then starts punching and kicking the cyclist before bystanders pull him away. A policeman then intervenes, holding the cyclist by his collar and walking him out of the frame while bashing him around the head.

It is not a terribly funny film, and, were it not for the fact that it cites the Lumière film, it might be mistaken for a documentary. It is interesting as a restaging of the violent historical transition from the age of mass transport to the age of privatised or individualised transport inaugurated by the bicycle (and it exemplifies early film-makers' cavalier approach to copying). However, it is also a clear example of the way that film comedy is often organised around an intransigent object, an uncontrollable machine, or what Tom Gunning terms a 'mischief device' – 'machines whose purpose is to stop things from working, or make them work in an explosive counterproductive way'.[19]

As this film of a cyclist ploughing into a crowd suggests, the bicycle lends itself well to film comedy. The history of representations of cyclists as antisocial nuisances ensures that the bicycle has always been understood as a 'mischief device', a catastrophe machine wreaking social disorder. The film invokes an already familiar figure of the careless, selfish male cyclist, the rogue 'scorcher' who rides at breakneck speed on pavements, crashing repeatedly into pedestrians and other vehicles. The crash is one of the most common motifs in comic depictions of cycling on film, reproducing the stereotype of the cyclist as a public menace engaged in a battle for the right to move through common space, and the bicycle as an antisocial weapon. Crashes also function as a formal device for assembling extended narratives that follow the conventions of vaudeville sketches, in which a series of arresting stunts are strung together with little regard for causal logic.

This is demonstrated by another contemporary Pathé film, *La Première Sortie d'une Cycliste* [*Her First Bike Ride*] (1907). An exuberant demonstration of the comedy of crashing bicycles, and also of the way that a narrative can be assembled through repetition and variation, it is an example of what Gerald Mast terms 'riffing' – the film built around 'the performers' tendency to reappear from gag to gag and the film's unceasing rhythmic motion. Pace and motion become unifying principles in themselves'.[20] It opens with a woman buying a safety bicycle (ironically enough) in a shop, and in the second shot she takes delivery of it in her house. She rides it out of the house and onto the street, colliding immediately with a top-hatted man and a maid who are in conversation. He attacks the cyclist with a nearby broomstick as she rides away and speeds off, head down, at a furious pace. Then, as if once she's moving she can't slow down or deviate from her course, she crashes repeatedly into every obstacle she encounters, and is attacked by the victims, who kick and punch her or set off in pursuit.

Along the way she crashes into a nanny with a pram, a square-bashing soldier, decorators working up a ladder, a group enjoying a picnic in a field, a herd of sheep, a horse and cart and, finally, in a head-on collision, an automobile. In the film's best gag, she is cycling frantically along a riverbank towards a bearded artist who is painting the picturesque scene on a large canvas. She bursts head first through the canvas, crashing into the artist, a self-reflexive joke that invokes the apocryphal stories of early film audiences who panicked at the spectacle of a train appearing to emerge from the screen. It is a formally simple film, consisting entirely of long shots, each shot constituting a complete scene, but it is very fast and physical (with male stuntmen in drag doubling for some of the women), with some impressively violent crashes. The film concludes with her escaping a group of pursuing soldiers and arriving back home with a bruised and bloody face, a black eye, a torn skirt and her brand new bicycle in pieces, the frame hanging around her neck, before she collapses on the floor.

There are numerous international variations on the 'crash and chase' format: Pathé's *Runaway Cyclist* substitutes a male novice for the female cyclist (although the film ends with him being lofted triumphantly onto the shoulders of his pursuers rather than battered to a pulp); in the American film *His First Ride* (Selig, 1907) a top-hatted tramp steals a bicycle that has been left outside a shop and crashes into a variety of bystanders, including a shoe-shiner, a shopkeeper, a surveyor and, finally, a pair of policemen, still chasing him into the distance as the film ends. *La Prima Biciclette di Robinet* [*Robinet's First Bicycle*] (1910) features the imbecilic protagonist as a trainee racing cyclist pulling his coach along on a trailer and followed on foot by two assistants, who rush to sponge and massage him each time he crashes, which he does with some acrobatic flair – although, even by silent screen performance conventions, he overacts dreadfully. In *Jock's Bicycle Chase* (Clarendon Film Company, 1911) a woman on the beach attempts to escape harassment by two men by renting a bike, but they pursue her on bikes, before a stereotypical Scotsman in a kilt eventually fights them off and proposes to her. French film *Slippery Jim* (Zecca, 1910) makes liberal use of special effects (including stop-motion animation, substitution splices and double exposure) in its account of a thief who goes on the run after being tied up inside a sack and thrown into the river to drown by the police, who are frustrated by his repeated success in escaping from their jail. After leaping out of the water he assembles a bicycle magically from parts folded inside his jacket and rides off. The police give chase, and he leaps onto the roof of a passing train, jumps and somersaults magically back and forth across a canal and then collides with one of the police officers, slicing him in two as he rides over him. A nearby bill poster uses his paste brush to stick the two halves back together.

The most refined of these films is the Italian comedy *Tontolini Ruba una Bicicleta* [*Tontolini Steals a Bicycle*] (1910), featuring the hugely prolific Ferdinand Guillaume, who ended his career performing in films by Fellini and Pasolini, but had established himself initially through the trickster characters Tontolini and Polidor; these featured in dozens of self-reflexive short slapstick comedies in a variety of potentially comic scenarios (as described in the titles), including a visit to the theatre, driving a car, going to the circus, winning the lottery and undergoing hypnosis. *Tontolini Ruba una Bicicleta* begins with Tontolini, a ragged-trousered precursor of Chaplin in torn hat and clown shoes, happening upon a bicycle that a telegram messenger has leant against a wall, casually looking around to make sure he is unobserved and then making off with it. Bicycle theft is a regular theme in early comedies, and, in this respect, *The Bicycle Thieves* (De Sica, 1948) is a reworking of a well-established cinematic trope. Indeed, the opening shot of *Tontolini Ruba una Bicicleta* is reproduced almost exactly in the final scene of De Sica's film, with the protagonist, Ricci, finally resorting to stealing a bike himself, having failed to retrieve his own. This appropriation – or theft – is an indication that the politicised aesthetic of Italian neorealism has deep roots in popular cinema.

After Tontolini steals the bike, a comical group of policemen, inept ancestors of the Keystone Kops, is summoned, and they march off in pursuit, along with the messenger. A nanny with a pram – a frequent target for these incompetent cyclists – and a wedding party join the chase after Tontolini crashes into them, and the film introduces a novel special effect when Tontolini rides into a wall and rebounds, now cycling backwards in reverse motion, so that he and the chasing group (including a horse and cart) are all travelling backwards. At the climax, having smashed spectacularly through a display of several hundred tins stacked invitingly on the pavement outside a grocery shop, Tontolini cycles magically across the surface of a pond while the pursuers all sink to their chests in the water. The final shot, which is spatially and stylistically distinct from the rest of the film, constitutes an apotheosis and shows Tontolini, floating against a black sky, looking back over his shoulder and still pedalling frantically, as if he has transcended the physical limitations of an earth-bound body and is now flying through space or another dimension.

More than any other film genre, slapstick comedy is concerned with the ballistics of bodily movement, the uncanny relationship between bodies, machines and other objects, and the variety of pleasurable ways in which this can be depicted.

Writing about the Keystone Studios films, a laboratory of slapstick screen comedy, Gerald Mast notes:

Figures ran after things they wanted to avoid, ran over mountains, over dangerous ledges, fields, beaches. If they didn't run they rode – in cars, in boats, on animals, on bikes. And they kept running from the start of the film until they smashed into something that stopped them.... By using human beings as projectiles and missiles, Sennett offered the conversion of people into 'Bergsonian' things.[21]

The bicycle is a particularly effective machine for converting humans into crash-test dummies, and the comedy of seeing cyclists flung around like puppets derives partly from the way that this captures our own experience of riding bicycles. From our first attempts to ride as infants, no matter how skilful we may be at handling a bike, the possibility of crashing is always present. As writer Paul Fournel observes, reflecting on the inevitability of collisions (in a passage that could be a commentary on life in general),

[e]very cyclist, even a beginner, knows that at any moment in his life he could have a rendezvous with a door. It could open in front of him at any time, from the right, the left, at the moment he least expects it, at a bend in the street, at an intersection, right in the middle of a straight and clear road.[22]

Cycling is characterised by a perpetual, vertiginous low-level anxiety – heightened when we are negotiating traffic and pedestrians – and so one of the pleasures of watching characters crash comically and painlessly on film is the cathartic release of tension.

Comedy and Complicity

As Jacques Tati observes, a central characteristic of laughter is its social function: 'Laughing together is easier than laughing alone.... The oldest spring of comedy is simply the pleasure that a group of people feel on being together.'[23] Comedy films are much funnier when viewed in a packed cinema, and one of the pleasures of comedy is the transient sense of community it generates. 'However spontaneous it seems,' Henri Bergson writes, 'laughter always implies a kind of freemasonry, or even complicity with other laughers, real or imaginary.'[24] The spectacle of suffering cyclists on the screen is thus ambivalently pleasurable, since it invites an identification with a familiar experience or sensation, but also implies a contemptuous superiority of the viewer over the unfortunate victim. 'In laughter, we always find an unavowed intention to humiliate, and consequently to correct our neighbour, if not in his will, at least in his deed.'[25]

Rather less bleakly, Mast observes that the demolition derbies of slapstick screen comedy are exuberantly iconoclastic: 'The greatest comedies of all throw a custard pie (sometimes literally) in the face of social forms and assumptions. The greatest film comedians are antisocial, but in this antagonism they reveal a higher morality.'[26] In the face of modernity's preoccupation with growth and progress, the destructive tendencies of slapstick comedians are deeply subversive. In their hands, the bicycle is a mischief device that travels round in circles, goes backwards, performs somersaults and falls apart, and only very rarely moves forwards. Although silent slapstick comedy is rarely realistic in its reliance on exaggeration, illogicality and a disregard for physics, nevertheless it can be an effective form of social commentary. While we might imagine history as a steady movement towards a more enlightened, just and equal society, film comedy reminds us how wildly optimistic this assumption is. Cinema and the bicycle are both marvellous symbols of industrial and scientific progress, but in the hands of these film-makers and comic performers what emerges is a perverse parody of a modern world peopled by efficient, skilled workers:

All social theories for human improvement, all attempts at social or technological progress, the unshakeable faith in reason, science, and social justice of our own century (and the two preceding it), are built on the assumption that human life is perfectible.... Comedy's assumption is the opposite: there is change, but not progress. Human and social life does not move unswervingly in one direction, in a line, but in a circle. Perhaps that is why so many of the greatest film comedies (especially those of Chaplin, Renoir, and Lubitsch) are circular.[27]

They are circular both in their refusal of the possibility of progress and in their reliance upon repetition, and the circular movement of the bicycle wheel symbolises this perfectly.

Performance Enhancement: Jacques Tati and the Bicycle

Scenes of comically inept cycling, hideously painful crashes or sublime acrobatics are all examples of virtuoso, technically accomplished screen performances. Although they affect us in different ways, making us laugh out loud, wince and close our eyes, or gasp, they make us similarly aware of our own bodies as spectators, inviting us to feel the sensations experienced by these twisting, folding, crumpling bodies, as they move in exaggerated, impossible ways. At the same time, they highlight the contrast between our own immobile frames and the disciplined bodies catapulting through screen space in front of us. As Alan Dale observes of Harold Lloyd, such stunts are impressively athletic:

[I]n the 1917 two-reeler, *Lonesome Luke on Tin Can Alley*, he rides a bicycle through a restaurant kitchen rolling over a counter on his back without unseating himself or taking his feet off the pedals. In these sequences Lloyd invents strange new Olympic events.[28]

However, it is Jacques Tati, more than any other film-maker, who approaches film comedy as if it were an Olympic sport. He explores the cinematic significance of the bicycle more systematically than any other major director, in a series of films that reflect upon the industrialisation and automation of modern life. From his second film, *Gai Dimanche* (1935), onwards, his films feature 'an amazing range of vehicles...as if from this point on Tati would never escape the contradictory passions attached throughout the twentieth century to the privileges and servitudes of individual mobility.'[29]

Although he directed only six feature films, his methodical approach to choreography and the relation between sound and image, and his preoccupation with film technology, ensured Tati's status as one of the most sophisticated directors of the twentieth century. He was involved in all stages of the production process, so that, as well as performing and directing, he wrote the scripts, edited, and devised the intricate sound design of the films. Whereas mainstream cinema is typically preoccupied with the psychological development of individual characters and the dramas of interpersonal conflict and intimacy, Tati's films are as interested in environments as they are in the bodies that travel through them; Brent Maddock writes: 'Tati's films are not so much stories or character studies as they are explorations of the systems and structures that make up society: architecture, transportation, the home, time-saving appliances and the vacation.'[30] The bicycle is one of the key vehicles through which Tati's films examine these systems and networks, as well as questions of national identity in post-war French culture, exposed to the forces of economic globalisation and Americanisation.

The bicycle also signifies a continuity between popular theatre and cinema comedy. Tati's performing career began with 'Sporting Impressions', a stage act in which he mimed several sporting activities, including ballooning, tennis, boxing and cycling.

Although 'Sporting Impressions' was not documented on film, it is reprised indirectly in his third extant short film,[31] *Soigne ton Gauche* [*Work on Your Left*] (Clément, 1936), a comedy about lethargic farmhand Roger (Tati), who is recruited as a sparring partner after a trainer notices him miming a boxing match. The film opens with a postman cycling frantically through the French countryside and then somersaulting into a farmyard to deliver a telegram. The following scene introduces

a group of children pretending to be newsreel reporters at the closing stage of the Tour de France, with an overgrown child – Jacques Tati – acting out the final sprint, the victory handclasp, and the winner's breathless speech into the toy microphone: a little world of make-believe sporting achievement.[32]

After the boxing ring collapses and Roger manages to knock out the formidable-looking champ, the film concludes with the children – who are still pretending to be a newsreel crew, 'filming' events with farmyard junk – conducting a post-fight interview with Tati. The Chaplinesque final shot shows the postman cycling into the distance, 'filmed' by one of the children. Framed by a child's perspective, the film finally suggests that the adult worlds of work, professional sport and film-making are all a matter of childish play and simulation, a theme that runs through all Tati's films.

Tati's next film, *L'École des Facteurs* [*The School for Postmen*] (Tati, 1946), places the figure of the rural cycling postman at the centre of the film. *L'École des Facteurs* is a film about the accelerationist impulse driving industrialised modernity and the application of Taylorist approaches to improve the productivity and speed of the rural postal service. The film begins with a military-style briefing as a shrill, uniformed official uses a blackboard to explain the schedule by which the postmen must deliver their mail to the mail plane, shaving off 25 seconds through 'extensive training'. The camera then pans around to show three postmen cycling on rollers. 'Work those calves, gentlemen!' he instructs, and leads them through 'an efficiency ballet', rehearsing the sequence of movements involved in delivering a letter.[33] To the instructor's exasperation, François (Tati) completes each sequence involuntarily by miming taking a swig from a glass, explaining that sometimes they're offered drinks. After being informed they are 'first-class graduates for distributing national mail' they are each sent off with a stack of letters, and the film proceeds with a string of slapstick gags. François grabs onto the tailgate of a passing truck, using it as a desk to sort and frank letters; he loses his bike when the gates at a level crossing lift it into the air; and he encounters a series of obstacles in trying to deliver letters, getting a letter stuck to his hand with glue, handing a parcel to the charcutier, who chops it in half with a cleaver, and chasing after his bicycle after it is accidentally towed away by a truck and heads off as if it has a mind of its own. He catches up with it outside Bondu's café, where the owner forces a glass of wine on him, before he dashes out at the sound of the mail plane flying overhead. He careers across country, causing a car crash, nonchalantly overtakes a peloton of racing cyclists and finally manages to hook his mailbag onto the tailplane of the taxiing aircraft, giving a thumbs-up as it flies away.

François is a comic caricature, unshaven, muttering indistinctly 'in an exaggerated countryside accent' that marks him out as a 'rural idiot',[34] wearing army boots and trousers and a jacket that are too short, emphasising his gangling frame. However, Tati's physical performance in this virtually dialogue-free film is deft and precisely timed, even as he goes through his frantic dance of hesitations, falls, collisions, pirouettes and missteps. The unruly bicycle is a prop for an acrobatic performance, and, beside Tati's tall frame, his bicycle looks comically small and fragile. The 16-minute film touches on several themes that become prominent in Tati's subsequent films, including nostalgia for the sleepy pace of pre-war life in the French countryside (*la France profonde*), the signs of Americanisation sweeping across Europe and the emergence of a militarised, 'scientific' managerial culture that treats employees as machines.

Jour de Fête and the Speed of Change

Tati's first feature film, *Jour de Fête*, is far more explicitly critical in its examination of questions of nationhood and modernity. This is evident even in the use of a new colour process to shoot the film, intended to make *Jour de Fête* both the first French feature film shot in colour and, crucially, a film made with a new colour process devised by a French company.[35] It was thus conceived, in part, as a patriotic demonstration of the competitive strength and technological advancement of the French film industry. Unfortunately for Tati, Thomsoncolor was a flawed technology, and the Thomson–Houston Electric Company closed the processing labs before the film was completed. The film-makers were able to avoid total disaster by releasing a black and white print from a second camera that Tati had, prudently, used as a back-up in case the new technology failed.[36]

Jour de Fête is an expanded reworking of *L'École des Facteurs*, and covers the 24 hours from the arrival of a travelling fair in the small village of Sainte-Sévère-sur-Indre, through the festivities of a holiday, to the dismantling and departure of the fair on the following day. Tati again plays François and reproduces exactly a number of the gags employed in the previous film, although the narrative focus of the film is distributed between François and the activities surrounding the fair. The events are framed with a running commentary offered by a hunched old woman, the village gossip, wryly observing the activities around her. The film opens with the early morning arrival of the itinerant fairground workers, towing a caravan and trailer behind a tractor. They install themselves in the village square and begin to set up the stalls and the carousel while the villagers emerge and begin to prepare for the festival, some of them attempting to erect a flagpole. François then appears, cycling along on his old Peugeot bicycle while trying to dodge a pursuing wasp. He is talked into helping erect the flagpole by two of the fairground workers, Roger and Marçel, who immediately recognise François as a figure of fun, and then proceeds with his route while a marching band assembles and the setting up of the fair continues. Delivering a letter to the café on the square, François repairs the pianola and joins in enthusiastically with the scrum of dancing people crammed into the café. He is offered a couple of glasses of wine by a villager, and then Roger and Marçel trick him by replacing his wine with cognac and encouraging him to down it quickly. Now drunk, François is called over to the cinema tent, where a documentary about the modernisation of the US postal service, *La Poste en Amérique*, is being screened.

After watching this film about the speed and heroism of American postmen through an opening in the canvas, and having been teased by some of the villagers ('What'd the Americans do with a mailman like you?'), a despondent François returns to the bar and resumes drinking, continuing on into the night. Later, the two fairground workers return to the bar and play another practical joke on him, giving him a black eye by tricking him into looking through a horn, before François wanders off muttering that he has mail to deliver. In a classic slapstick sequence, François, who is by now blind drunk and weaving all over the road, attempts to cycle on his route in the dark, climbing astride a fence thinking it's his bike, crashing into an apple tree, which showers him with fruit, and then a bush – where he is once again bothered by the wasp. After being shot at by a farmer he has roused from sleep, he climbs inside a cattle truck and slides the door shut.

Waking the next morning as the truck is shunted into a railway siding, François retrieves his bike, throwing the insult 'English!' at one of the railway workers, and rides back to the square, where he encounters Roger and Marçel. Picking up where they left off the previous night, they begin to advise him on American postal techniques. Persuading him to sit on a bicycle on their carousel, they show him how to jump on and off a moving bicycle, swinging his postbag around his neck as he does so. François cycles back to the post office, where he realises, seeing his reflection in his locker mirror, that he has a black eye from the previous night's prank. Irritated by this, and also by the slow pace of his two colleagues silently franking letters in the office, he declares: 'The Americans are right. Speed! Speed!' and heads off to deliver his letters at full pelt in a sequence reproduced more or less exactly from *L'École des Facteurs*, with sometimes identical composition and locations. 'François is delivering American-style,' the baker's boy observes, and several bystanders shout: 'Allez, allez!' when he passes, as if they are spectators at a race. Struggling to follow the baker's boy on his motorcycle, pedalling fast with his head down, François finally cycles straight off a bend and into the river. The film concludes with the crooked old woman giving him a lift back into town on her cart as he explains: 'I just wanted to be fast.' 'The Americans can do as they please,' she responds, 'but the world won't turn any quicker!'

François joins some villagers gathering hay in a field, and one of them sends a young boy to finish François's route, reiterating the theme that adults are really just oversized children. François pauses from collecting hay to watch the fairground convoy travel past the field, and, in the final shot of the film, the boy, wearing François's cap and bag, skips along behind the wooden horses projecting from the back of the trailer. The film thus concludes with a restatement of the idea that the adult world is really – or, at least, should be – a matter of child's play.

Cyclical Rhythms

Circularity is a central motif in *Jour de Fête*. It is evident in the narrative structure of the film, which loops back on itself so that at the end of the film we return to the beginning. Recounting events across 24 hours, the film describes the village during one revolution of the Earth, while the film's protagonist, François, makes his living doing 'rounds' or circuits of the area. Circularity is a visual motif too, articulated by the carousel at the centre of the village, travelling in circles but moving nowhere, and, most of all, by the spinning wheels of François's bicycle. Circularity is also a feature of the film's history, since *Jour de Fête* is not an autonomous work but belongs to a series of iterations. Beginning with Tati's 'Sporting Impressions' act, which itself originated in after-dinner performances he gave at social gatherings with his rugby club, Tati's comedy cycling routine is reiterated in *Soigne ton Gauche, L'École des Facteurs*, the three versions of *Jour de Fête*, a stage version, *Jour de Fête à L'Olympia* (1961), and the short film *Cours du Soir* (1967). In *Mon Oncle* (Tati, 1958), meanwhile, the protagonist, M. Hulot (Tati), is out of step with the pace of modernisation and Americanisation taking place around him, and this is indicated by his choice of vehicle: a French

45cc VéloSoleX motorised bicycle rather than the gleaming, streamlined Chevrolets, Oldsmobiles and Studebakers that fill the streets around him.

If circularity and repetition are a feature of Tati's approach to film-making and comic storytelling – as David Bellos observes, most of Tati's physical gags are done twice,[37] always with a slight variation the second time around – they are also features of the mechanics of the worlds depicted on screen. As the sardonic fairground worker, Marcel, observes of the villagers' failure to erect the huge flagpole, 'I don't think they were in rhythm', and, in one respect, this observation applies to many of the characters in the film, who move at varying speeds and frequencies. François, a loner with no immediate family or friends, moves at a different rhythm from the world around him, as symbolised by his singular, rubber-legged polka-dancing to the pianola in Bondu's café. He has an ambivalent social status within the village, since he is teased by some of his villagers, but is also treated with indulgent compassion.

Tati's initial portrayal of him as a uniformed, self-important buffoon resembling the wartime leader of free France, General Charles de Gaulle, lends the film a satirical edge, but, while François displays a laughable lack of self-awareness or physical coordination, over the course of the film he emerges as a positive figure of nonconformity. In some respects *Jour de Fête* is a gentle, nostalgic comedy presenting an image of France as timeless and rural, its economy organised around agriculture rather than industry. However, while it offers a comforting depiction of village life, with everybody knowing one another, in contrast to the alienated condition of urban modernity, the film is concerned with the threat to this way of life, identifying the threat as automation and Americanisation.

The arrival of the fair disrupts the rhythms of the village, and this is encapsulated by the cinema tent screening American films, thereby representing the threat to a ravaged French film industry posed by the thousands of US films that a liberated French population now had access to. The films screened are a western, *Les Rivaux d'Arizona*, starring 'Jim Parkers' and 'Gloria Parson', and the postal documentary, the propaganda film that prompts François to speed around the village 'American-style' the following day. We see only glimpses of the film, which include shots of men being lowered from a helicopter, picked up by a low-flying plane, performing stunts on motorbikes and posing on stage in a bodybuilding competition. The documentary's voice-over predicts that '[i]n the future each postman will spend an hour a day in training' for delivery by helicopter, declaring: 'Nothing stops the Yankee postman. If the road ends, he flies.' The voice-over continues: 'In some cases a mailman can be a hero'; and, over shots of bodybuilders posing in briefs, the commentary observes: 'Each year in Oklahoma a competition is held to find the sexiest Apollo in the US Mail. Ladies, would you like your mailman to ring your bell dressed this way?'

The final section of *Jour de Fête*, in which François races around the countryside at breakneck speed, demonstrates the incompatibility between the traditional tempo of French village life and machinic American efficiency (while also affording an opportunity to enjoy Tati's virtuoso bike-handling). As François accelerates, his deliveries become more erratic, and he slaps an envelope on one man's head, sticks letters under a door knocker and a horse's tail and drops a letter down a well, in a man's hat and into the funnel of a threshing machine. Finally, he tosses a parcel containing a pair of new shoes onto the butcher's chopping block, which is sliced in two by the butcher, who is busy cutting up meat. François continues to race around, shouldering his bike and heading across country, overtaking a peloton of cycle racers – once more an essential feature of the French countryside after the reintroduction of the Tour de France in 1947 – eventually coming to an undignified halt in the river. Whereas, in *L'École des Facteurs*, Francois successfully achieves the efficiencies demanded by his supervisor, managing to reach the airfield in time to attach his mailbag to the departing plane, in *Jour de Fête* he fails. He cannot maintain the heroic rhythms and tempos of the modern American postal service or the cyborg-like integration with machines, but this failure constitutes a rejection and ridiculing of the productive regime he aspires to. When he encounters a couple of US military policemen lounging by the side of the road on their jeep, François picks up the receiver of a broken telephone strapped to the front of his bicycle and pretends to be speaking to somebody in New York. Amazed at this spectacle of new technology, the two soldiers follow François in the jeep before veering off into a field in their astonishment. Ridiculously, these Apollos are tricked by the sight of somebody pretending to have a conversation with a broken phone. In the restored colour version of the film, François mutters: 'To hell with the Americans!' as he rides away.

The film concludes with a rejection of time-saving, the cult of productivity and the subordination of the individual to the dehumanising, rationalised rhythms of industrial modernity. As Michel Chion observes in his study of Tati's films,

François on his bike meanders his way through lines, curves, detours. Yet the letters he carries manage to reach their destination. The day he follows a straight bee-line doesn't promise better results. Catastrophe lies waiting around the corner. [...] The person expecting the letter risks not receiving it, because the straight line leads François right into a river.[38]

The film's argument is crystallised in a single shot in which a large black car screeches to a halt as François is pushing his bike across the street in the centre of the village. François stops, glaring at the impatient driver, who is revving his engine, and then slowly walks forwards, forcing the driver to wait until he has passed. In the context of this film, the bicycle symbolises tradition, continuity and the nonchalant French character, while the car symbolises speed, change, modernity and aggressive Americanisation.

Jour de Fête won the prize for 'Best Scenario' at the 1949 Venice International Film Festival and the Grand Prix at Cannes in 1950, although its reception was mixed, since it was released at a moment when war films were becoming a staple of French cinema.[39] Moreover, French cinema had been dominated since the 1930s by a mode of '"intimate realism" [that] concerned itself with the family unit and its day-to-day activity. No explorations were made, as in the Italian Neorealism, of man in connection with his society.'[40] Tati's film, by contrast, was a unique fusion of silent slapstick comedy with an ethnographic documentary of French rural life in the village in which he spent several months during the war to avoid forced labour, and in which almost all the village inhabitants appear on screen (except, ironically, the village's 12 postmen, who were employed as technical advisers).[41]

The parallel identified by Brent Maddock between Italian neorealist cinema and Tati's film is instructive. Like the classics of neorealism, *Jour de Fête* was shot on location with non-professional actors and on a restricted budget, and, as with the contemporaneous work of directors such as Roberto Rossellini and Vittorio De Sica, Tati's film is concerned with working-class experience in post-war (post-fascist) Europe, and with the complex networks of social relations that constitute a community. The cycling postman personifies the communications infrastructure that ties the community together as he delivers produce, parcels and death notices. He is also a convenient device through which to explore this community, since he provides the narrative pretext for introducing a wide variety of characters. While the film's politics is non-partisan, it is underlined by a humanist sympathy for ordinary people. There are no heroes but, instead, a broad variety of characters and types, many of whom are prejudiced, impatient or ungenerous, and this unsentimental depiction of the village undercuts the possibility of a simplistic nationalistic discourse. As David Bellos recounts, *Jour de Fête* was shot against the background of the 1946 Blum–Byrnes agreement, which revised the pre-war protectionist quota system that restricted the numbers of foreign films imported into France.[42] This revived concerns about cultural and economic imperialism that have preoccupied European film industries and critics since the First World War, and helps to explain *Jour de Fête*'s surprising bitterness at the presence of Americans and elements of US culture on French soil: 'It heaps ridicule on America barely two years after the final defeat of the greatest evil France and Europe had ever known. Who could guess from watching this film that less than three years before the shoot began the Gestapo still had an office on the main square of Sainte-Sévère?'[43]

However, there is an ambivalence underlying this resentment or anxiety, evident in the fact that what the film offers as a rejoinder to the figure of the muscular, militarised, technologically augmented US mailman is François. Rather than an airborne 'Apollo', he is an ungainly, inarticulate and earthbound figure who struggles to control his bike, or even to repair a puncture, who is teased and patronised by his neighbours but who nevertheless aspires to be as fast as an American. Far from a rejection of American cultural imperialism, he is the embodiment of the fusion of French and American cinema. In one of the film's final gags, François cycles over a patch of wet tar and comes to a halt, his wheel spinning in the tar until the road worker tosses a shovelful of sand onto the tar; François's tyre then finds some grip, and he shoots off. It is a scaled-down repetition of a gag from *The General* (Keaton, Bruckman, 1926) in which the wheels of Keaton's locomotive are spinning until he throws dirt on the tracks to provide some friction. François's modest emulation of the speed and power of the American mailman is doubled by the film-makers' modest emulation of the spectacle of Hollywood cinema.

The parallels between Italian neorealism and *Jour de Fête* extend beyond thematic and historical affinities. From this film onwards, a distinctive feature of Tati's cinema is an almost complete reliance upon wide or long shots. Maddock suggests that this approach is a sign of Tati's background on the stage, the director effectively treating the film frame like a proscenium arch, but it has a broad political significance in so far as it affords the spectator a greater freedom to decide where to direct her attention: 'In his democratic concept of comedy, he believes the audience should not be forced into watching only what the director wants them to watch.'[44] While François is a hero of sorts, the film is equally interested in what is taking place around him, and, indeed, in Tati's subsequent films the protagonist, M. Hulot, has an increasingly marginal role.

As André Bazin observes, a striking feature of post-war Italian cinema was a new realism or authenticity that was an effect, in part, of similar stylistic choices. Whereas 'classical' cinema relies upon a complex montage of long, medium and close-up shots to direct the spectator through the narrative and through the screen space, neorealist cinema relied upon long takes and long shots in presenting stories to the spectator. As a result, '[i]t is no longer the editing that selects what we see, thus giving it an *a priori* significance, it is the mind of the spectator which is forced to discern...the dramatic spectrum proper to the screen.'[45] And so, although there would seem to be a gulf between the polemical documentary aesthetic of neorealist films such as *The Bicycle Thieves* and the gentle slapstick of Tati's cinema, the films invite us in quite similar ways to study and reflect upon the environments of the modern world and the individuals trying to navigate them.

3

The Hard Labour of Cycling

Figure 3.1
Bruno (Enzo Staiola) proudly watches his father, Ricci (Lamberto Maggiorani), preparing for his first day in a new job in *Ladri di Biciclette* [*The Bicycle Thieves*] (De Sica, 1948) (© Produzione De Sica/Kobal/REX/ Shutterstock)

On Your Bike

Cycling is work. No matter how fit the cyclist and how light the machine, riding a bicycle demands physical effort. In *Bad to the Bone*, a magic realist novel about cycle racing, doping and serial killing, James Waddington suggests that 'a racing cyclist [is] a protein machine that converts carbohydrate into heat and energy at an exorbitant rate. Matter to movement. Sweat 'n' spirit. Shit 'n' dreams.'[1] This mechanistic analysis of the corporeal economy of cycle racing applies equally well to any form of cycling. When we cycle, our bodies convert food and drink into heat and movement; whether we are transporting goods, travelling somewhere or riding on a stationary exercise bike, cycling involves building muscle, burning calories, raising the heart rate and disciplining the body, preparing it for further work, as well as enjoying the pleasures and physical pain of labour.

As is documented in many films, the bicycle is also a means by which people can do work in the economic sense, 'the contractual exchange of a certain amount of productive time for a wage.'[2] Among the various meanings the image of the bicycle conveys, perhaps the dominant connotation is work. The first film, which shows a number of cyclists among the workers leaving the Lumière factory in Lyon, cements the association between work and the bicycle. This image reaches its apotheosis in an American factory-gate film from 1899, showing

nearly a hundred employees of the Detroit drug firm Parke-Davis leaving work – on bicycles. Upright women in dresses and high-collared shorts make up a surprising number of the bicycle commuters, mixed in among men in suits, ties and hats.[3]

Tracking the movement of bicycles across cinema allows us to see the variety of ways in which work is conceptualised and the way that concepts of work shift historically. However, the bicycle has an ambiguous significance with regard to work, since, although it is firmly associated with employment, it also promises escape from work. This is indicated by the documentary *Spare Time* (1939), directed by Humphrey Jennings for the GPO Film Unit. A poetic record of the range of leisure activities undertaken by labourers in heavy industry such as coal miners and cotton mill workers, the film includes a short sequence showing Sheffield steel workers riding into the countryside on their bikes and drinking in a country pub. Reflecting on the emergence of the expressions 'free time' and 'spare time', Theodor Adorno proposed that the belief that there are areas of everyday life in capitalist society that are 'autonomous' was misguided. Rather, the temporary escape from wearying, physically damaging labour allows people to work harder, making it possible for them to do this work by offering them brief intervals of recovery.

Free time is shackled to its opposite.... [F]ree time depends on the totality of social conditions, which continues to hold people under its spell. Neither in their work, nor in their consciousness do people dispose of genuine freedom over themselves.[4]

Cycling, like other leisure activities, enables some of us to cope with work.

Tracing the cinematic history of workers on bicycles allows us also to track the changing nature of labour across the last 120 years – in Europe and the United States in particular – as an industrial economy underpinned by resource extraction and manufacturing gives way to a post-industrial information and service economy. This is embodied by the twin figures of the factory worker, riding to and from work, and the bicycle messenger. However, as is suggested by the Vietnamese film *Cyclo* (Hung, 1995), which is about an orphaned teenager who makes a hard living as a 'cyclo' – bicycle rickshaw – driver in the punishing heat of Ho Chi Minh City in the 1990s before joining a gang when his vehicle is stolen, these transformations take place at different speeds in different places.

The Cyclist (*Bicycle-Ran*)[5] (1989), an early film by Iranian new wave film-maker Mohsen Makhmalbaf, is one of the most single-minded examinations of the work of cycling in cinema.[6] It tells the story of Nasim, an impoverished, taciturn Afghan immigrant in Iran who scrapes a living by digging wells with his son, Jomeh, but cannot afford to pay the bills for his wife, who is dying in hospital. It transpires that he was a cycling champion in Afghanistan who 'once rode three days around the clock', but now he is middle-aged and weary. A businessman and former circus ringmaster learns of this and, realising the potential for lucrative exploitation when Nasim tries to borrow money, organises a seven-day endurance trial. As he explains to a colleague, 'I've found a real desperate guy. He was made to bet on. He's a former champion.... His wife is dying.' He provides Nasim with a bike – a black Flying Pigeon, the Chinese bicycle that was emblematic of the egalitarian agenda and ethos of selfless labour underpinning Mao Zedong's Cultural Revolution – and Nasim begins to ride, first of all in small circles around a pond in the organiser's yard, and later, after a sabotage attempt, around a town square. The organiser sells tickets and people begin to gather, some selling food and trinkets or playing music while a medical team stands by, taking urine samples and preparing food supplements in their ambulance. There are various attempts to disrupt the feat, including slipping Nasim Valium, puncturing his tyres and offering him money to give up, but, when he falls off his bike on the third night, his friend jumps on the bike in disguise since the referee has also fallen asleep, allowing the exhausted Nasim to recover. By the fifth night he is using matchsticks to keep his eyes open while Jomeh throws water over him and slaps him repeatedly. He manages to keep going until the seventh day, an IV drip attached to his bike by this point, and upon completing the feat he is mobbed by spectators and journalists with cameras, one firing questions at him, including 'What's your opinion about prosperity?' and 'What was your motivation?' However, it is far from a euphoric climax, since at the film's end he continues to ride in circles while Jomeh tries to persuade him the race is over, and his wife struggles to reach an oxygen mask from her hospital bed.

Makhmalbaf's film depicts cycling as draining physical labour and draws a parallel between Nasim's feat of endurance and the punishing work done by other Afghan labourers in Iran, digging wells and ditches (in between trying to avoid police raids on their accommodation). The desperate misery of the immigrants' situation – a recurrent theme for Makhmalbaf – is made explicit early on when Nasim attempts suicide, placing his head under the wheels of a bus. Although the scenario was based on Makhmalbaf's childhood memory of seeing a Pakistani cyclist trying to ride for ten days to raise money for flood victims in Pakistan, it is a film about cinema that invokes *The Bicycle Thieves* with its focus upon the relationship between depressed father and tolerant, loving son. It also includes a scene in which Jomeh sits in a café watching *They Shoot Horses, Don't They?* (Pollack, 1969), a New Hollywood film about a Depression-era dance marathon in which contestants danced until they dropped, competing to win a cash prize. Moreover, rather than offering reassuring narrative closure, in a classic avant-garde gesture, the final shots of the film lay bare the illusionistic mechanism of film-making, showing us the crane-mounted film camera that pans to follow Moharram Zaynalzadeh (Nasim) as he cycles around it. We are left not with a sense of satisfaction but, rather, with the impression of perpetual motion, the final moments of the film implying that Nasim, the camera operator and the reels of film inside the camera will continue to revolve indefinitely. This sense of constant motion conveys powerfully the rootless, nomadic subjectivity of the migrant labourer, and so the bicycle is a perfect symbol for this experience of continual, anxious social, cultural and geographical displacement.

The degrading pointlessness of Nasim's cycle labour is emphasised by the motif of circles running through the film; rather than making any progress, Nasim rides around endlessly in small circles, echoing the motorcycle wall of death that we see in the film's opening, the circular well shaft that Nasim is digging, the tyres of the bus and, of course, the wheels of his bicycle. The panning camera, spinning around inside the wall of death and following Nasim's relentless and painfully slow movement, places further visual emphasis on the spectacle of unremitting effort, suggesting also a connection between professional sport and punishing manual labour.

As well as *requiring* the cyclist to work, the bicycle also *enables* women and men to work in various ways. Bicycles allow people to commute greater distances to work, or to travel in search of work, and, historically, this increased mobility played a role in urban expansion. In Vietnam (or French Indo-China) in the early 1900s, for example,

The bicycle transformed everyday life, making it possible for low- and middle-level clerks and functionaries to work in the private and public offices in central Saigon and Hanoi and still live further out, thereby encouraging the development of suburbs and the integration of the rural hinterland into the economic activity and social patterns of the city.[7]

One of the most dynamic depictions of the bicycle's role as enabler is in the opening scenes of *Kuhle Wampe, or: Who Owns the World?* (Dudrow, 1932). Written and co-directed by Bertolt Brecht, the film portrays the desperate, punitive conditions of some residents of 1930s Berlin, centring upon one family who are evicted from their apartment and are forced to live in 'Kuhle Wampe', a tent colony outside the city. A demonstration of Brecht's interest in producing intellectually and politically engaging artworks through formal experimentation and the use of popular modes, the film consists of four sections interspersed with songs and montage sequences. In the opening chapter, 'One Unemployed Man Less', a montage of shots of the city and newspaper headlines recording rising unemployment is followed by shots of scores of people, mostly on bicycles, gathering by the roadside. A newspaper man arrives and is mobbed by the crowd, which is waiting for news of the latest vacancies. Groups of them then hare around the city, cycling from one factory to another in a literal race for jobs, the shots of speeding bicycles functioning as a symbol of the desperation to find employment. Indeed, when the son throws himself from a window after being harangued for his laziness by his father (who, ironically, is himself unemployed), we see another image of frantically pedalled bicycles, and then a shot of his own bike hanging from the empty apartment ceiling. There is also a shot of his wristwatch laid on the window sill, a sombre symbol of mortality and the tyranny of rationalised time management he has escaped. This section dramatises the way that the bicycle mobilises the labourer, enabling him to work, but, as Brecht writes, 'the film shows the search for work as work itself'.[8] Even in the face of mass unemployment, in a society dominated by what David Frayne terms the 'work dogma', non-work is not a viable option.[9]

Although *Kuhle Wampe* is concerned with the aftermath of the global economic crisis of the 1920s, the motif of the unemployed cyclist retains its currency. *The Middle of the World* [*O Caminho das Nuvens*] (Amorim, 2003) tells the story of a Brazilian family who cycle 2,000 miles to Rio de Janeiro in search of work: Romão, Rose and their five children on four bikes, the youngest of whom is a baby. Romão, a former truck driver, describes himself as 'a man of destiny' and will not settle for a job that pays less than 1,000 reals, an unrealistic ambition for an unskilled labourer. Thus, their journey in this road movie is motivated as much by masculine pride as by economic reality. Throughout the film the rest of the family find ways of earning money along the route, singing, playing music, making hammocks – even stealing from a church donation box – but Romão remains preoccupied by self-pity, complaining to Rose: 'I'm not a man if I can't provide for my wife and kids. How can you put up with a man who doesn't give you a decent life?' At the same time, he is a distant father who is indifferent to his family's wretched situation. 'I can't stand the road anymore,' Rose tells him as they apply for a job in the Caminho das Nuvens resort, performing on stage for tourists as 'real Pataxo Indians'. 'I can't stand the bicycles. I can't stand seeing the kids go hungry.' However, Romão cannot stand the humiliation of performing ethnicity, and walks off stage at the first show. They eventually arrive in Rio de Janeiro, and in the final scene they look out over the city from beneath the statue of Christ. However, with his family having spent six months travelling to Rio, washing in rivers, camping in empty houses and bus shelters, encountering violent drifters, begging and starving, it seems that the perpetually disgruntled Romão is now thinking about pressing on to Brasília.

Bicycles are the contraption through which family relations are mediated, the means by which the self-important but useless father imposes his will on his reluctant family, but, as in *Kuhle Wampe*, this machine for mobilising the labour force and conveying the unemployed to work is also the object of energy-sapping work. Whereas road movies are typically preoccupied with free movement, *The Middle of the World* proposes that roads, like many public spaces, are socially stratified. For this impoverished family, consigned to the hard shoulder, travelling along the open road is dangerous and tedious.

As well as transporting women and men to the workplace, bicycles have also been important tools for various jobs, enabling postal workers to deliver mail more speedily, soldiers to undertake reconnaissance and cover ground more quickly than on foot, policemen and women to patrol the streets, street merchants to sell ice cream and peanuts over greater areas, and delivery workers to transport bread or meat.[10] In the most clichéd image of national occupations, Breton farmers, the French 'Onion Johnnies', crossed the Channel to Britain to peddle their wares on bicycles from the 1920s through to the post-war period. In American silent comedy *Bill Henry* (Storm, 1919), the naïve protagonist even tries to make a living selling 'electric vibrators' before his bicycle is destroyed by an over-stimulated customer. In Britain, health workers used bicycles to visit patients and clients, and in the UK TV series *The District Nurse* (1984–1987) and *Call the Midwife* (2012–2017), set in the 1920s and the 1950s and 1960s respectively, the figure of a female health worker travelling through towns and the countryside on a bicycle is a recurring motif of these period dramas, a sign of a slower, more compassionate and more feminine past.

Bicycles were also used by colonial administrators in India and other imperial outposts to travel between hill stations and offices.[11] In this context, the bicycle was a prestigious, expensive import that functioned as a tool of colonisation. It symbolised colonial occupation and violence, surveillance and racialised social inequality as well as the relative advances of European industrial technology, although bicycles were quickly superseded by motorcycles and automobiles, both for the greater ease and comfort they offered and for physical protection from resentful locals. In India and across Asia, the development of bicycle rickshaws in the 1930s and 1940s also allowed cyclists to operate a taxi service for paying passengers. In the dynamic Hong Kong action film *Pedicab Driver* (Hung, 1989) the low social status of the bicycle rickshaw driver in 1930s Macau is evident in the milieu of criminal gangs, prostitution, gambling and vicious street fighting, although of course, as with many films starring prolific actor-director Sammo Hung, historical accuracy is less important than a blend of broad comedy, sentimentality, stunts and beautifully choreographed fight sequences. The setting is the pretext for some innovative stunts, including a wild downhill chase as the gang boss's car chases the hero's pedicab, as well as comic shots of Hung's wobbling backside.

Writing on the conjunction of cycling and labour in cinema, Lars Kristensen observes that bicycle work is typically represented as different from other forms of oppressive work because of its orientation around physical mobility: '[I]nstead of being positioned behind the immovable machine in the factory building, the worker *on* the bicycle machine performs life as it unfolds. The bicycle worker comes across as free while the factory worker appears to be chained.'[12] This idea of oppressive industrial labour is strikingly represented in the first scene of *Saturday Night and Sunday Morning* (Reisz, 1960), one of the influential films of the British New Wave of the late 1950s and early 1960s, a cycle of films that addressed working-class experience (primarily that of young men) with an aesthetic that blends documentary authenticity with the formal playfulness of the *nouvelle vague*. The film opens with a shot of the dark, noisy interior of a factory, where scores of men work at rows of machines receding into the distance. The camera tracks in on the young protagonist Arthur Seaton (Albert Finney), who is cutting metal axles on a capstan lathe, and, over a documentary-style montage showing Arthur's hands operating his machine and the various figures bustling along the cramped aisles around him, his voice-over commentary declares a stubbornly defiant, 'self-limiting' approach towards this physically damaging work:

Fourteen pound, three and twopence for a thousand of these a day. No wonder I've always got a bad back.... No use workin' every minute God sends. I could get through in half the time if I went like a bull, but they'd only slash my wages, so they can get stuffed. 'Don't let the bastards grind you down'; that's one thing I've learned.... I'd like to see anybody try to grind me down. That'd be the day. What I'm out for is a good time. All the rest is propaganda.

This arresting opening is followed by a title sequence showing workers streaming out of the factory on foot and on bicycles (although the supervisor rides a motorcycle and sidecar). Seaton rides his racing bike over cobbled streets past soot-blackened Victorian terraced houses overshadowed by huge chimneys and a gasometer. In one respect the bicycle is a means of escape from work, as Seaton rides home on Friday evening hoping for 'a good time' over the weekend, but it is also the reason for the work he does; as it happens, the shooting location for this depiction of oppressive industrial labour was the 60-acre Raleigh bicycle factory in Nottingham, where Alan Sillitoe, the author of the 1958 source novel, had worked as a teenager – as had his father. The company is not named directly in the film (although Arthur's supervisor carries a tray with the firm's name stencilled on it in the opening scene), but it is nevertheless significant that a bicycle factory symbolises the soul-crushing monotony of industrial work. This imagery is a cautionary reminder that the potential of the bicycle to liberate and mobilise the rider depends partly upon the immobility and invisible exploitation of the women and men who manufacture the vast majority of bicycles that are ridden around the world. It is the concealment of this labour that allows the bicycle to take on the status of fetishised commodity and symbol of freedom.

The images of 'ground-down' factory workers are a striking contrast to the images of Raleigh workers in the promotional documentary *How a Bicycle Is Made*. This short film documents the stages of manufacture of the bike from design to assembly, emphasising the firm's cutting-edge technology and the expert efficiency of the employees. The voice-over's claims that a worker loading hubs with ball bearings 'can fill over 1,000 hubs a day' and that '[t]hese girls are so expert that they can fit a tyre and a tube in 50 seconds' are, as Seaton might observe bitterly, propaganda celebrating British industrial might. The irony that the machine that frees the rider is manufactured by a system that grinds down the labourers who make it is heightened by the historical centrality of the bicycle in the development of mass production techniques. As discussed earlier, the system of continuous production with alternating shifts was pioneered by Pope's Manufacturing Company when Edison was commissioned to electrify the Columbia bicycle production line at a Connecticut factory, and so it is entirely apt that a bicycle factory is the site of industrial labour in this film, since Pope's factory was the prototype for the intensive manufacturing systems adopted internationally from the late nineteenth century onwards.

Saturday Night and Sunday Morning has an ambivalent poignancy as a document of Britain's increasingly distant industrial past, since, along with much of the United Kingdom's manufacturing base, the Raleigh bicycle factory shown in the film has closed down, the buildings long since demolished, British bicycle manufacturing having been rendered 'uncompetitive' by the availability of cheaper labour overseas. As Vivanco observes, in the 1980s traditional manufacturing models in Europe and the United States were

supplanted by a new style of manufacturing based on globally dispersed networks of suppliers, manufacturers and distributors, distantly removed from the markets in which those goods are sold.... As a result of this offshoring, today 99 percent of the bicycles sold in the U.S. are imported from China or Taiwan...and approximately two thirds of the 130 million bicycles produced globally each year are made in Chinese factories.[13]

Raleigh bicycles are still sold from Nottingham, but the firm closed the frame-making plant in 1999,[14] auctioning off the laser cutters and frame-welding robots, and in 2002 it closed the assembly plant where workers had built bikes from imported components.[15] The firm now concentrates on the design, sales, import and distribution of bikes, which are made entirely in Asian factories. Raleigh was established in 1886, at the beginning of the bicycle boom triggered by the safety bicycle, and so the history of the firm is coextensive with the history of the modern bicycle's fluctuating popularity. The company's history is also a barometer with which to measure the growth and post-war decline of Britain's manufacturing industries. If *Saturday Night, Sunday Morning* were made today, either Arthur Seaton would be working in a sales office or Amazon-style distribution warehouse (before driving home) or he would be a poorly paid Chinese, Taiwanese, Sri Lankan or Indonesian factory worker.

'No Bike, No Job'

As with any job, bicycle-related work is not just a means of earning money but is also a sign of social identity. In the 1990s, for example, European and American urban bicycle couriers acquired the status of brave, anti-materialistic individualists moving within a counter-cultural community, rather than, say, low-paid, alienated and exploited manual labourers doing physically dangerous piece work. They were epitomised by the frenetic, drug-damaged raver 'Tyres'[16] in the UK TV comedy series *Spaced* (1999–2001) and the tough female protagonists of cyberpunk science fiction, such as the genetically modified soldier Max Guevara in James Cameron's near-future dystopian TV drama *Dark Angel* (2000–2002) or Chevette Washington in William Gibson's Bridge series of novels (1993–1999). By contrast, in 1930s Vietnam, the operators of 'cyclos' were regarded as abject 'human horses' and were the subject of regular press campaigns and legislation to eradicate them from the streets.[17]

Lars Kristensen suggests that '[t]he use of the bicycle results in two types of productivity: external material gains, such as relieving human workload or actual monetary income, and well-being from physical fitness.'[18] The most celebrated film to explore the potentially productive relationship between cycling and work is undoubtedly *The Bicycle Thieves*. Although it is concerned with the precarity of working-class life in impoverished post-war Rome, the film has had a pervasive influence on world cinema. Indian director Satyajit Ray, a key figure in the development of the naturalistic, non-commercial 'parallel cinema' movement, recalled the impact of viewing the film when visiting Britain in 1950:

Within three days of arriving in London I saw *Bicycle Thieves*. I knew immediately that if I ever made *Pather Panchali*...I would make it in the same way, using natural locations and unknown actors. All through my stay in London, the lessons of *Bicycle Thieves* and neorealist cinema stayed with me.[19]

Woody Allen, meanwhile, reflected glumly in 2015 that '[y]ou always set out to make *Citizen Kane* or to make *The Bicycle Thief* and it doesn't happen', suggesting that the film has become a globally recognised shorthand for high-quality cinema.[20]

The film's influence is attributable partly to its radical embrace of 'realism', casting non-professional actors, shooting on location in Rome and eschewing formulaic narratives to show the desperate struggle of people to survive in contemporary Italy. It demonstrated that the cinema could find drama and profundity in life's mundane details. The most well known of the 'neorealist' films produced by Italian film-makers from 1942 through to the mid-1950s, it exemplifies the movement's investigation of realist cinema's political potential and film-makers' preoccupation with the city – especially with the city as a space undergoing transformation – and urban life, working-class experience and societies in transition following the trauma of war.

The film opens with a group of men crowding around a government employment office waiting to see whether any jobs are available. The protagonist, Antonio Ricci, is offered the position of poster hanger with the proviso: 'No bike, no job. It's a condition of employment.' He promises he will get one, and, shortly afterwards, his wife Maria takes their wedding sheets – a gesture that quietly symbolises the destructive effect of poverty on intimacy – to a vast pawn shop, exchanging them for Ricci's battered bike, a Fides (Latin for 'faith'). He receives his assignment at the headquarters of the bill-posting company, and, in a brief moment of playfulness and intimacy, Maria sits on his crossbar, smiling, while they ride through the city.

Early the following morning Ricci leaves for work with his son, Bruno, who has been polishing his dad's bike proudly. After dropping Bruno at the petrol station where he works on Saturdays he cycles happily to his new job among the hordes of cyclists filling the streets. A squadron of cyclists leaves through the gates of the poster warehouse, ladders over their shoulders, and a colleague shows Ricci how to hang a poster – an image of Rita Hayworth in *Gilda* – before kicking a child who is begging on the street next to them, passing details that highlight the gap between the glamorous world of Hollywood cinema and the tough reality of urban life. Ricci sets out by himself, but shortly afterwards a young man steals the bike he has propped against the wall while he is up a ladder hanging a poster. Ricci gives chase but the thief escapes through the busy traffic.

On reporting the theft to the police, Ricci is told: 'Look for it yourself', and this establishes the theme of the abandonment of the poor by the state. At the local Communist Party headquarters a shop steward, Baiocco, agrees to help him, and the following morning, at dawn, Bruno and Ricci meet Baiocco, who is supervising the despatch of road sweepers and dustcarts, and they head for the Piazza Vittorio market, which is packed with stalls selling bicycles and bike parts. Baiocco explains: 'We'll look for it piece by piece, then we'll put it together', but, although they find one stall holder repainting a similar frame, the serial numbers don't match, and so Bruno and Ricci move on to another market to continue their search. There Ricci spots the thief handing money to an old man, and he and Bruno give chase, losing the thief in a lab-yrinth of back streets before coming upon the old man. Ricci badgers and threatens him, following him to a church, where volunteers offer food, shaves and haircuts for the poor – a makeshift welfare system – but the old man gives Ricci the slip during Mass and disappears.

After visiting a clairvoyant in desperation, Ricci comes, miraculously, face to face with the thief and gives chase, cornering him in a brothel. They are pushed out onto the street by the women, and Ricci threatens to kill him, but a crowd begins to form, closing in around them threateningly, and a gangster in pinstripe suit and shades begins challenging Ricci. The young man starts to convulse and has an epileptic fit, and shortly afterwards Bruno arrives with a policeman, who takes Ricci to search the empty, dilapidated one-room flat the boy shares with his mother.

Ricci storms off, and he and Bruno come to a square outside a football stadium, where they sit forlornly on the kerb. As the stadium empties, the roads fill up with peo-ple on foot and on bikes, including a peloton of racing cyclists, who streak past them. Clearly wrestling with his conscience, Ricci gives Bruno money for a tram home, and attempts to steal a bike propped against a wall. Several men give chase but, unlike the thief who stole his bike, Ricci is caught by his coat-tails. As his son watches, Ricci is slapped, shouted at and frog-marched to the side of the road. While the men dis-cuss taking him to the police station, the bicycle's owner notices the tearful Bruno and relents: 'I don't want to bother. The man has enough trouble.' In a terribly bleak con-clusion, father and son trudge silently down the street past rows of gleaming bicycles and bustling traffic, both of them now crying. In the final shot they are walking away from the camera, and are subsumed into the jostling crowd.

For film theorist André Bazin, the importance of neorealist cinema was that it dem-onstrated the aesthetic richness and sophistication of realism in cinema. Films such as *The Bicycle Thieves* demonstrated for Bazin that 'there is no "realism" in art which is not first and foremost profoundly "aesthetic"'.... Realism in art can only be achieved in one way – through artifice.'[21] Despite the 'photographic nature of the medium', reproducing reality involves more than simply pointing a camera at the world and exposing film. Moreover, what was revolutionary about neorealism, for Bazin, was the way in which the use of long takes, wide-angle lenses and location shooting allowed the spectator's eye to explore the space within the film frame. Whereas, in Hollywood films, the sound design, lighting, composition, choreography, focus, camera movements and cutting work in concert to steer the viewer's eyes towards particular areas of the frame, a neo-realist film gives the spectator a democratic freedom to decide where to look.

Bazin argues that the film's success in replicating the textures and density of reality meant that it 'is one of the first examples of pure cinema. No more actors, no more story, no more sets, which is to say that in the perfect aesthetic illusion of reality there is no more cinema.'[22] The film's political power rests also in the relationship between this aesthetic of disappearance and the absence of a simplistic polemical narrative. For Bazin, Italian cinema expressed 'a revolutionary humanism', exemplified by a refusal to frame the story in moralising terms.[23] Ricci is abandoned in an indifferent, godless universe, unable to find justice, guidance or the narrative resolution promised by Hollywood storytelling conventions. At the same time, the film refrains from demonising any characters, regarding them all with a measure of sympathy. The thief is revealed to be poorer than Ricci, living in a slum and suffering from a debilitating medical condition, and his wretched elderly accomplice relies on handouts to survive. The concluding scene, in which Ricci is driven to theft, makes clear that crime is not a moral failure but a consequence of circumstances and the vicious cycle of poverty wrought by a combination of Fascism and years of war, which has turned people with similar interests violently against one another, wrecking both families and communities. Unlike a propaganda film, it offers neither a solution nor a reassuringly optimistic vision of the future.

In retrospect, it seems clear that, in his enthusiasm for the film, Bazin overstates the film's formal radicalism and its distance from classical cinema. Loosely adapted from a novel, *The Bicycle Thieves* draws on film melodrama in its narrative focus upon a family and the Oedipal drama of the strained father–son relationship. It uses music, sound and editing artfully to underline the emotional drama of Ricci's plight, and even makes reference to film comedy, citing *The Kid* (Chaplin, 1921), Chaplin's sentimental study of an impoverished father and adopted son, and the knockabout slapstick short *Tontolini Ruba una Bicicletta* [*Tontolini Steals a Bicycle*]. Moreover, as Elena Lombardi observes, although the film is engaged with a critical documentation of contemporary experience, the narrative is 'a modern embodiment of the ancient and metamorphic theme of the quest.'[24] As the bicycle's brand name, Fides, suggests, *The Bicycle Thieves* is a film about faith, and, for Ricci, retrieving the lost object means happiness and closer family relations, food, virility and a useful life. Recovering the bicycle is the means by which Ricci can earn money, entering the circuits of productivity and labour relations, and, as Lombardi observes, the bicycle's significance is stressed throughout:

In addition to the key sequences at the bicycle market and the stadium, where one is truly made 'bike-sick', in all outdoor sequences after the theft there is at least one bicycle zipping through. While this is certainly a 'realistic' portrayal of transportation in post-war Italy, it is also a constant reminder of the alienated and commodified condition of what the object stands for: human labour.[25]

Rather than a touristic view of Rome as a picturesque ancient city, it appears in the film as a site of labour and a centre of commerce, and it is significant that Ricci's job is advertising. Like Jacques Tati's postman, he is a communication worker, whose role foreshadows the emergence of a post-industrial knowledge economy.

Recycling, Reframing and Global Circulation

The Bicycle Thieves has been immensely influential upon film-makers around the world partly because it demonstrates that a formally sophisticated, moving artwork can be made using very limited resources, and partly because of the translatability of this film fable of mobility, masculinity and economic precarity. The variety of recyclings and citations of De Sica's film testifies to this, some films replacing the bicycle with equivalent vehicles that serve a similar purpose. For example, in the Jamaican film *Rockers* (Bafaloukos, 1978) the protagonist, Horsemouth, is a drummer struggling to make a living in a Kingston shanty town, a self-described 'sufferer' in Rastafarian patois. He scrapes together the money to buy a 175cc motorbike to augment his income by distributing records from Joe Gibbs' pressing plant to record shops, declaring: 'I-Man gonna be the hardest salesman around town.' The bike is stolen that evening when he visits an open-air dance in order to sell a new record, but he locates it in a warehouse where a local gangster stores stolen goods, and he and his friends get revenge by emptying both the gangster's own house and warehouse, and then, like Robin Hood and his gang, leaving the stolen goods in the streets for the people living in the ghetto to help themselves. *The Bicycle Thieves* provides the narrative and thematic chassis for this account of the impoverished lives of Rastafarian Jamaicans, but *Rockers* takes the fusion of fiction and documentary further than De Sica. Shot on location with non-professional actors and an extraordinary array of Jamaican musicians playing themselves in the main roles – including Leroy 'Horsemouth' Wallace himself – the film documents the commercial networks through which roots reggae music circulated in the 1970s (as Horsemouth moves between music rehearsals, recording studio, pressing plant, record shops, sound system dances and gigs), as well as the hand-to-mouth existence of the urban poor in Jamaica's capital.

The Bicycle Thieves is also the model for the first film by Senegalese director Ousmane Sembène, a 20-minute black and white short shot with non-professional actors and using voice-over dialogue rather than synchronous sound.[26] Already established as a successful novelist, Sembène turned to film-making in the 1960s in the belief that cinema had a greater transformative political potential thanks to its wider reach. Films, he felt, 'could become the vehicle "par excellence" for the creation of a modern form of African culture able to transcend artificial frontiers and language barriers'.[27] One of the first films by a black African director, and 'the first black African film seen internationally by a paying audience', *Borom Sarret* [*The Cart Driver*] (1963) depicts the experiences of a desperately poor cart driver working in Dakar, Senegal's capital, transporting people and cargo around the dusty outskirts of the city, the 'native district', with a horse and cart.[28] Most of his passengers are too poor to pay, and the driver tells himself consolingly: 'We'll wait for God's mercy', although he gives most of the money he earns to a charismatic 'griot' storyteller in the street. After conveying a heavily pregnant woman and her indifferent partner to the maternity hospital, and a dead baby to the cemetery, where its grieving father is barred from entering the cemetery since, as a foreigner, he doesn't have the correct documents, the driver reluctantly agrees to take a sharp-suited man 'uptown'. Although carts are banned from this area of town, which consists of apartment blocks, grand colonial buildings, and tree-lined, tarmacked boulevards, the driver decides to risk it. Inevitably, he is pulled over by a policeman, his passenger leaves without paying and his cart is impounded since he can't afford the fine. 'It doesn't matter that my ancestors were heroes', he reflects, walking home with his horse, Albourah, a silent substitute for Bruno.

Now I have nothing. What am I going to tell my wife? What am I going to give her? Yesterday it was the same thing. The day before, too. This is jail. This is modern life. This is the life in this country. I might as well die.

When he arrives back at his shack, his wife hands him their baby and leaves, announcing impassively that they will have food to eat.

Described by Nwachukwu Frank Ukadike as 'unquestionably an African masterpiece', this bleak film portrays the inequalities of life in urban Senegal with stark simplicity. The cosmopolitan, 'uptown' environment, which resembles a European city, is contrasted with the driver's neighbourhood, a dusty shanty town marked by death, immigration, abject poverty (as the driver observes when approached by a severely disabled man crawling on hands and knees, 'What could I say? There are so many beggars. They're like flies.') and humiliation, as the ending implies that his wife is selling sex in order that they can eat. This spatial distinction represents the newly independent country's transition from a traditional society to a 'modernised', post-colonial society, and it emphasises the difficulties and costs of this shift.[29] The cart driver is unwelcome uptown, the horse and cart an incongruous, atavistic trace of an indigenous society, and he observes on his return home: 'This is my neighbourhood, my village. I feel good here. Not like up there. Here, there is no police officer.'

However, Andrea Dahlberg suggests that the sentimentality of De Sica's film is absent from Sembène's, which is far more critical of its hapless protagonist:

[H]e can be seen as a traditional man unaware that he is now living in a radically new form of society.... He is resigned to the plight of others and seems unable to empathize with them. His lack of awareness of the power of his own actions and the new social context he inhabits has dehumanized and demeaned him.[30]

One of the most striking signs of his resistance to dynamic social change is his attitude to women. When his pregnant passenger rests her head on his shoulder he complains in the voice-over about 'modern women', but the end of the film reveals his financial dependence upon his wife, remaining hypocritically silent when she sets out to earn some money through prostitution.

Thus, Sembène uses De Sica's film as an aesthetic and politically progressive template for his first low-budget experiment with decolonised film-making that 'puts into play the type of neocolonial critique that will provide a foundation for Sembène's entire body of work'.[31] In relocating the European film to Africa, in a gesture of transnational 'theft', Sembène explores issues of modernity, colonisation and social inequality. However, with an ending that highlights oppressive gender relations, it also foregrounds an aspect of social injustice that remains unaddressed by De Sica's film.[32]

The East German film *Das Fahrrad* [*The Bicycle*] (Schmidt, 1982) also explores questions of inequality through the staging of a bicycle theft. The film centres on single parent Susanne Becker, who works at a metal press but struggles to pay the rent. Her life is boring, repetitive and draining; 'One day's like another,' she tells her friend in a joyless nightclub. 'All the same mess.' The following day she quits her job and finds herself cycling around the city, Halle, looking for work, but with no qualifications she is unable to get hired. Her neighbour, Mrs Puschkat, later reassures her, invoking the symbol of a spinning wheel: 'The world revolves. We sit in our rooms. The world revolves. And we act as if it had nothing to do with us. Well, it's God. Somebody must be in control.' After getting drunk at the nightclub she is followed and raped, and the next morning decides to take the advice of a friend, and pretends her bike has been stolen, claiming 450 Marks from the insurance company. Unfortunately, shortly afterwards she runs into the policeman to whom she'd reported the theft while cycling with her daughter through the city. Charged with 'simulating a crime' and 'fraud against socialist property', she relies on a new boyfriend, Thomas, who has a senior role at the factory where she now works at an assembly line, to arrange for her case to be referred to a Communist Party 'grievance committee', at which she will be treated more leniently. However, Thomas, who has pulled in a favour to help Susanne, returns from work furious at having been saddled with responsibility for a problematic project: 'Now I'm left to bail out.... It was a real frame-up.' The film finishes on an uncertain note, with Thomas watching as a laughing Susanne teaches Jenny to ride her bicycle, pushing her in circles around a fountain until Jenny sets off unsteadily by herself, the very image of the revolving world mentioned by 'Granny Puschkat'.

Perhaps unsurprisingly, given its depiction of contemporary East Germany as an alienating, institutionalised environment, the film met with a hostile response. The Ministry of Culture raised objections; the general director of the state-owned film studio, DEFA, distanced himself from the project (having previously approved it); its release was delayed; the reviews were 'unfairly devastating', according to screenwriter Erika Richter; and the film was not circulated internationally. It is visually striking, representing the interiors of factories and offices as gloomy, drab, institutional spaces that compound the listlessness and dissatisfaction of Susanne. Richter suggests that the uneasy response to the film was occasioned by 'the power and the violence of the visual'; the only colourful space, providing some visual relief, is the nightclub, but this is also a space where Jenny goes to drink, and it is after leaving there that she is raped.

Das Fahrrad tells a depressing story about the sense of young East Germans in the 1980s that they had no future, consigned to unrewarding, uncreative work, and disregarded by the older generation. Directed and written by women, it also tells a depressingly familiar story about gender inequalities. Susanne seems determined to live an independent life, and the happiest sequences are those in which she is cycling and reading with her daughter; she lies about the bicycle theft only after Jenny falls ill and Jenny's estranged father refuses to give her money for medicine, and, although Thomas agrees to help, he is patronising and resentful throughout. 'You can't even grasp basic things,' he snaps, telling her: 'We're all responsible for ourselves.' Of course, Susanne is responsible for Jenny too – indeed, she is one of the few characters who must balance self-interest with care for another – but Thomas is so bitter at having agreed to help Susanne that he tells her in one of the final scenes that Jenny is certain to become a thief herself.

Most recently, the American film *A Better Life* (Weitz, 2011) uses De Sica's film as a template for a story of contemporary immigrant experience in the United States. The protagonist, Carlos, is a Mexican 'illegal' working as a gardener in Los Angeles. He buys a large pick-up truck in the hope that he can earn enough money to afford a lawyer in order to get legal citizenship, and move with his son Luis to a better area away from the predatory gangs at his school. Soon after buying the truck with a loan, a day labourer employed by Carlos steals it. Although Carlos and Luis eventually retrieve the truck, Carlos is subsequently arrested and deported, while Luis undergoes the initiation ritual of taking a beating to join a local gang. In the film's final shot, Carlos has joined a group who are crossing the border from Mexico illegally, telling them: 'Let's go home.' Made by a Hollywood director, the melodramatic film is stylistically slick, but eschews the understated irony of De Sica's film. The bleak conclusion of *The Bicycle Thieves* is softened with an optimistic coda, but *A Better Life* shares the compassionate humanism of the earlier film. Its sympathies lie with Carlos and his son, who are presented as innocent victims of a brutalising combination of poverty, racism, institutional indifference and hypocrisy.

By contrast with this Hollywood humanism, one of the earliest and darkest – both thematically and visually – recyclings of *The Bicycle Thieves* is the Spanish film *Muerte de un Ciclista* [*Death of a Cyclist*] (Bardem, 1955). A bitter, satirical critique of bourgeois self-interest and moral cowardice, the film takes the figure of the anonymous cyclist as an archetype of the worker or everyman. Virtually invisible in the film, the cyclist nevertheless remains an accusatory presence throughout, reminding the film's protagonists of their complicity with a social system founded on inequality, injustice and violence.

The film opens with a long shot showing the distant figure of a cyclist disappearing over the brow of a hill at dusk as a swerving car appears and comes to a halt. The titular death takes place out of sight, with no drama, no spectacle. The couple in the car pause to examine the fatally injured cyclist but quickly decide to drive away, the wheel of the bicycle still spinning at the bottom of the frame. We soon learn that one of the reasons they fled is that they are conducting an illicit affair and they would have risked exposure in reporting the incident, but the damning implication is that, from their elite perspective, the death of a factory worker is of little significance; Juan is a university professor and Maria José is the wife of a wealthy businessman. As the film unfolds, Juan becomes consumed by guilt, going as far as posing as an insurance agent to visit the cyclist's wife. He hands in his resignation and tries to persuade his lover to join him in surrendering to the police. 'We'll be masters of our own destiny,' he promises her. 'We have to purify ourselves, become clean and good again.' Returning to the scene of the killing – a battlefield where Juan had fought in the trenches during the Spanish Civil War – they stop to study the landscape en route to the police station, before Maria José gets back in the car and runs Juan over. She is racing back home to her husband in the dark and rain when, with grim dramatic irony, she swerves to avoid a cyclist, crashes through a wall and flies off a bridge. The film ends with her lifeless body hanging out of the wrecked car in the gully, while, pointedly, the cyclist rides off to find help at a nearby house.

Death of a Cyclist was made during a period in the early 1950s when General Franco's fascist dictatorship was undergoing limited liberalisation, attempting to establish better relations with the rest of Europe and the United States, but Spanish cinema was still subject to state censorship and cultural conservatism – a repressive, hypocritical situation that was deeply frustrating for film-makers, including the director/writer, and Communist Party member, José Antonio Bardem. However, while the import of foreign films was carefully controlled, the state-run film school in Madrid gave students access to films that were not licensed for public distribution, and Bardem, along with his contemporaries, had been strongly influenced by a week's screening of Italian films in 1951. As a result, 'film-makers from both the left and the right looked to Italian neo-realism as a model, setting it in opposition to Hollywood conventions and using this dialectic to structure many of the key films of the period.'[33] Thus, *Death of a Cyclist* reproduces the thematic and stylistic features of Alfred Hitchcock's Hollywood films of the 1950s, with chiaroscuro lighting and a score that recalls Bernard Herrmann, but then undercuts this aesthetic, and its ideological association with bourgeois values, by interlacing it with the deep-focus cinematography of neorealist film, emphasising the characters' relationship to their physical and social environment. This formally disruptive technique is reinforced by the film's disorienting tendency to cut abruptly between scenes, and this 'dialectic opposition' of clashing aesthetics became the basis for the emergence of the 'New Spanish Cinema' in the late 1950s and 1960s.

Capitalism, Migrant Labour and Theft

Beijing Bicycle (Wang, 2001) demonstrates that De Sica's film remains a template for socially committed film-making half a century later, and the bicycle a powerful symbol of struggle. The director, Wang Xiaoshuai, is associated with the 'sixth generation' of experimental Chinese film-makers who emerged in the 1990s. As Jian Xu writes, '[w]ith a small budget, a microscopic lens trained on everyday urban life, and a disdain for the historical epic or national allegory that so engaged their older, more illustrious colleagues,' they 'developed their own forms and styles of filmmaking to attend

to the specific contemporary issues brought about by the country's rapid modernization' as the socialist state tentatively embraced market capitalism.[34]

In particular, one of the themes addressed by the 'sixth generation'

is that of the newly emergent subaltern class in the city, following the increased social mobility
brought about by market forces. This new subaltern class consists of millions of migrant workers from the countryside, the majority of whom are peasants coming to the city to sell their
labour.... Nomads of subjectivity, they linger in a liminal space in which they belong neither to
the country nor to the city.[35]

As in Makhmalbaf's *The Cyclist*, the bicycle is the perfect symbol of this nomadic
subjectivity.

Wang's film tells the story of 17-year-old Guei, who has travelled to Beijing in
search of work. He is hired as a cycle courier along with several other rural migrants,
and, after being 'cleaned up' with a haircut and a uniform, is presented with a new
German mountain bike, for which over 80 per cent of his earnings will be docked until
he has paid for it. After just over a month Guei has earned enough to take ownership
of the bike, but, when collecting a package from a bath-house, he emerges to find his
bike has vanished. In despair, he forgets to deliver the letter, and is fired the following
morning. His boss agrees to give Guei another chance if he can find the bike, but asks,
'Do you know how many bikes there are in Beijing?' Shortly afterwards Guei is caught
stealing a bike by a security guard and has to be freed by a now furious manager,
who tells him: 'Don't bother me again.' In a parallel plot thread, Guei's bike has been
bought by teenage boy Jian with money he stole from his father. After Guei's friend, a
shopkeeper from his village, recognises Jian's bike, Guei follows Jian and steals it back,
before crashing into a truck, allowing Jian and his friends to retrieve the bike.

The film then follows the repeated attempts by both boys to retrieve the bike as the
bike changes hands back and forth, and Guei is beaten up by Jian's gang. Eventually,
after a lengthy stand-off, Guei agrees to share the bike with Jian. The two of them
exchange it every day, and continue on this basis for a while until Jian realises that the
schoolgirl he had hoped to impress with this expensive bike is going out with a cooler
older boy, Da Huan, an expert stunt rider who sports shades, ear-ring and dyed hair. In
revenge, Jian ambushes Da Huan, hitting him with a brick, and afterwards tells Guei to
keep the bike: 'I don't need it any more.'

In the film's climax, Da Huan and his gang of friends chase the two boys through
the labyrinth of narrow hutongs running between the old buildings and courtyards,
Guei on the bike and Jian on foot. They are cornered and set upon in a courtyard,

where Jian is beaten unconscious. The gang disperse, but, as Guei stumbles out of the courtyard, he finds one of them still stamping on his bicycle with glee. Distraught and sobbing, he knocks the thug out with a brick, hoists the mangled bicycle onto his shoulder and walks away. The final shots, in which Guei walks through crowded, traffic-clogged streets in slow motion, echo the conclusion of *The Bicycle Thieves*, in which Bruno and Ricci disappear into the crowd.

Although Wang, known in China as the 'bicycle director', has claimed 'many times that his *Beijing Bicycle* is actually under no direct influence of *Bicycle Thieves*, and even is rather discontented with the juxtaposition', the parallels are obvious.[36] While it is stylistically slick, Wang's film retains the device of a series of characters brought into contact by the bicycle, which constantly changes hands, and also a plot that is propelled by chance encounters. Like De Sica, Wang shot on location in Beijing with non-professional actors in the lead roles, and this lends the film a sense of authenticity, underlined by geographic particularity in its depiction of the complex of bustling streets, vacant lots, unfinished high rises, tree-lined riverside walks and the maze of old residential buildings surrounded by new office blocks and apartments. As Huang Zhong observes, 'many films of the Chinese Sixth Generation directors, particularly their early works, often draw inspiration of some Italian neorealist films'.[37] Most of these film-makers attended the Beijing Film Academy, where they were exposed to foreign films, as well as to film theory, and so were also influenced by Bazin's writing on realist cinema. However, *The Bicycle Thieves* has a deeper historical significance within Chinese cinema history as 'the first Western European film to be dubbed' for release in China in 1953.[38] Among the reasons for this was a political message that could be readily appropriated to articulate the values of Chinese Communism; a lobby card from its release describes the film as 'reflecting the poverty and hunger of the miserable life, in the unjust system of a capitalist society, of the broad working populace'.[39] However, this synopsis also rewrites the film's bleak, open ending with propagandistic optimism: '[W]hen [Ricci] sees that Bruno is crying, he suddenly feels that there is still hope; in this miserable society, Bruno still understands him, sympathizes with him. For Bruno's future he has to continue to live.'[40]

Like *The Bicycle Thieves*, *Beijing Bicycle* describes a society in transition and the direct impact of social transformations upon some of the poorest inhabitants: migrant workers and children. Like the Italian film it also retains a certain ambiguity, an approach that remains unconventional in early twenty-first-century Chinese cinema: 'That the film makes no clear statement...is itself a critical stance that is relatively new in mainland Chinese filmmaking.... The ambiguity affords room for thinking so that the impact of the contradictions of social life may register.'[41] Indeed, for Xu, the director's 'ambiguous mode of inquiry is more productive and ethical than would be an approach aimed at providing definite answers' with regard to the problems posed by China's rapid transformation to a post-socialist, globalised market economy.[42]

Another reason why *The Bicycle Thieves* lends itself to appropriation by Chinese cinema is the symbolic importance of the bicycle in Chinese culture in the second half of the twentieth century. Although bicycles were initially viewed with scepticism as expensive imports, and the first factories were Japanese-owned, the establishment of Chinese bicycle factories in 1930 and the nationalisation of the bicycle industry in 1949, with loans available to bike buyers, meant that the bicycle, in various forms but especially the black, single-speed Feige (Flying Pigeon) and Yongjiu (Forever) roadsters, became an increasingly visible symbol of contemporary China.[43] In the words of Edward J. M. Rhoads: 'In the first four decades after the Communist Party came to power in 1949, bicycles were the primary mode of transportation for most urban and many rural Chinese.'[44] Paul Smethurst writes: 'The PRC reached its [annual] production target of one million bicycles by 1958' and '[t]he bicycle finally reached all Chinese towns and cities by the mid-1970s', Chinese leader Deng Xiaoping having promised to put a Flying Pigeon in every home.[45] However, whereas the bicycle once symbolised equality, national unity and collective effort, one of the transformations hinted at by the film is the shifting status of the bicycle as a marker of social class. In Beijing, in particular, car ownership is rising rapidly, since, as elsewhere, the car remains a symbol of individual affluence and social progress. Whereas, '[i]n 1986, bicycles made up 63 per cent of transport on the roads [, by 2014] they accounted for just 15 per cent.'[46] Guei's expensive mountain bike thus has a tandem significance, both as a sign of his low status as a migrant worker and as a sign of a cultural shift in China of the bicycle from purely functional machine to a leisure apparatus. One dimension of the film's ambiguity is represented by the bicycle's symbolism of past and future – a vehicle that continues to signify social movement or transition.

Bicycles and the Information Economy

Like Ricci, Guei is a communication worker. Bicycles – like radios, computers and mobile phones – are communications media conveying messages and materials from one location to another, with modern bicycle couriers connected to mobile phone and computer networks. Bicycle couriering is therefore the perfect subject for cinema, a means by which the medium can reflect upon itself. A film about bicycle messengers is, effectively, a self-reflexive film about the processes and mechanisms of communication, and so it is perhaps unsurprising that the first bicycle messenger appears on film at least as early as 1910 in the slapstick comedy *Tontolini Ruba una Bicicleta*, which depicts a wild chase after Tontolini steals a telegram messenger's bike.

In his essay on bicycle work, Kristensen suggests that the two principal types of bicycle-based labour depicted in cinema are couriering and racing, although he observes that 'the position of racing has been overlooked as work-related by academic accounts'.[47] However, what is a racing cyclist whose colourful clothing and vehicles are entirely covered with corporate logos if not a bicycle messenger? Indeed, as Bernard Vere observes of cycle racing in the early twentieth century, '[b]icycle manufacturers, the sporting press and top riders enjoyed a symbiotic relationship', and this relationship extends well beyond specialist reporting as races such as the Tour de France – which was itself conceived as a promotional device for the newspaper *L'Auto* – became increasingly popular during the twentieth century.[48]

The bicycle messenger is cinema's perfect protagonist. She is the visual articulation of cinema's preoccupation with the moving body and the city, and offers the pleasurable spectacle of a technically adept performance, of muscular, supple interaction with a machine, as she negotiates routes through the streets. In her autobiographical account of working as a cycle courier, Emily Chappell suggests that the romance of couriering rests on couriers' incongruity in the context of a modern city:

Cycle couriers are splendidly anachronistic figures – in an age where almost everything is mechanized and digitized.... [S]eeing actual human beings on bicycles darting among the traffic to deliver packages seemed almost equivalent to spotting Roman chariots racing between the buses on the Euston Road.[49]

The bike messenger is identified with an intriguing, romanticised subculture marked by specialised slang, individualism (expressed partly through clothing, tattoos and piercings) and social marginality (as couriers are usually non-unionised subcontractors, working on their own for low pay and minimal security).[50] Former courier Jon Day recounts:

Bicycle couriering tends to attract the forgotten, people who have fallen through the cracks of the system: migrants flying under the radar.... Some are merely dedicated cyclists unable to pursue a career in the professional racing peloton through lack of talent or dedication. But most are running away from something.[51]

In this sense, the bicycle represents both the possibility and foreclosure of the desired escape, as the cycle courier returns repeatedly, Sisyphus-like, to the dispatch office.

The bicycle messenger's job also lends itself to tense narrative drama, since it is physically dangerous, involves fleeting contact with an array of different characters and movement between separate social spheres, from high finance to the criminal underworld, and, like the plot of a thriller, is organised around fixed deadlines.[52] Collecting and delivering packages potentially places riders, inadvertently, in the midst of conspiracies and criminal networks, as they could find themselves carrying stolen money, jewels, drugs or secret codes, and so it provides a convenient narrative pretext. More generally, the messenger's activity is a dramatic visualisation of the circuits and flows of capitalism. As Day recalls,

I was beguiled by the wonderfully straightforward economies of the job. As a courier it is easy to see what, precisely, you are being paid to do: earnings are measured in miles – the distance theory of value. Carry a package from one postcode to another and you get paid accordingly. If it needs to go further or get there quickly you are paid a bit more.[53]

For all the romanticisation of the messenger's maverick status (which is equally seductive to riders and outside observers),[54] and an intoxicating sense of individual freedom and fluid movement, the bicycle and the rider remain intrinsic components of the economic system, consigned to what Jeffrey L. Kidder describes as 'dirty work' or 'edgework'.[55]

Cycle couriers skirt the edges of many films about modern cities. For example, *Taxi* (Story, 2004), the US adaptation of the 1998 French film, opens with the courier protagonist Belle (played by pioneering rapper Queen Latifah) careering through New York on her mountain bike, riding through Macy's department store, down into the subway and across the Brooklyn Bridge in order to set a speed record on her last day at work (before beginning a new career as a taxi driver). Documentaries and feature films about bicycle messengers comprise a minor subgenre that is complemented by a small body of novels and autobiographical texts. The fiction films range from low-budget independent films such as *2 Seconds* (Briand, 1998), *Faster!* (Ullrich, 2010), *The Cyclist* (John Lawrence, 2013) and *The Alley Cat* (Ullrich, 2014) to Hollywood films such as *Quicksilver* (Donnelly, 1986), *Premium Rush* (Koepp, 2012) and *Tracers* (Benmayor, 2015). They are consistent in their depiction both of the subculture of bicycle messengers – the impression of a tight, defiant community of riders, the precarious financial status of the messengers and the sense of the job as a temporary refuge – and in the mise en scène of the shadow city as viewed from the rider's perspective: a colourful labyrinth of underpasses, alleys, traffic-clogged streets, crowded sidewalks, warehouses, shabby apartments, foyers and busy courier offices. Although stylistically different, the films share several formal devices in their depiction of cycling to empha-sise speed of movement. These include low-angle travelling shots, kinetic point-of-view shots threading through lines of queueing cars, close-ups of parts of the bicycle and the rider's body, and high-tempo music.

The Reconfigured City

The city is reconfigured in these films, which represent it not as a vast agglomeration of enormous buildings and suffocating masses of people trapped in gridlock but as a network of pathways, through which a rider possessing almost magical knowledge and specialised physical skills can move at high speed. It is a space of mobility rather than stasis, and the bicycle emerges as the perfect machine for navigating urban spaces. These routes are invisible to most of us but the bicycle messenger is an ultra-flâneur who studies the city with a particularly acute gaze (as demonstrated by the motif of dynamic point-of-view shots in every film about bicycle messengers), scan-ning the space for possibly better routes. The image of the rider zipping down alleys, through plazas, across pavements, down flights of stairs and through underpasses, tracing the physical networks of the city, implies the presence of other, related invis-ible networks – criminal organisations, financial systems, security services, data net-works. The city, the figure of the bicycle messenger reminds us, is a space of networks overlaid on networks, simultaneously virtual and physical. Indeed, like red blood cells transporting oxygen through the body's circulatory system,

bicycle couriers carry everything and anything the city needs to function. Couriers carry physi-cal objects that haven't yet been replaced by images or data streams: bundles of legal papers tied together with their jaunty pink ribbons; video tapes and DVDs from production compa-nies to edit suites; jewellery and clothing samples from East end sweatshops to West End PR companies; blood and urine samples from hospital to hospital; contracts from production companies to talent holed up in Primrose Hill mansions; forgotten keys or mobile phones from pubs or strip clubs to offices; congratulatory bottles of champagne from agents to the stage doors of West End theatres.[56]

At the same time that the bicycle messenger appears to move through the city with an enviable lightness and autonomy, she also embodies the subjection of the individual to the unrelenting pressure to meet deadlines. For the messenger, the city is an abstracted space whose expanse is measured in both time and distance, and travelling through the city involves a race against the clock. From this perspective, the city is also reconfigured as an actively hostile space littered with the mobile obstacles of pedestrians, large, slow-moving vehicles and aggressive drivers.

The feature-length documentary *The Godmachine* (Steffen, 2007) is a comprehensive global survey of the transnational bicycle messenger subculture in the early twenty-first century, alongside the message that bicycles should replace cars in cities. Interviewing riders in different cities around the world, the film documents various races and social events organised by couriers, including critical mass rallies, street parties, illegal races and official competitions that attract riders from around the globe. Jan Steffen follows riders on their sometimes hairy routes with his camera, and interviews messengers working in different cities, recording their accounts of the experience of riding bikes for a living and the attractions of the job. For New Zealander Mike Nailer, this edges into mysticism, as he describes bicycle riding as 'the creation of energy', lending the film its hyperbolic title.

Shooting the Messenger

Quicksilver is the film that establishes the template for the bicycle messenger subgenre. Starring Kevin Bacon, whose previous film, *Footloose* (Ross, 1984), made him a star, it tells the story of a cocky, exceptionally successful stockbroker who makes a tremendous loss in a single day, wiping out his parents' savings in the process. Having been outpaced by an African-American bicycle messenger while taking a taxi to work at the beginning of the film, Jack Casey (Bacon) quits and takes a job as a cycle courier with the Quicksilver messenger company. Wearing a beret dropped by the courier in the opening scene (and, like him, riding a Raleigh), he starts a new life among this motley group of colleagues with his girlfriend Rand, a dancer and socialite whose name, an allusion to the incoherent libertarian philosopher and novelist Ayn Rand, signifies the aspirational desires that will eventually draw her away from her downshifting boyfriend.

The tensions in their relationship are evident from her first appearance, when she is rehearsing in the apartment and he does his best to distract and interrupt her. While she dances he cycles in circles around her, performing gymnastic tricks until she relents and climbs on board the bike with him and he rides over to the bed, tossing her onto it. This flirtatious parrying in an otherwise sexless film invokes the scene in New Hollywood western *Butch Cassidy and the Sundance Kid* (Hill, 1969) in which Butch Cassidy (Paul Newman) cycles around a farm with Etta Place (Katherine Ross) balanced on the handlebars.[57] The bicycle is the mediator of the relationship between Casey and Rand, but this collapses after a gallery private view when she leaves in a limousine with some rich clients and he refuses her instruction to leave his bicycle and join them. Casey chooses the bicycle – and fellow female courier Terri – over his partner.

The ethnically diverse, almost entirely male group of couriers is mostly identified by nickname, and, for all of them, bicycle work is a temporary or part-time occupation. If, as Kathi Weeks observes, 'the workplace is a key site of becoming classed', the film suggests that the relationship between class and occupation among bike messengers is particularly complex.[58] Apache used to work for the mayor, Tour de Franz is a ballet dancer, Teddy Bear is saving up to go to college while Educated and Dedicated were formerly college professors. Voodoo (Lawrence Fishburne), we are told, is 'not too particular what he carries, and for who', and falls out with one of his clients, Gypsy, who is shown selling guns from his car. When Jack and Voodoo compete in a race through the city, navigating through the steep streets and Chinatown of San Francisco, Voodoo is deliberately run over by Gypsy.

In order to raise some cash for another courier, Hector, and to repay his parents, Jack reluctantly returns to the stock exchange, where he demonstrates that he still has the requisite nerve, making $38,000 in a day. As the film progresses, Terri is sexually harassed and assaulted by Gypsy, leading to a confrontation outside the courier office in which Gypsy shoots one of the couriers and runs over their bikes. Terri escapes while Jack lures Gypsy away on his bike, and a breakneck car/bicycle chase ensues (capturing both the danger of the job as well as every cyclist's sense that every driver is out to get her) until Jack tricks Gypsy into driving his car from an upper floor of an unfinished office block, bringing it crashing to the tarmac. The film ends with Jack and Terri together on the street. Now wearing a suit and tie, he has been fielding job offers while she, also smartly dressed and made up, has enrolled on a paramedic trainee programme. Unable to decide where to eat, they go to Hector's hotdog stand, the business he set up with the money Jack earned for him.

Earlier in the film, Jack explained the attraction of the job to a former colleague who was trying to persuade him to return to finance:

[N]ow all I'm responsible for is me. I pick up here, I deliver there. It's simple. Nobody worries, nobody gets hurt. I pay my rent. I got a coupla extra bucks. If I need more, I work a few more runs. Look: when I'm on the street I feel good, man. I feel exhilarated. I go as fast as I like, faster than anyone. The street sign says, 'One-Way East', I go west. They can't touch me.

It is an expression of transgressive individualism, the pleasures of speed and the American national myth of the frontier, but, as Kristensen observes, the notion of the bicycle courier's freedom rests on a contradiction:

[T]he economy that these urban warriors refuse to take part in is actually upheld by their bicycle work [even though] the romantic view of bicycle couriering sees it as free and outside mainstream work, such as factory or office work. The bicycle couriers' work is seen as nonwork which means work that is enjoyed rather than endured.[59]

This equation of physical freedom with social freedom or agency is echoed in *The Godmachine* by Ercan Tursun, a messenger working in Hamburg, who describes '[t]his feeling…of being free, being on the street and having total freedom. You are your own boss; when you're riding…all you are is happy.' However, while Jack sees a clear distinction between his new mobile job and the constraints of his previous occupation, the freedom offered by couriering is not equally accessible. As cynical African-American rider Voodoo explains, the street is not an autonomous zone but a marketplace: 'The street is free enterprise. You work your side. I work mine.' The severely restricted freedom offered by the unpoliced, unregulated street is the free-dom to do business with no differentiation between legal and illicit trade. In that sense, there is an equivalence between his two jobs, with Jack having moved from one trading floor to another. However, this mobility is not distributed equally, and thus it was Terri and Voodoo who find themselves pressured into working for Gypsy while Jack, protected by the cultural capital of middle-class white masculinity, is able to enjoy the simple pleasures of slumming it as a low-paid worker.

(Non-)Work and (Un-)Freedom

Messengers may extol the freedom their job offers them, but the bicycle courier exemplifies a troubling model of post-industrial neoliberal labour in which the boundary between work and leisure is erased, as work extends beyond the confines of the working day and leisure too becomes capitalised and exploitable. Kristensen writes: 'Neoliberalism packages this as a fashionable lifestyle, a desirable living condi-tion for a free individual. And, true to the dictum, compared to his previous life as a broker, Casey believes in his happiness.'[60] However, as German philosopher and cul-tural theorist Theodor Adorno observed presciently, 'unfreedom is gradually annexing "free time", and the majority of unfree people are as unaware of this process as they are of the unfreedom itself.'[61] On the one hand, this is evident in the ways that work penetrates free time – with mobile devices that make it difficult for workers ever to leave work at the end of the working day – and, on the other hand, it is evident in the ways that leisure activities are incorporated into work – as represented in the job of the bicycle messenger, in which the pleasures of cycling are co-opted and exploited by low-paid, unregulated piecework.

Nevertheless, while Casey may have been persuaded by his own comments, *Quicksilver*'s reactionary ideological framework precludes the possibility that such modest aspirations can be the basis for a happy life. The film ends with him wearing a business suit and preparing to resume his former job. Having been rescued by him, Terri is at his side, appropriately feminised in a skirt and high-heeled shoes, rather than clad in the androgynous jeans and army-surplus jacket she has worn throughout the film, and embarking on a suitably feminine job in the caring profession of medicine. The final shot is a freeze frame showing their Hispanic friend Hector, who was also rescued (financially) by Jack, bowing gratefully as Jack and Terri wait to be served by him. The antithesis of the radically open ending of *The Bicycle Thieves*, it is a particularly unpleasant image that summarises Hollywood cinema's insistence upon ideological and narrative resolution. The trio are happily resuming their gendered, racialised roles after a brief foray into a more equal but abject and dangerous environment.

More modest in scale, Marie Ullrich's low-budget independent films *Faster!* (2010) and *The Alley Cat* (2014) counter the celebratory depiction of messenger culture in the exhilarating thrillers *Quicksilver*, *Premium Rush* (Koepp, 2012) and *Tracers* (Benmayor, 2015). The protagonist of Ullrich's films is a muscular woman, the androgynously named Jasper (Jenny Strublin), and they emphasise the inequalities of working the streets. Although they convey the exhilaration of cycling through Chicago effectively – *Faster!* even cites the famous chase sequence from *The French Connection* (Friedkin, 1971) beneath the elevated railway – they make clear that Jasper is far from free. In *Faster!* she is sexually harassed by businessmen in a lift and manhandled by a receptionist, has to argue with clients for a decent rate and, finally, is hit by a car, which also destroys her bicycle. For Jasper, the apparent freedoms of this occupation do not extend to liberation from gendered norms.

While they depict the cycle courier community in familiar terms, as a colourful collection of cool nonconformists, dreadlocked slackers, dope smokers and tattooed hipsters, Ullrich's films emphasise the alienating bleakness and physical dangers of this 'edgework'. Uniquely among the titles discussed above, Ullrich's films suggest that, even though messengers have a specialised knowledge of the city, and move through urban spaces in a particularly deft and efficient way, nevertheless the female cyclist is exposed to the same hazards as any women moving alone through the city. There is little sense of the pleasures of free-flowing movement or of the mastery of urban space.

The accounts of messenger culture offered by the cyclists interviewed in *The Godmachine* emphasise its sociality and camaraderie. Kevin, a New-York-based messenger, likens it to a 'family', but also reflects, in a rueful echo of Arthur Seaton's monologue at the opening of *Saturday Night and Sunday Morning*, that

I've seen over the years, like, ten, fifteen guys die. Messengers, you know? I've seen girls get wracked up. [...] It's kinda like this – like a big machine, you know, and people get grinded up in it every once in a while.

It is a telling comment, challenging assumptions that the shift from industrial production to a 'knowledge economy' or 'information economy' results in emancipation, equality and the end of work. The cycle couriers populating these films remind us of the vast army of workers doing poorly paid, physically dangerous, sometimes deadly work in order to keep the modern city moving. Indeed, the films discussed throughout this chapter remind us that the bicycle has an ambiguous significance, representing both the promise of freedom and the relentless grind of punishing physical labour.

4

Sport and Performance Machines

Figure 4.1
Lance Armstrong (Ben Foster) racing in the Tour de France leader's yellow jersey in *The Program* (Frears, 2015) (courtesy of StudioCanal)

Cyborgs and Mega-Machines

Sport is an intrinsic element of contemporary life. Its social significance extends from children's education to international relations. It is a crucial means through which ethics and morality are taught and continually rehearsed, and, whether or not we play sports or follow them ourselves, they play a crucial role in shaping our sense of belonging to an imagined local, national or international community of spectators, the extent to which we conform to or deviate from conventional gender categories and our sense of our own bodies. Jean-Marie Brohm suggests:

Apart from the act of labour, the dominant and fundamental way man relates to his body in state capitalist society is through sport – inasmuch as it is through the model of sport that the body is understood in practice, collectively hallucinated, fantasised and individually experienced as an object, an instrument, a technical means to an end, a reified factor of output and productivity, in short, as a machine with the job of producing the maximum work and energy.[1]

Examining the ideological function of modern sport from the late nineteenth century onwards, Brohm argues that it has an alienating effect, encouraging us to see our bodies as mechanisms whose principal purpose is the generation of surplus value. Invoking the imagery of dystopian science fiction, he suggests that

sport might be regarded as a sort of mega-machine within which performance-machines, a superior form of automaton as it were, operate in a symbolic world of figures, computers, curves, stop-watch times and quantified energy.... Sport embodies the totalitarian dream of a system run on completely cybernetic lines, developing sporting 'cybernetropes', to borrow H. Lefebvre's expression, destined to serve as guides for the human race.[2]

Contemporary cycle racing is perhaps the clearest expression of this machinic ideal, the rider following a scientifically designed training and nutrition programme, riding a computer-designed and engineered bicycle that is configured to maximise power output and wearing computer-designed clothing to minimise drag. 'The entire technocratic ideology, whether in its imperialist or Stalinist form, of the good machine – cybernetic, productive and functionally integrated – is expressed in pure form in sport: the experimental science of human output.' Given that the term 'cybernetics' is derived from the ancient Greek term *kybernetes*, meaning 'pilot' or 'steersman', the cyclist is also the purest example of the cyborg.

Although it is widely seen as a corruption of the sport's ethical integrity, doping follows the same instrumental logic, using scientific knowledge to extract as much energy from the cyclist's body as possible. 'If cyclists see themselves as biological racing machines,' observes a contributor to the documentary *The Armstrong Lie* (Gibney, 2015), then Lance Armstrong's doctor/supplier '[Michele] Ferrari was one of the world's greatest mechanics'. This image of the cyclist as performance machine finds its purest literary expression in Alfred Jarry's absurdist 1902 novella *Le Surmâle* [*The Supermale*], which recounts the staging of a 10,000-mile race between a locomotive and a five-man bicycle by an American chemist to promote 'Perpetual Motion Food'. The riders' legs are linked by aluminium rods, and they continue riding even after one of them dies from exhaustion, his decomposing body still fuelled by the miraculous food. At this point the distinction between the locomotive and the human–bicycle coupling begins to vanish, the rider reduced to a component of the machine.

This disturbing fantasy foreshadows the way that modern sport reproduces and crystallises dominant social values, as sport, science and commerce are inextricably enmeshed. Preoccupation with sporting records, for example, represents both a rationalising desire to quantify any and all human activities and modernity's irrational belief in unlimited progress; Hibai López-González writes:

The direction of sport is always forward and any future sportsman is predicted to achieve further records than his predecessors. World and regional records are broken and that is believed to be the *telos* of the game. The main advantage of the idea of progress is that it can be easily extrapolated to basically every sphere of the society, that is how deeply ingrained the concept is in the minds of modern citizens. We can progress in school, at work or in our familial situation.[3]

The integration of sport into contemporary society in various forms is a consequence of its mediation, which is so significant to its composition that Lawrence A. Wenner uses the neologism 'MediaSport' to emphasise this co-dependency. It has become such a powerful cultural force that, for Michael R. Real, '[i]gnoring MediaSport today would be like ignoring the role of the church in the Middle Ages or ignoring the role of art in the Renaissance; large parts of society are immersed in media sports today and virtually no aspect of life is untouched by it'.[4]

The Passion of the Professional Cyclist

Competitive cycling is the perfect subject for dramatic cinema, and some of the earliest glimpses of bicycles on screen are depictions of road races in Lumière *actualités*. One short film shows scores of mustachioed riders – and one woman, Mme Vialette – rolling out of Lyon through clouds of dust along a sun-dappled road lined with trees and spectators at the beginning of a one-day race on 12 July 1916. It is at once a rare glimpse of an alternative possibility of desegregated sport with women competing alongside men in the same races, and at the same time a reminder of the historically embedded gendering of cycling cultures. As David Herlihy puts it, although '[w]omen have participated in competitive cycling since its inception…it was not until the second half of the twentieth century that official annual track and road titles were established.'[5] The first Olympic road race for women was only introduced in 1984 and the first track race in 1988, while '[t]he International Olympic Committee excluded women from its numbers until 1981.'[6] A century after the Lumière film it is depressing to read British champion cyclist Victoria Pendleton's complaints at the 'corrosive culture' of British cycling, characterised by misogyny and disableism, which led her to abandon cycling for horse racing,[7] while her team-mate Jess Varnish observes that the sexist culture of the national cycling team is maintained through a 'culture of fear' that silences critics.[8]

In its various forms – road, track and off-road racing – competitive cycling offers the viewer the voyeuristic pleasures of scrutinising athletic bodies in motion, and film intensifies the spectatorial pleasures of viewing sport, allowing us to study details of faces and bodies in slow motion, in intimate close-ups, from various angles and repeatedly. For instance, the short film of Scottish track racer Craig MacLean, *Standing Start* (McDowell, Pretsell, 2013), intercuts footage of MacLean racing in a velodrome, riding on static bikes mounted on rollers and lifting weights, and has a fetishistic focus upon the cyclist's massive, muscular legs. As well as objectifying the (male) athlete's body, cycle racing also invites us to identify with the struggles, failures and euphoric successes of individual cyclists, often through an emphasis upon the hard work, personal sacrifices and self-inflicted physical damage involved in competitive cycling, especially at professional level. This is typically underpinned by a narrative strategy of hyperbole, emphasising the historic significance of particular competitions or encounters and stressing the allegorical register of certain events, hill climbs inviting inevitable allusions to the myth of Sisyphus. Invocations of Greek myth permeate the imagery and verbal commentary associated with contemporary sports events, reinforcing the equation of athletic accomplishment with masculinity.[9]

The documentary *Moon Rider* (Dencik, 2012) exemplifies this preoccupation with physical struggle, as it details the suffering experienced by young Danish cyclist Rasmus Quaade as he attempts to establish himself as a professional rider. Shot on digital video and Super 8 film (implying a generic link to classic cycle race documentaries), the film emphasises the extreme demands cyclists place on themselves. 'I want to get as close to dying as possible,' Quaade explains, and we later see him pass out at the end of a time trial. The title refers to the extraordinary distance Quaade calculates he will have ridden in preparation for the under-23 world time trial championships: 379,000 kilometres, the distance to the Moon. As *Moon Rider* suggests, in cycle racing demonstrating endurance is almost as important as winning. Indeed, in contemporary sports coverage, '[i]njury is presented as entertainment, as spectacle. Television cameras regularly frame injured players and slow motion replays are used to allow viewers to see how an injury occurred and commentators to estimate the location or extent of the injury.'[10] This sadistic aesthetic – the expression of 'a political economy of licit cruelty' – is shared by most films about cycling sport.[11] The capacity to suffer – or simulate suffering – is a crucial skill or performance technique for athlete/actors, and this cruel aesthetic has a clear commercial logic: 'In short, blood sports trigger primal anxieties, and consumerism comes to the rescue with a quick fix.'[12] For Jean-Marie Brohm, it has a darker function still: 'Sport represents a veritable *ideological apparatus of death....* [I]t legitimizes all the current forms of torture and ill-treatment by exorcising them on "another stage" – on the sports field (which, by the way, is often the scene of acts of physical terror and torture, as in the Santiago stadium after the Coup d'Etat in Chile).'[13]

Domestique Labour

Questions of ethics are at the centre of the comedy *Le Vélo de Ghislain Lambert* [*Ghislain Lambert's Bicycle*] (Harel, 2001), a detailed pastiche of the rise-and-fall biopic. Following the conventions of the genre, it recounts the career of a moderately successful Belgian cyclist (an authentically wiry Benoit Poelvoorde) in the 1970s, condemned to ride in the shadow of his unbeatable compatriot Eddy Merckx. 'This movie is not the story of a champion,' the introductory voice-over explains, 'for the stories of great people are to be found in an encyclopaedia. The character of Ghislain Lambert can't be found anywhere.' The film proposes that sport's fascination lies in this potential for identification with athletes whether they are stars or anonymous women and men. This voice-over accompanies stock footage not of victorious cyclists but of riders crashing spectacularly, grimacing with pain, bleeding and writhing, and the physical hardships and misery of professional cycling are the film's focus. It documents the frustrations, banal duties and humiliations of riding for a professional team as a 'water carrier' or 'domestique', the team members who ride in support of stars such as Merckx. While touring, their 'directeur sportif' confiscates their shoes so that they can't leave the hotel to meet women, leading them to sneak out at night, hobbling awkwardly on their rigid cycling shoes and cleats.[14] Meanwhile, Ghislain's mundane duties include working as a door-to-door salesperson for the team's second-rate sponsor, 'Magicrème'. In a culture in which doping is tacitly condoned, Lambert embraces it enthusiastically, albeit with some comic practical difficulties, as his team-mate accidentally injects a double dose into his buttocks, sending him racing off like a rocket before collapsing into a ditch, delirious and convulsing. Lambert is later exposed and sacked, going on to end his career with some brief celebrity as the 'lanterne rouge', the last man in the field in the Tour de France.

As this fictional portrait suggests, cycle racing shares the celebration of individuality that is at the centre of mainstream cinema, stressing the conflicts between the ambitions of an individual rider and a restrictive institutional system. This is sometimes dramatised through the tense relationship between the rider and the team, the theme of the first Japanese anime selected for the Cannes Film Festival, *Nasu: Summer in Andalusia* (Kosaka, 2003), produced by Studio Ghibli.[15] The typically exquisite animation depicts European cycle racing with loving detail, centring on Spanish rider Pepe Benengeli, competing in the Vuelta a España. Pepe opts to ignore the instructions of the directeur sportif to ride in support of the team leader after overhearing that the sponsor wants him sacked, setting out to win the stage himself. The peloton is a metaphor for society in which riders are in constant communication with those around them, continually renegotiating their relationships with one another, forming fleeting alliances, observing fealty to their team leaders and conducting minor races as they move back and forth through the pack. This is captured visually in fluid CGI sequences simulating the helicopter shots used in TV coverage, in which the riders form into echelons to protect themselves from the wind. Viewed from above it is clear how the competing cyclists also work cooperatively. Questions of honour and loyalty, moral compromise, altruism and self-interest, corporate power and the colonisation of everyday life by commerce are all articulated through the relationship between the rider and team.

This confrontation between idiosyncratic individual and implacable institution is dramatised in the melodramatic biopic of record-breaking racing cyclist Graeme Obree, *The Flying Scotsman* (MacKinnon, 2006), in which the amateur rider clashes continually with the Union Cycliste Internationale (UCI) over the acceptability of his self-built, radically innovative bicycle designs. The film draws a parallel between the bipolar cyclist's lifelong experience of bullying and his vindictive treatment by the international cycling organisation, which changed its rules to prevent Obree from competing with his bike for the one-hour record. *The Flying Scotsman* raises the question of what a bicycle is, and how far it can mutate before it is no longer recognisable, and it also offers a window onto a vanishing world of sport as the province of gifted amateurs. Obree is a bicycle repairman, and his key rival for the hour record, Chris Boardman, personifies the new culture of professional sport, dominated by corporate investment and the application of scientific analysis and computer-aided engineering in the pursuit of 'marginal gains' in speed and efficiency, rather than relying upon the cultivation of particularly talented individual riders.[16]

Biopics and documentaries, such as *Pantani: The Accidental Death of a Cyclist* (Erskine, 2014), also emphasise the way that the world of professional cycling is populated by celebrity riders with distinct characters and easily identifiable physical characteristics. In *Le Grand Boucle* (Tuel, 2013), a cheerful comedy about an unemployed man riding the route of the Tour de France, the protagonist, François, and a rapper, Âme Strong,[17] compete over their connoisseurship by testing their knowledge of cyclists' nicknames. As with film fandom, cycling fandom can involve a fascination with the intimate details of an athlete's psychology and personal life, the 'star system' of professional cycling emulating that of commercial cinema and involving the 'manufacture' of charismatic characters through 'candid' interviews, product promotion, press conferences and makeovers.

Despite the team-based structure of most road racing, competitive cycling (like many sports) reiterates a capitalist discourse of individualism through the insistence that 'success' is primarily a matter of determination – the triumph of the will. Garry Whannel observes of the parallels between sport and capitalism, 'Both are competitive, both reward winners, and in both the majority are losers.'[18]

Heroes and Villains

Cycle races lend themselves to narrativisation by film-makers in various ways. Individual races are self-contained narratives organised around the quest for a goal, and these independent narratives are woven into a complex mesh of ongoing narratives that include the progress and decline of individual riders, the unfolding of a sequence of races across a season and the historical development of the sport. Consequently, as documents of staged performances, sport documentaries have an interstitial status, located somewhere between fiction film and *cinéma-vérité*. Like concert movies or filmed stage plays, they remind us of the inadequacy of the commonplace assumption that the documentary is, or should be, an objective record of reality.

Interviewed in 2003 about filming cycle racing, Danish director Jørgen Leth reflects:

I always thought it was a fantastic sport with great stories, and I always thought it deserved bet-ter than lousy sports journalism. I thought it deserved to be sung about in big, epic films.... So, I'm simply telling the stories that I see in the sport, and I know that I'm projecting certain val-ues into the sport, but I think they are there.... I'm talking about mythological values, and the heroes and villains, and the good and the bad.... For me, it's...the material of great storytelling.[19]

Leth's dismissal of journalism is less persuasive now that television coverage of certain cycling races is so comprehensive, incorporating high-resolution video from a dynamic constellation of cameras on helicopters, motorcycles and cars, and even 'onboard' cameras mounted on the racers' bicycles, all relayed instantly by satellite. The superimposition of continually updated statistical data on the screen, accompa-nied by an almost continual audio commentary, reinforces the impression of omni-scient, panoramic visuality, the sense that this density of data ensures that we can see (and know) everything that is happening. However, the crucial distinction between cinema and journalism lies not so much in cinema's superior narrative capacity as it does in the medium's limited capacity to reproduce the experience of contingency. While cinema is perfectly suited to restaging the ritualised drama of sport, what it *can-not* reproduce is liveness – the ever-present possibility of unexpected occurrences and the viewer's sense of participation in a collective event. Although a documentary can record a surprising event, such as the disruption of the Paris–Roubaix race by striking print workers in Leth's *A Sunday in Hell* (Leth, 1976), or Ole Ritter's failure to break the hour record in *The Impossible Hour* (Leth, 1974), once it has been recorded and is replayable it becomes a component of the filmed narrative, as if it had been scripted and staged. As Hibai López-González argues, sport's theatrical spectacle involves 'the tension between the scripted elements of the show and the open-to-improvisation ele-ments of it. A fully theatrical version of sport would have been perceived as a forgery, a deception of the sports ethos.'[20] Viewed on screen – and especially in retrospect – the distinction between accident, improvisation and rehearsed action becomes increas-ingly indiscernible – and in some cases, perhaps, the full, stage-managed, deceptive theatricality of sport also becomes visible – and the thrill of spectatorship is muted. Leth is correct that cinema can enhance the narrative drama of sport, but in so doing neglects the gripping contingency of the viewing experience.

Media Sports

In a broader sense, competitive cycling is already thoroughly mediated – a spectac-ular attraction designed for consumption through various media, both 'live' in real time and in retrospect through newspapers, periodicals, radio and television, as well as literary and autobiographical accounts. One feature of the current bicycle boom is the substantial shelf space in bookshops given over to biographies and autobiographies of famous – or undeservedly obscure – racers, histories of classic races, memoirs of passionate fandom, anthologies of sports journalism, tourist guides to cycling the routes of races, lavish collections of photojournalism and glossy, fetishistic photographic celebrations of racing bikes, racing jerseys or even promotional memorabilia. Films of bicycle racing are one instance of this rich cycle of recontextualisation and renarration. As Josh Malitsky observes, one consequence of this is that contemporary sport documentaries typically acknowledge that the history of a particular sport is also the history of its mediation, and so 'contemporary sports documentaries continually assert that *knowing about sport* requires knowing about and through media'.[21]

In other words, there is a co-constitutive relationship between modern sport and media. This is particularly evident with the Tour de France, which was first staged in 1903 as a promotional stunt to boost newspaper sales:

Georges Lefèvre, the cycling editor of *L'Auto-Vélo*, a sporting daily, hatched the concept…to upstage his paper's chief rival, *Le Vélo*. Headed by the tireless promoter Pierre Giffard, *Le Vélo* was already running two races, Paris–Bourdeaux and Paris–Brest–Paris. As Giffard had discovered, the buildup to and coverage of the races themselves provided an excellent means to sell newspapers. Lefèvre's boss, Henri Desgranges, agreed to try out the idea of a grand 'stage race' that would last several weeks and attract the top racers.[22]

The form of the 'Tour' is shaped by the commercial demands of publishers, offering readers an extended narrative of daily updates covering the subplots of passing rivalries, intrigues and conspiracies, minor contests and diverse environments, from pancake-flat sprint stages and time trials to lofty 'queen stages'. As Paul Fournel has commented, 'in bicycle racing…the day-to-day narrative of a race is very good for a reader, is always very easy to digest'.[23] However, the promotional value of cycle racing extends well beyond news titles. Indeed, one reporter observed that 'every labourer in France…remembers the name of the winning make when he has to buy a new bicycle'.[24] However, if it was good for a reader of daily newspapers, it is even better for a film or television viewer, who can watch in it real time.

The media–sport interrelation was also crucial to the emergence of cinema, since sport provided early film-makers in different countries with both subject matter and a pre-constituted audience. As film historian Luke McKernan observes, Muybridge's experiments with moving pictures initially 'came into being through a problem of

chief interest to the horse racing community.'[25] However, McKernan continues by challenging the technological determinism of film historians, who understand cinema as
the product of a series of technical experiments, and proposes that 'one may even go
as far as to say that the mere mechanical construction of a film projector has been
overestimated, and that it was boxing that created cinema.'[26] McKernan is drawing a
distinction here between a restricted concept of cinema, as the technical apparatus
of film-making, and a broader concept of cinema, as a component of modern culture and society. This argument is based on the prominence of sport, gymnastics and
dance in early American films, and the particular popularity of boxing films, which
led to the first feature film, directed by Enoch J. Rector in 1897 (in a 63 mm widescreen
format), a two-hour record of the heavyweight world championship fight between Jim
Corbett and Bob Fitzsimmons. Boxing is eminently filmable, since the action takes
place within fixed boundaries, and McKernan suggests that the boxing film is the stylistic and thematic source of American film: 'In the early American boxing film we
can see the very birth of American cinema – realism and drama, newsfilm and fakery,
commercialism, populism, professionalism, two protagonists battling within the perfect staging, the ring.'[27]

Films about cycle racing thus belong to a history of sport films as old as the medium
itself. While boxing was especially significant in American cinema, '[o]ther sports
filmed to some degree or other in Britain by 1900 were golf, cycling, polo, cycle polo,
water polo, wrestling, gymnastics, and of course the perennial favourite, the Oxford
and Cambridge boat race.'[28] Prolific Lancashire film-makers Sagar Mitchell and James
Kenyon produced many films featuring cycling, athletics, rowing, rugby and football,
for example, in documenting Edwardian life in Britain and Ireland. A 1901 film of the
amateur Manchester Muratti Cup race, the ten-mile 'Race of Champions', shows the
riders setting off chaotically from the start line on the Fallowfield velodrome; shots
showing the spectators pressed into the terraces alongside the track, and the winner,
Roland Jansen, being carried aloft on the shoulders of the crowd, who are capering
in front of the camera (both in excitement at the result and at the novelty of being
filmed), give a good sense of the popularity of the sport.[29]

Of Myth and Men

While cycle racing continues to provide rich material for film-makers from which to
fashion dramatic narratives, the most acute reflections upon the meaning of cycle racing are those of cultural critic and literary theorist Roland Barthes in a short magazine

essay from the mid-1950s, 'The Tour de France as Epic', and in *What Is Sport?*, the voice-over commentary he wrote for a Canadian documentary, *Le Sport et les Hommes* [*Of Sport and Men*] (Aquin, 1961). *What Is Sport?* examines the fascination the 'prodigious spectacle' of the Tour de France holds for French audiences, alongside sections on bullfighting, motor racing, ice hockey and football. His commentary is an analysis of cycling's significance as a cultural activity that elicits impassioned identifications and interpretation from audiences, written with the passion of a cycling fan. He writes with celebratory excess, going as far as to propose that, when riders find themselves slowing to a standstill on the forbidding Mont Ventoux stage, 'certain collapses have assumed a "Hiroshimatic" character.'[30]

Discussing the relationship between sport and nation, Barthes observes that the Tour offers viewers '[d]elicious rides followed by great combats, that free rhythm of serious efforts and amused idleness, so characteristic of the French: drama, humor, emotion.'[31] It also compounds a sense of national identity for French audiences, schooling them in the history and geography of their country.

The race describes the physical expanse of the country as riders trace a route linking towns and cities, tourist destinations and historic landmarks. While other sports may be understood as expressions of national character, none is as comprehensive as road racing. This is equally evident in *Wyscig Pokoju 1952. Warszawa–Berlin–Praga* [*Peace Race 1952. Warsaw–Berlin–Prague*], the documentary of the so-called 'Tour de France of the East' by Dutch auteur Joris Ivens, which uses a film of the multi-stage race to document the modernity of eastern European cities (and the damage done to them during the war), the productivity of socialist industry and agriculture (through shots of huge factories and farms) and the unity of Eastern bloc countries under socialism. As well as a survey of the country, Barthes suggests, in terms familiar from commentaries upon sport, the Tour is also a military campaign:

It is in the setting of a great war that a whole army of followers will play the part of the general staff and the commissariat. This army has its generals who stand, eyes fixed on the horizon. It has its light cavalry [...] it has its thinkers [...] its historians...and its press correspondents.

It also, and especially, has its commissariat, its heavy convoys loaded with supplies, machines or food.[32]

The Tour, Barthes observes, is the object of continual storytelling in which the 'war' is reframed in grandiose terms: 'There is the narrative of the day's epic, which the Tour broadcasts across all France, for the Tour has its writers...its inspired poets.'[33] What gives this spectacle such resonance is the sense that the cyclists are not competing against one another so much as the stubborn inertia of matter, the gravitational pull of the Earth: '[M]an must conquer not man but the resistance of things.'[34] Consequently, it is the mountain stages that bring the existential stakes of the race into focus, reinforcing the notion that this competition is a measure of an individual integrity:

The severest ordeal that nature imposes on the racer is the mountain. [...] But this conquest is so arduous that a moral man must commit himself to it altogether; that is why – and the whole country knows this – the mountain stages are the key to the Tour: not only because they determine the winner, but because they openly manifest the nature of the stake, the meaning of the combat, the virtues of the combatant.

The end of a mountain stage is therefore a condensation of the entire human adventure.[35]

As Tour veteran Louison Bobet concludes in Louis Malle's poetic documentary *Vive le Tour* (1962), '[w]ithout mountains there'd be no Tour de France'. Barthes proposes that the race takes place on a conceptual as well as a material plane, and his broader thesis is that sport is more than a simple physical competition; it is defined by its symbolic richness and metaphorical potential. 'Muscle does not make the sport.... What wins is a certain idea of man and of the world, of man in the world. This idea is that man is fully defined by his action, and man's action is not to dominate other men, it is to dominate things.'[36] It is, therefore, an exploration of ethics, but it is the expression of 'an ambiguous ethic', since it places equal value on both morality – exemplified by 'a racer's *sacrifice* to his team' – and realism – since the importance of winning dictates that '*[t]here is no place for sentiment in the Tour*'.[37]

Like theatre, sport offers a shared social experience. However, a key difference between these two modes of performance rests in the relationship between performers and audience: '[E]verything happening to the player also happens to the spectator. But whereas in the theater the spectator is only a voyeur, in sport he is a participant, an actor.'[38] This sense of participation, enacted most obviously by the tens of thousands of people who assemble along the race route every year for the briefest glimpse of riders streaking past – and who are just as important in *Vive le Tour* as the riders themselves – explains people's passion for this 'useless combat'.[39] Spectators of sporting events are active and expressive, as we see with the festive crowds of people who gather on the mountains to eat and drink and roar encouragement or abuse, to douse the riders with water and run alongside them, giving them a helpful push as they labour up the slopes. 'To watch is not only to live, to suffer to hope, to understand but also, and especially, to say so – by voice, by gesture, by facial expression.... [I]n a word, it is to communicate.'[40]

As an epic narrative, the Tour is an example of a contemporary myth. Myths, for Barthes, are not falsehoods but stories that circulate through various cultural contexts, including advertising, fashion, design and sport, shaping our understanding of the world, determining the dominant vocabulary, values and meanings that are available within a particular social context. Myth, therefore, has an ideological function, and the repetition of certain myths works to 'naturalise' or 'reify' certain concepts or social structures, by insisting, for example, upon the central importance of sexual difference, competition and individualism. An example is the idea that sport is timeless, emerging directly from classical Greece and Rome, rather than from industrial modernity. In fact, it was invented alongside the safety bicycle and the film camera. Brohm notes:

'[M]odern sport' appeared with the advent of large-scale industry during the period of the rise of English capitalism in the 18th and 19th centuries. The development of sport went hand in hand with that of world capitalism. The first Olympics in Athens in 1896…, those in Paris in 1900, in Saint Louis in 1904 and in London in 1908, were all in fact sporting appendages of Universal Exhibitions where the economic world powers were gathered.[41]

The language of sports commentary and promotional media, which emphasises the epic resonance of certain sporting events (and the preoccupation with historical precedents and traditions), encourages our acceptance of this racialised, gender-segregated arm of industrial and post-industrial capitalism as a timeless, universal and therefore inevitable human activity.[42]

In the Vicinity of Jørgen Leth

Roland Barthes' account of cycling's epic theatricality could be an instruction manual for films about competitive cycling. Danish director Jørgen Leth's films about cycle racing similarly emphasise the dramatic, mythic dimension of the competitions he films. Although Leth established himself as an experimental film-maker, poet and novelist – and is best known internationally as the subject of Lars von Trier's *The Five Obstructions* (2003) – his passion for cycle racing led him to make several films (and a collection of writing) on the topic, and he is a popular Tour de France commentator on Danish TV. He was involved for a time in the 1980s with the development of a Hollywood film on the Tour, *The Yellow Jersey*,[43] initiated by veteran producer/screenwriter Carl Foreman, and intended to star cycling fan Dustin Hoffman. Leth was employed as a consultant on the strength of his documentary of the Paris–Roubaix race, *A Sunday in Hell*, but was promoted to director after Hoffman fired the director

Michael Cimino. Leth got as far as shooting second-unit footage during the 1986 race before Cannon Pictures, which had taken over the project, went bust, and it was cancelled along with all the other films that were in development.[44]

Leth's first short cycling film, *Eddy Merckx in the Vicinity of a Cup of Coffee* (1973), is, as the title suggests, a fascinating exercise in juxtaposition: '[I]t takes place near paper and coffee,' the voice-over explains. The black and white film intercuts shots of Leth sitting behind a desk in a TV studio reading his poems to the cameras – 'poems about water, fire, war, silence, the scent of roses, bright lights at night and other depraved stimulants' – with Super 8 footage Leth shot as a spectator at the 1970 Tour de France, the year Merckx won the second of five victories. The film has a self-reflexive voice-over commentary, also delivered by Leth, describing what we are seeing and hearing. It is a critique of the radically incoherent form of television in which entirely unrelated material is presented in a disorienting and unbroken stream: news, adverts, soap opera, sports broadcast, discussion programmes, and so on. It also mocks the hyperbolic conventions of sports commentary: Mont Ventoux is described as 'a classical stage for martyrs', while '"les pavés" [the cobbled farm tracks of northern France] is a classical terrain where much can be gained and everything can be lost'. The commentary also highlights the banal redundancy of TV sports commentary that presents a description of what is on screen as psychological insight. Over shots of the 'almost intolerably ambitious' Merckx recovering after a stage, Leth observes,

He doesn't just want to win. He wants to win gloriously. It's a testament to his greatness that he respects the traditions and his own role in the epoch. Did he win as beautifully as someone like Coppi did in his day? That is his yardstick. I can study his face. He smiles. He eats a cake.

Leth's spare poetry is characterised by a fascination with bodily experience and the senses, and a structural interest in language that is paralleled in his films' experiments with cinematic form. His verse has a stylistic preoccupation with the repetition of words and phrases, using them in different combinations so that we become increasingly aware of the sounds of the words as they are emptied of meaning. The strategy of juxtaposition invites us to see a relationship between the two elements of the film, finding a strange poetry in what he terms the 'radiant clichés' of sports commentary. 'There's no such thing as tactics any more,' Leth observes over images of Mont Ventoux. 'It's only about each man's legs, wheels, gears, mind and stomach.'

Leth made a further three documentaries about cycle racing (alongside films about tennis, table tennis and pelota), and, while they are all more conventional, the earlier film is a model for the later films: all make a feature of Leth's distinctive dispassionate voice-over, they all regard Merckx (a cyclist who has won more professional races than any other rider and whose aggressive approach was characterised by strength and endurance, riding as hard as he could until his rivals fell away) as a superhuman figure, and all the films understand cycle racing as thoroughly mediated. That is to say, these are not presented as objective records of a sporting event. Instead, they acknowledge that the presence of cameras is an intrinsic element of the event, the film-makers participating in an entertainment conceived and staged for the spectator.

Stars and Water Carriers (1974) is a feature-length film about the 1973 Giro d'Italia, which covered 3,746 kilometres in 20 days, but the film also provides the viewer with a critical anatomy of professional cycle racing. The film explains the tactics of road racing and racing techniques – such as cycling in an 'echelon' formation to shelter from the wind, and braking 'in short jolts' to avoid destroying the brake pads on fast descents – and the riders' daily routines of meals, massages, team talks and interviews, but also reveals the organisational infrastructure of the race that TV sport coverage typically overlooks. The first shot of the race uses a long take and a telephoto lens[45] – a recurrent motif in Leth's bicycle films – to show not just the riders but the huge column of vehicles preceding and following the cyclists through the main street of a town. 'The long procession is set in motion,' the voice-over explains: 'the publicity caravan, press and TV, the police escort, officials, radio vans, and so on.' As the peloton of riders comes into view, rather than naming the individual riders and team sponsors, Leth observes that they consist of '[m]ostly Italians, of course, but also quite a few Belgians, Dutch and Spaniards. A few Frenchmen, West Germans and Swiss, and one Luxembourger, a Swede and a Dane.' He then explains, as the vehicles continue to pass the camera, 'Behind the riders are their team cars, 28 in all, two for each of the 14 teams. The cars contain team bosses, mechanics and masseurs. The procession ends with the ambulance and the broom wagon [the van that collects those riders who are too exhausted to continue]'.

From the title onwards – which describes the hierarchical relationship between the team leaders, whose job is to win races, and their team-mates, who 'get paid to help, not to shine' – the film reminds us repeatedly that professional cycling is a business. *Stars and Water Carriers* features a great deal of footage of the race, mobile cameras following riders closely through various stages, sometimes picking out particular riders, such as Giovanni Battaglin, José Manuel Fuente, Felice Gimondi and Francesco Moser, or significant passages, such as a contest between Merckx and Manuel Fuente on a mountain stage, or Danish rider Ole Ritter's time trial ride. These sequences resemble TV coverage of stage races, but the film presents us with a necessarily condensed account of the race, and is less interested in the result of the race than in the grand spectacle of cycle racing. Rather than climaxing with the awards ceremony, Merckx having won the 'general classification' with the fastest time overall, the film instead cuts anticlimactically from the sprint finish at the end of the final stage to a sequence in which Ritter packs his luggage into the boot of a car outside a hotel and drives away. 'A race has been run,' the voice-over says. 'He has said goodbye to the team. Now he's ready for other races. A man with a bicycle. And a bag full of contracts.'

Performance, Passion Work and Profit

Elsewhere, in a section introduced with the intertitle 'Money', shots of the convoy of vehicles passing through a town and out into the surrounding countryside are accompanied by an explanation of the financial basis of the race and the salaries of professional riders:

The towns pay for the privilege of being a dot on the race map. Most expensive is being a stage's destination and therefore the centre of all attention for 24 hours. The route is not planned without an eye on the financial side. Giro d'Italia is a national feast and a profitable private business.... It's all based on media coverage. The whole of Italy is glued to the TV for 22 days.

Leth goes on to provide a breakdown of the budget and the variety of sponsors, from sausage makers to mattress manufacturers. The riders constitute '140 human billboards', but, while some of them scrape a living,

Eddy Merckx is the best-paid rider ever. He earns at least 3 million kroner a year, a million of which is paid as a fixed wage by the sausage factory. The rest is starting fees and prize money. His fixed price for getting on a bike is 15,000 kroner a day.

For Leth, this demystification of the business of cycling does not detract from the sport's authenticity or integrity, since the film regards cycle racing as a form of public theatre. As the film shows a team of riders assembling for the start, stretching their muscles and warming up, the voice-over explains,

It's their job to participate in a ritual play of great beauty and depth. They're actors on a classical stage. The bicycle race: Giro d'Italia. A drama about the old virtues: bravery, stamina, sacrifice, courage, honour, pride, and so forth.

As the riders set off, Leth continues, 'The actors embark on new plots.... Into a new set of scenery, where the play can continue.' For Leth, athletes are professional performers, and they correspond to the colourful 'lexicon' of types catalogued by Barthes, which includes 'ardent warrior', 'formidable ghost', 'intractable jailer', 'actor' and 'traitor'.[46] It is their skill as performers that makes cycle racing so compelling.

In the film *A Sunday in Hell* (1976) – Leth's documentary of the Paris–Roubaix race, a European one-day 'classic' known as the 'Hell of the North' – his hyperbolic commentary stresses the melodramatic extremes the performers push themselves to. 'Each year this is where Dante-esque scenes are played out. Incredible hardship, martyrdom.... This hell is home turf to the Flemish supermen. An exclusive affair where only the strong survive.' As the film shows the riders negotiating the hazardous cobbled farm tracks, Leth comments: 'Within a few kilometres the peloton has been blown to smithereens. The merciless elimination process has begun.' He goes on to warn: 'A mishap on this first stretch of pavés can be fatal.' This is the cliché-ridden, overemphatic language of breathless TV and radio commentary, a fusion of literary, philosophical, religious and martial imagery, although Leth's tone remains comically cool, as if he is narrating a public information film. *A Sunday in Hell* observes that a key task of these athletes is *performing passion*. More than other forms of competitive cycling, and many other sports, road racing requires its participants to suffer, pushing themselves repeatedly to a point of utter exhaustion.[47] Indeed, during a mountain stage in *Stars and Watercarriers*, when Fuente and Merckx are racing head to head, Leth observes with relish, 'This is the decisive phase. This is the decisive moment of suffering. This is when it really starts to hurt.'

This is why the mountain stages of the Giro, the Tour, and the Vuelta a España, and the relentlessness of the hour record, are so fascinating; they test these performers to a point at which their composure and their discipline start to disintegrate. It is the point at which, as Leth says of Ole Ritter as he struggles up a mountain, we see 'the pain as an icon'.

I suspect this is a key reason why cycling fans are upset by doping: it is not that it exposes the inauthenticity of the sport, since this is well known,[48] but that it reduces the visible suffering of the riders, denying us the sadistic pleasure of watching them pedal themselves into the ground. It is not so much a display of skill that we demand, as what Barthes terms, in relation to 'all-in' professional wrestling, a 'performance of suffering'.[49] How fitting, then, that the steroids, hormones and stimulants used by athletes are 'performance enhancers', and the drug prescriptions 'scripts'. Professional cyclists are – to appropriate Annette Hill's description of pro wrestlers – passion workers, and, in so far as they are performers, we want 'method' actors who will go all the way for their art.[50] Brohm writes that '[t]he sporting legend is above all else a story of the pain barrier, of going to the limits of endurance, of being drunk with "animal" fatigue and of getting a kick out of bruises, knocks and injuries', and cycling epitomises the mythic function of sport more than any other.[51] However, for Brohm, the effects of this mythic spectacle are socially repressive; with its enervating emphasis, sport, like religion for Marx, is 'a *libidinal substitute* and a sublimation of aggressivity',[52] leaving participants and spectators drained of revolutionary energy, opiated and satisfied with an intolerable social status quo.

Although Leth is an experimental director, these films are relatively conventional, chronologically organised sports documentaries. Some generic elements are missing, such as interviews to camera, comprehensive histories of the event and biographies of key competitors, but, although they draw attention to the economics of road racing, 'Leth's films shy away from a political interpretation, since there is no clear division between the exploiters and the exploited'.[53] An exception is the scene in *A Sunday in Hell* when the race is interrupted by striking print workers, protesting against redundancies at the newspaper *Le Parisian Libéré*, one of the race's sponsors. The chanting protesters block the road, dumping piles of newspapers into the riders' path. 'A professional cyclist is a living billboard. Why not borrow some space for solidarity?' Leth asks on the commentary, as we see a protester stick a flyer over the logo on a rider's jersey. Over a disturbing shot of dozens of police wielding truncheons and rifles, Leth observes drily that industrial action has been going on for some time and '[t]he race organisers are not exactly unprepared'. Kristensen notes that, while 'the strikers are making a direct link between the bicycle race and an uneven labor system...in Leth's portrayal, there is no alignment of the riders with those aggravated by the race sponsor'.[54] This is true to an extent, although, as noted above, his films stress repeatedly the way that financial interests shape cycle racing, and also the ways in which the riders' understanding of their own roles is shaped by fantasy. Over a shot of Ole Ritter slumped in bed after a bad day that will mean his demotion to a supporting role – downgraded from star to water carrier – the voice-over explains: 'This is the face of disappointment. This is how a rider looks when he has lost a number of illusions.'

Leth's films offer some of the most comprehensive accounts of cycle racing in documentary cinema. They convey the ways in which it is sustained both by extremes of passion and idealism and by mundane financial arrangements. They also acknowledge that the films themselves are components of the spectacle of the bicycle race – not simply representations of the event, but a constitutive aspect of the races. They provide the spectator with intimate access to the stages in similar ways to TV coverage, with cameras in cars and on motorbikes capturing key moments. In addition, the films take us inside hotel rooms and restaurants, allowing us to watch riders relaxing, receiving massages, eating and discussing tactics. This culminates, in *A Sunday in Hell*, with a final sequence in which Merckx and the other naked riders wash in communal showers while fielding questions from a scrum of reporters and camera operators.

Hard Men and Homosociality

This foregrounding of cyclists' bodies draws indirect attention to another feature of Leth's films – and the culture of sport cycling more generally – which is an uncritical celebration of masculinity. This is expressed through a sadomasochistic preoccupation with pain, endurance, strength, control and a martial ethos, but the preoccupation with masculine power also extends to an erotic fascination with the male athlete's body. The grimy, wiry bodies on display in Leth's films are less obviously aestheticised than those in Leni Riefenstahl's monumental *Olympia* (1938), the archetypal sports documentary,[55] which includes a dreamily erotic scene in which naked male athletes enjoy an early morning lake swim before massaging and bathing one another in a sauna.[56] Nevertheless, Leth's reflections upon his interest in Merckx make clear that the film-maker was seduced by the cyclist: 'I was fascinated by him as a man. He has this Asiatic face, high cheekbones, very central eyes – "bedroom eyes", with long eyelashes. He is handsome in a very unorthodox way. The close-ups were almost sensual.'[57] The homoeroticism Leth finds in the world of competitive cycling is attributable partly to the almost wholly homosocial culture of the sport, which crystallises a broader historical tendency of cycling cultures, and of sport more generally. Toby Miller observes:

Sports allow men to watch and dissect other men's bodies in fetishistic detail, a space for staring without homosexuality alleged or feared.... The fetish of admiring body parts...gives a scientistic pleasure and alibi. A man who is lifting weights gives off signs of pleasure-pain akin to facial correlatives of the male orgasm, a sight otherwise denied men who define themselves as straight.[58]

In terms of the gendered coding of the body, the cyclist's body is ambiguous in so far as racing cyclists – especially road racers – are often as thin as possible (to maximise their power-to-weight ratio, allowing them to climb hills with less effort), and so perhaps the pleasures of men studying other men's bodies become more markedly complex. Obsessed with diet and calorie intake, a top road racer appears emaciated during the racing season, ribs, muscles and veins all visible under the taut skin; in conjunction with shaved legs (to make massages less painful and the cleaning of wounds easier and to reduce aerodynamic drag, but also, no doubt, for aesthetic reasons) and revealing, skin-tight clothing, their bodies are an unusual mix of signifiers of masculine strength, a narcissistic preoccupation with appearance, and feminine slenderness. Miller suggests that sport is 'a site of struggle over contemporary definitions of masculinity', but, in spite of the potential semiotic confusion written on the cyclist's body, cinema displays little interest in using the bicycle as a means of redefining and expanding masculine categories. Minor, but generally non-progressive, exceptions can be found in US film comedy, in which the bicycle is a sign of masculine inadequacy or immaturity.

Professional cycling is emphatically a 'man's man's man's world', in which men travel, work, socialise and sleep together (in shared hotel rooms and tour buses). Removed from the distractions of family and partners, other men – 'soigneurs' (assistants), masseurs, chefs and doctors – typically take care of the cyclists' bodies. Notably, one of the few distinct female voices in Leth's cycling films is that of a striker disrupting the race in *A Sunday in Hell*. Joining in with the chants of the crowd, she wrestles with one of the cyclists, pushing through the picket line, and explains furiously to another protester that she has children to support. In so far as women can penetrate this exclusive world, it is either as 'podium girls',[59] adoring fans – such as the woman who snatches a rider's cap at the end of the race – or a disruptive force, intruding into the man's world and spoiling everybody's pleasure.

In describing the homosocial world of professional cycling, Leth's films are a component of the complex, continuous multi-media representation of sport that works to shape the culture and mythology of contemporary sport and to interpret and fix its meanings. Professional cycle racing is an example of what, as already mentioned, Lawrence A. Wenner calls 'MediaSport', a field of social activity in which competitive events support the operations of a transnational commercial and political infrastructure principally dedicated to generating income – and, as Toby Miller observes, '[m]edia sports have been staggeringly masculinist. Most nations dedicate less than 5 per cent of press coverage to female athletes, and what there is frequently condescends and trivializes.'[60] He goes on to suggest that '[t]he most widely read segment of newspaper, the sports pages, routinely give greater attention to animals than women.'[61] This systematic sexism goes hand in hand with homophobia, which frames the gay male athlete as a particularly troubling figure, whose 'presence in the theater of sport ruptures cultural associations among masculinity, athleticism, hardness, toughness, and heterosexual potency'.[62] Paradoxically, this preoccupation with strength reveals that '[h]egemonic masculinity's idealizations of "manly men" are extraordinarily fragile constructs. Made of myth, these ideals are constantly contradicted by reality, and, as a result, they constantly require aggressive reaffirmation', and many of the films discussed in this chapter are engaged with this task of reaffirmation.[63]

The Myth of Merckx

In this regard, *La Course en Tête* [*Head of the Field*] (1974), by French documentarist Joël Santoni, is an interesting counterpart to Leth's films. A documentary portrait of Merckx, it follows him from the 1973 world championships in Barcelona, which left the beaten rider in tears, through a series of races in 1974, including the Giro d'Italia documented in *Stars and Water Carriers*.[64] Santoni was reading Roland Barthes' *Mythologies* when his friend Louis Malle suggested he make a film about Merckx, and Santoni recalls that *Mythologies* 'was my guide'[65] and that, when filming the cyclist,

I was not there as a journalist, to ask questions. I was there to capture images of this world and one of its main actors, Eddy Merckx. I was trying to catch this myth all the time, this moment of building a mythology and how people relate to this. That's what the film is about.[66]

Santoni's poetic film uses several strategies to capture the construction of a myth. It opens with a montage of excerpts from bicycle films, ranging from a 1901 Pathé trick film by Ferdinand Zecca of a fantastic flying bicycle/dirigible hybrid and a Lumière film of trick cycling from 1897 through to newsreel footage of races. This introduction locates Santoni's film within a representational history of cycling that blends documentation with fantasy indiscriminately. The chronological organisation of the film is unclear and fragmented, as it cuts back and forth with no clear indication of the temporal relationship between shots and sequences, and it makes only sparing use of voice-over narration and captions to guide the viewer. The effect of this, in combination with the insertion of stills and stock footage (and even illustrations and frames from comic books), is of a dense mosaic of mediated images of Merckx. This montage of monochrome and colour images of variable resolution, exposure and contrast also draws the viewer's attention to the rich textures and grain of film itself, making an aesthetic feature of the differences between different qualities and ages of the film stock from which it is assembled. Indeed, the opening telephoto shot of the convoy of riders and vehicles slowly approaching the camera is accompanied by a whirring sound that could be the distant sound of vehicles on tarmac but could, equally, be the sound of a film projector. One of the most remarkable stylistic features of *La Course en Tête* is the use of radically incongruous music to accompany the footage of cycle racing. Along with Jelly Roll Morton's New Orleans jazz, the film makes extensive use of arrangements of Renaissance music by David Munrow, along with Munrow's own compositions. Although the music, played on early instruments, seems initially to be a bizarrely anachronistic choice, much of it is dance music with rhythms that complement the cycling sequences perfectly, while the more majestic, courtly passages emphasise the ritualistic aspect of cycle racing, and the theatricality of sport (as well as an understanding of road racing as a European sport).

Another remarkable feature of the film is the narrative's orientation around the perspective of Claudine, Merckx's wife. Merckx was a reluctant interviewee who hated media attention, an impression confirmed by a sequence showing him squirming uncomfortably in various press and TV interviews. In place of revealing interviews with Merckx, audio interviews with Claudine provide a framing commentary, elaborating on Eddy's feelings and thoughts, but also reflecting on her own concerns. Alongside Santoni's commentary, her observations guide our interpretation. While *La Course en Tête* reiterates the idea of professional cycling as a passion play, it also emphasises the physical dangers and the frailty of the riders as well as their strength and courage. Over images of Merckx struggling through snow and the mud of Paris–Roubaix, Claudine observes: 'Cycling is a job like any other, but I prefer not to watch each race while he is suffering so much.' She relates that she is frightened when he is track racing after an earlier crash in which the rider in front of him died from a fractured skull, and a brief sequence of Merckx racing in a velodrome is followed by a gruesome sequence of crashes as riders slide across tarmac into crash barriers and spectators, are buried under high-speed pile-ups and writhe on the ground, bloodied and in pain. The soundtrack to this sequence is a chorus of wailing, groaning voices.

Rather than treating Merckx as a solitary, superhuman figure, *La Course en Tête* depicts him as a father and partner. The film's titles introduce Merckx as 'the champion' before introducing his wife, father-in-law and children, like the credits of a TV soap opera. We see Merckx at home eating and watching TV with his family, playing with his children and taking them to the fair; in one knowing sequence, shots of him watching his daughter riding a bicycle on a merry-go-round bracket footage of him racing in a velodrome, implying that, even at Merckx's level, cycle racing is an extension of child's play. Moreover, whereas Leth's film celebrates the heroic sacrifices made by riders for their team-mates, Claudine makes clear that racing depends on other mundane, less visible sacrifices and unacknowledged domestic labour:

I'm often sad when he goes out and I am left alone. On Saturday afternoons I see couples out walking and think, "Here I am, all alone." When a man works in an office he leaves in the morning and returns in the evening. It's very different when you say goodbye to him for four weeks.

Her presence in the film is a reminder that 'unpaid women's work, such as ferrying players, mending uniforms, and so on, is the sine qua non of most sport.'[67] Furthermore, Claudine reflects on the dangers of a rider such as Merckx identifying with the mythical persona of the champion:

When you are a star you always have an image. Looking thoughtful and having breakfast in bed. With the dog or on skis. All for publicity. But glory never lasts. It would kill him to think of the day he must retire.

This acknowledgement that success is transient and the athlete's body infirm is developed further through a reference to Merckx's failure of a dope test. After Claudine's observation that the distress of losing the 1973 world championships meant 'he can never resign himself to losing. Whenever he does it's the beginning of the end', we see a series of shots and stills of Merckx racing and crossing finishing lines triumphantly. The film then cuts to a shot of him emerging unsteadily from the Controllo Medico office at the 1969 Giro, followed by a TV interview in which the tearful cyclist protests: 'I have always been an honest sportsman.' Although the test result, which saw him disqualified from the Giro, was overturned by the UCI allowing Merckx to ride in the 1969 Tour shortly afterwards – and Merckx has claimed he was framed after refusing to 'sell the Giro' and throw the race[68] – the film underlines the link between doping and ambition, a subtext more or less absent from Leth's films.

Both directors' films feature wordless sequences in which shots of racing cyclists are accompanied by music, capturing the kinetic poetry of the sport, as well as the costly spectacle and logistical complexity of professional cycling. Television sports commentary shares with radio commentary a fear of 'dead air', and so such contemplative opportunities simply to watch athletes are extremely rare in sports coverage. This is a key way in which these films diverge from journalistic coverage.[69] Eschewing standard formal devices such as 'talking head' interviews – since both film-makers understand the bicycle to be the cyclists' most revealing medium of communication – they are hybrid films situated 'in the vicinity of' conventional documentaries and international art cinema. They are also both marked by a degree of ambivalence with regard to the sport: seduced by the spectacle, but fully aware that this is a performance staged for the cameras and that the film crews are participants rather than observers of these events. In distinguishing their work from the formal blandness and naïve aspiration to objectivity of 'journalism', both Leth and Santoni acknowledge that documentary cinema is a dynamic fusion of myth-making and demystification.

Lance Armstrong and the Problem of Truth

Questions of myth-making and what Barthes calls the 'problem of truth' are personified by Lance Armstrong, one of the most infamous examples of the athlete as performer, or spinner of stories. The feature film *The Program* (Frears, 2015) explores a number of the themes discussed in this chapter, including the commercialisation of the sport, the function of journalism, celebrity culture, the self-destructive effects of training and competition, and drug-taking. The biopic is a dramatised account of Armstrong's career from 1993 through to 2013, when he appeared on the Oprah Winfrey talk show and confessed to doping. Armstrong (played by Ben Foster, in a very precise imperson-ation) explains to Winfrey at the end of the film, 'This story was so perfect for so long. You win the Tour de France seven times, you have a happy marriage, you have children. I mean, it's just this perfect mythic story – and it wasn't true.'

The Program follows Armstrong's initial rise, racing in Europe after winning the world championship, his setback when diagnosed with brain, testicular and abdomi-nal cancer in 1996 and his return to professional cycling in 1998. With the assistance of the (aptly named) Italian physician Michele Ferrari, Armstrong puts together the 'blue train', a team sponsored by the US postal service (as if in a rejoinder to the stubbornly anti-American cycling postman in Jacques Tati's *Jour de Fête*). Armstrong informs them they are adopting the titular doping programme to win the Tour de France, and he begins winning Tours, but suspicion about the basis of his success begins to mount. The film is based on an account of Armstrong's career by *Sunday Times* journalist David Walsh, and Walsh is a key character in the film, drawing attention to the ubiq-uity of doping in the professional peloton in the wake of the scandalous discovery by customs officers of a suitcase of steroids and syringes in the car of a Festina 'soigneur' at the French–Belgian border in 1998, which was followed by police raids. Disgusted by the extent and the obviousness of doping, Walsh later tells his editor: 'I have no interest in going up a mountain to watch chemists compete.'

As the film progresses, and Armstrong continues winning, he fights running battles to protect his name, bullying another rider, Filippo Simeoni, who testified against Ferrari, into silence. He complacently instructs an obsequious official of the World Anti-Doping Agency in Geneva after he has tested positive for erythropoietin

(EPO), the hormone at the centre of Ferrari's programme that stimulates red blood cell production, 'You should do whatever you think is best for the integrity of cycling.' An international celebrity by that point, having published a best-selling autobiography, and established the Lance Armstrong Foundation to raise money for cancer sufferers, Armstrong understands his crucial role in raising cycle racing's international profile; as his bullish agent Bill Stapleton explains to the investigator, 'Lance is single-handedly transforming your shitty little Eurosport into a global brand.' Stapleton threatens Armstrong's former team-mate Frankie Andreu over Andreu's wife's testimony about Armstrong's drug use, and Armstrong successfully sues *The Sunday Times* for libel over one of Walsh's articles.

After retiring in 2005, having won an unprecedented seven consecutive Tours, Armstrong returns to professional racing in 2008. A comic sequence showing Armstrong shooting embarrassingly bad TV adverts, followed by a grim corporate speech at the '1st National Aircon Sales Awards 2008', makes clear the comparative attractions of racing for this incorrigible performer: the addictive appeal of winning, but, more importantly, the accompanying celebrity. Ignoring the warning of his former directeur sportif and accomplice, Johan Bruyneel, that '[w]e got away with it for a long time', Armstrong decides to start racing again. This fatal scenario is familiar from crime dramas in which a reluctant thief is coaxed out of retirement for one final catastrophic heist, and the narrative follows this trajectory closely. In this case, his downfall is bought about by Floyd Landis, a former US Postal Service team-mate who embraced Armstrong's doping programme with naïve enthusiasm. Armstrong refuses Landis a place on his new team, since Landis has recently tested positive for testosterone after winning the 2006 Tour. Landis, a devout Mennonite Christian troubled by guilt and hurt by Armstrong's rejection, goes on to confess everything at a US Anti-Doping Agency (USADA) hearing.

Armstrong manages to reach a disappointing third place in the 2009 Tour before USADA issues a lifetime ban. His reaction to USADA's impassive panel members cycles rapidly through anger, disavowal and despair: 'I can clean up the whole sport without your help because you're a bunch of amateurs!' he yells, before declaring desperately:

I can't get up in the morning unless I have something to live for. That's training. Competition. I'm not training because I enjoy it. I'm not training because I want to stay fit. It's my whole – my whole life. It's what I do.

The film ends, as it opened, with shots of Armstrong riding uphill, breathing hard, although unlike in the opening Armstrong is no longer wearing the yellow jersey of the Tour de France leader.

Aptly enough, director Stephen Frears' first feature-length production, *A Day Out* (1972), was a nostalgic TV drama about a Sunday ride into the country by four members of Halifax's cycling club in 1911, foreshadowing *The Program* in its preoccupation with masculinity, a theme running through Frears' work alongside questions of national identity. Although *The Program* is concerned with the controversies of doping in professional cycling, the film is most interested in the figure of Armstrong and his story's symbolic richness. Frears directed a TV movie[70] about the supreme court negotiations following Muhammad Ali's refusal of the draft to fight in Vietnam, but *The Program* has more in common with his commercially successful film portraits, *Florence Foster Jenkins* (2016), *Philomena* (2013) and *The Queen* (2006).

As Armstrong acknowledges to Oprah Winfrey, this is an archetypal narrative of a protagonist whose fall from grace is a direct consequence of his own ambition and overconfidence. Screenwriter John Hodge's previous screenplay was the kinetic thriller *Trance* (Boyle, 2013), about the theft of a painting from an auction house, and, as a film about a multi-million-dollar criminal conspiracy that gradually falls apart, *The Program* follows the same heist film conventions. Like the gangsters of *Scarface* (De Palma, 1993) and *Goodfellas* (Scorsese, 1990), Armstrong over-reaches himself, deluded by drugs and wealth to believe that he is invulnerable. 'I'm Lance Armstrong, and he's fucking no one!' he roars at his agent when he learns of David Walsh's whistleblowing article. Indeed, Armstrong is an improbably perfect cinematic character. A Texan with a name that could not be more phallic, he is the very epitome of heteronormative American masculinity.

He also epitomises American individualism, the self-created figure who wills himself to succeed after receiving the opportunity for a second act, and he achieves success by assembling a team to engineer his transformation. These include his agent and his directeur sportif, Johan Bruyneel, whose job includes administering drugs, cheerily hooking the team up to intravenous drips. Most importantly, though, Armstrong's team includes the physiologist, Ferrari. Armstrong initially offers himself to Ferrari, declaring: 'I want to be one of your guys. I want to be on whatever program they're on.' Ferrari goes on to explain to Armstrong, in a commentary that applies to modern sport more generally, 'This is not just running up a hill in the hope of getting fitter. This is science.' However, Ferrari is not an unassuming lab technician but an evangelist, who recalls that his first encounter with EPO at a nephrology conference 'was like a vision, a heavenly vision, when God spoke to Paul. That is how it felt to me. Lacryma Christi.' Evoking the deranged scientists peopling Universal horror films of the 1930s, Ferrari rhapsodises: 'No longer were we confined to the limits of physiology. Now we could alter physiology. No longer confined to Earth, now we had learned to fly.'

The Program is a portrait of determination, and there is little sense that the Armstrong depicted here is troubled by guilt. In the opening scene, set in a café in 1993 before Armstrong's first Tour, an interviewer observes that many riders experience the race as 'an odyssey into pain and suffering, ...an almost religious experience. Eventually you arrive at a point of enhanced self-awareness, and I was wondering: do you think about that?' 'Well, I just love to ride my bike,' replies Armstrong with a shrug. The film proposes that, for Armstrong, having almost died from cancer and the aggressive treatment of the disease, the attraction of cycle racing was not the ecstasies of passion endured by many professional cyclists but the satisfaction of winning; 'I never want to be that close to losing again,' he tells Bruyneel.

The Program also makes clear that, for Armstrong, success involved the construction of a persona alongside the reconstruction of his body; he was a skilled performer, at ease in press conferences and promotional appearances, relishing the opportunity to occupy the stage. Speaking at a charity dinner for his Livestrong Foundation, he recalls being in hospital recovering from surgery and willing himself to walk along the corridor, even though he was stumbling and disoriented, dragging an IV drip. 'I didn't give up, because it's worth it.... Inside each and every one of us is something more potent, more powerful than any drug on the face of the planet.... It's called the will to survive.' Crucially, when the scene he describes occurred earlier in the film, the unstable Armstrong had to be helped into a wheelchair by nurses, while deliriously insisting he was the world champion; however, as he goes on to tell the audience with the slightest of smiles, 'we are all the authors of our own life stories, so go out there and write the best damn story you can, and live it, and be strong'. For the Armstrong depicted in this film, as for Leth, Santoni and Barthes, cycle racing is a narrative medium and the cyclist is a storyteller. As he tells his future wife when she approaches him after the speech, 'I just tell 'em what they want to hear'.

Early on in the film David Walsh complains to colleagues: 'I used to believe in this sport, and Armstrong is killing it', but the film is far more ambivalent in its attitude to Armstrong and professional racing's permeation by drug-taking. Indeed, the film seems to echo Paul Fournel's observation that doping is almost inseparable from the sport:

It's commonly said that racers dope because it's a hard sport, but their sport is also hard because they dope. The milieu of racers is a doper's milieu, and the serpent of doping endlessly bites its own tail. The lie is too old, and the hypocritical abyss they've allowed to open between the official line and real practices is too enormous ever to be done away with.

In the peloton, refusing to dope means refusing to 'do the job'; it's like refusing to train or get a massage.

[...]

Doping itself has become a form of high-level competitive sport. They should do dope checks on the docs.[71]

The narrative focus on Armstrong ensures that he emerges as a sympathetic character simply because he is the most fully developed. However, the film's ambivalence about doping is unsurprising, since Armstrong's drive to do whatever it takes to win is consistent with the ethos of a sport that celebrates riders' physically self-destructive efforts, and with cinema's celebration of heroic masculinity and self-destructive physical excess. In this respect, the Armstrong depicted in *The Program* remains a quasi-heroic figure whose single-minded drive to succeed would be a commendable attribute in most films. As novelist James Waddington writes in a magic realist novel about the Faustian pact between cyclists and dealers, '[a] drug, whatever it is, its effect is to allow the body to spend itself recklessly, sometimes fatally so'.[72] Drug-taking is a pure form of expenditure or consumption, and, as the documentaries of Jørgen Leth and Joël Santoni make clear, expenditure is precisely what we expect of professional cyclists.[73] Moreover, as Paul Fournel observes,

[t]he bike is in itself a form of doping.... It's the tool of natural speed; it's the shortest path to the doubling of yourself. Twice as fast, two times less tired, twice as much wind in your face. It's all right always to want more.[74]

Secrets and Lies

The Program is focused on the athlete rather than the sport, and, as a consequence, the sense of Armstrong's betrayal of the sport's ethical ideals is muted. Investigative documentaries *The Armstrong Lie* (Gibney, 2013) and *Stop at Nothing: The Lance Armstrong Story* (Holmes, 2014) are far more damning in their account of Armstrong's career.

Stop at Nothing combines stock footage along with interviews with the cyclist's former friends and colleagues, as well as journalists and lawyers. Unlike *The Program*, Holmes' film proposes that Armstrong tried to manipulate races from early on in his career, beginning with a 1993 race in Philadelphia in which the young rider paid his rivals to let him win the million-dollar prize. The Armstrong described in this film is not just shameless in pursuit of success but is also a vicious, exploitative bully, ready to use threats and slander to silence or discredit opponents. One solicitor suggests that Armstrong might be a 'clinical sociopath'.

The sense of betrayal recounted by Armstrong's former friends and colleagues, as well as the outrage of journalists such as Paul Kimmage and David Walsh, is stronger in *The Armstrong Lie*. This betrayal is shared by the director, campaigning documentarist Alex Gibney, an Armstrong fan who had intended to film an account of Armstrong's comeback in the 2009 Tour. However, after Armstrong appeared on TV in 2013 to confess to doping in all his successful Tours, the focus of Gibney's film shifted. Armstrong agreed to a further interview, although the director was uncertain '[w]hether he wanted to try to make things right, or whether he still wanted to influence my story'. One of the most astute observations, made by a journalist interviewed by Gibney, is that '[t]he gift that he has, that gets overlooked, is his gift as a storyteller, his gift as a manager of his own storyline'.

Armstrong himself makes a similar point to Gibney in an interview recorded shortly after taping the Oprah Winfrey show: 'There are these two complete opposite narratives. The only person that can actually start to let people understand what the true narrative is is me. And you should know that better than anybody.' One of Gibney's interviewees observes of Armstrong's story: 'This is not a story about doping; this is a story about power', and power for Armstrong is a matter of shaping the narrative.

It is clear in both documentaries that Armstrong relished the visibility that came with success, and it is also clear from the quantity of stock footage incorporated into both films that, as an amateur and professional racer, Armstrong has lived his life on camera. Being a racing cyclist involves being a public spectacle, and this extends to the intimately intrusive dope-testing regimes. *The Armstrong Lie* shows a pair of UCI doping control officers arriving unannounced one morning at his house to take blood and urine samples in front of his young daughters, and then, the following morning, a USADA officer arrives at his house, again without warning, to perform the same tests. It is a disturbing insight into the lack of privacy available to professional athletes, whereby their body must be made humiliatingly, intimately available to official strangers at any time. Brohm warns that modern sport offers us a testing ground for the biopolitical techniques that will bring about a rationalised, totalitarian surveillance society, as '[t]he sports and medical authorities, reigning hand in hand over a system governed by the logic of competition and productivity, inevitably give birth to a strengthened judicial and police apparatus'.[75] As the Armstrong films suggest, professional cycling is the perfect experimental laboratory for the quantification and monitoring of the body conducted by a partnership between medical institutions, judicial systems and supranational corporate bodies.

While the Lance Armstrong depicted in these films is often dislikable, he is nevertheless a fascinating personification of the ideological contradictions of contemporary sport's celebration of individual achievement. 'The hero of this ideology,' writes Brohm, 'is the "self-made man" who attains the heights of performance on the basis of his own merit and through his own efforts: social advancement is possible after all.'[76] Armstrong understood what was required of him, and set about unsentimentally transforming himself into a performance machine that could occupy the heroic role at the centre of this narrative of the self-made man. The appeal of cycle racing, like all sport, rests on its symbolic richness, its mythic potential, and so the stories told by *The Program* and the other films discussed in this chapter are more than just accounts of individual athletic achievements or particular sporting events; they are allegorical narratives about how we accommodate ourselves to the demands placed on us by friends, families, employers, changing technologies and society at large.

5

Riding like a Girl

Figure 5.1
Ahoo (Shabnam Tolui) at the head of the bicycle race in *The Day I Became a Woman* (Meshkini, 2000)

Published in 1895, at the peak of the cycling boom and the birth of cinema, Frances E. Willard's *A Wheel within a Wheel* is an account by the American temperance and suffrage campaigner of learning to ride a bicycle at the age of 53. Interlacing autobiographical and philosophical reflections with a description of the practical process of learning to ride a safety bicycle, this slim book is a quietly moving testament to the emancipatory potential of the new machine.

After the strain of a life devoted to 'the indoor realm of study, teaching, writing, speaking' had led to 'a mild form of what is called nerve-wear', and 'sighing for new worlds to conquer', Willard decided to take up cycling.[1] Willard was attracted to the bicycle as a temperance reformer, since it 'is the vehicle of so much harmless pleasure', by comparison with the ravages of alcohol, requiring the rider 'to keep clear heads and steady hands'.[2] In addition to its moral value, she saw the bicycle as a social leveller, since it was affordable to people who would never be able to afford a horse, and was a machine that both 'peasant and prince must master...by the democratic route of honest hard work'.[3] Importantly, Willard was enthusiastic about cycling because it offered physical freedoms that were typically unavailable to respectable adult women. Having grown up in the country, she recalls experiencing the transition to womanhood as the unjust imposition of physical confinement:

I 'ran wild' until my sixteenth birthday, when the hampering long skirts were brought, with their accompanying corset and high heels, my hair was clubbed up with pins, and I remember writing in my journal, in the first heartbreak of a young human colt taken from its pleasant pasture, 'Altogether, I recognize that my occupation is gone.'[4]

In the course of patiently learning to ride her machine (fondly dubbed Gladys) and learning 'the location of every screw and spring, spoke and tire, and every beam and bearing', Willard 'found a whole philosophy of life in the wooing and winning of my bicycle'.[5] She discovered in cycling an instructive analogy with human experience, seeing in the bicycle wheel an echo of both the rotating Earth and 'the wheel of the mind'.[6] Successful cycling requires the development of skills and qualities that have a much wider application, and she relates that she

began to feel that myself plus the bicycle equaled myself plus the world, upon whose spinning-wheel we must all learn to ride, or fall into the sluiceways of oblivion and despair. That which made me succeed with the bicycle was precisely what had gained me a measure of success in life – it was the hardihood of spirit that led me to begin, the persistence of will that held me to my task, and the patience that was willing to begin again when the last stroke had failed.[7]

For Frances Willard, cycling was both a rich metaphor for a way of being in the world and as a means of being in the world *differently*. For all the book's gentle humour, evident in the captions accompanying the photographs of Willard attempting to master Gladys, the emancipatory potential of the bicycle is clear: '[N]o matter how one may think himself accomplished, when he sets out to learn a new language, science, or the bicycle, he has entered a new realm as truly as if he were a child newly born into the world.'[8] Reflecting on the social impact of this technologically driven renaissance, she observes that the spectacle of women engaged in athletic activities is having a transformative effect on assumptions about gender difference: 'The old fables, myths, and follies associated with the idea of woman's incompetence to handle bat and oar, bridle and rein, and at last the cross-bar of the bicycle, are passing into contempt.'[9] She suggests that the sight of a woman on a bike will be far more effective than campaigns, such as those mounted by the British Rational Dress Society, to liberate women from the constraints of incapacitating skirts, crinolines and corsets:

An ounce of practice is worth a ton of theory; and the graceful and becoming costume of woman on the bicycle will convince the world that has brushed aside the theories, no matter how well constructed, and the arguments, no matter how logical, of dress-reformers.[10]

At the book's conclusion, she reflects that she was prompted to master the bicycle by her love of adventure, but also 'from a love of acquiring this new implement of power and literally putting it underfoot.'[11]

Speed, Power and Rational Dress

The image of a well-dressed woman on a bicycle is one of the most enduring symbols of the social transformations taking place in industrialised countries at the end of the nineteenth century, and of the demand for greater rights and political representation for women. As Clare Simpson observes, since female cyclists were regarded as eccentric and unfeminine, 'women on bicycles generally became associated with the image of the New Woman, who was equally unconventional.'[12] The safety bicycle was the power tool of the Suffragettes and the 'New Woman', its novelty captured in two early 'actualities' by British film-makers. Robert W. Paul's 30-second *Hyde Park Bicycling Scene* (1896) shows a busy, tree-lined road filled with cyclists on safety bicycles (including a twin-seater 'sociable') weaving around horse-drawn carts, female cyclists clearly outnumbering the men. Cecil Hepworth's 75-second *Floral Parade of Lady Cyclists* (1899) documents a ride on a dusty London road by female members of Catford Cycling Club. Following a horse-drawn wagon carrying a brass band come dozens of women cycling past the small group of onlookers, some of them racing past the camera. Although it is not a very formal display – some of the riders have their jackets draped over the handlebars – all the women are dressed in heavy skirts and hats, ranging from simple straw boaters to lavish flower-bedecked hats with veils.

These films testify to the fact that 'the popularity of bicycling for women reached its zenith in the 1890s, so that in 1896 more women's bicycles were manufactured than men's'.[13] As well as simply documenting this fashion, these films contributed to the popular stereotype of the 'New Woman', satirised in H. G. Wells' *The Wheels of Chance*. When Wells' protagonist, draper's assistant Hoopdriver, encounters a young bourgeois woman on a bicycle during his cycle trip to the south coast, he is bewildered to find that she is wearing bloomers: 'And the things were – yes! – *rationals!* Suddenly an impulse to bolt from the situation became clamorous.'[14] As Patricia Marks observes, such abject responses to the phenomenon of the 'New Woman' reveal a curiosity with this group of middle-class women demanding more access to education, greater mobility and a louder political voice, but they also express an 'entire panoply of concern about a changing feminine mythology'.[15] Beth Muellner notes:

Late nineteenth-century women bicyclists were viewed as independent, youthful and emancipated, and were inscribed in the popular imagination as such through the proliferation and public display of advertising posters, postcards and stamps.[16]

These images are an indication of the speed with which manufacturers and retailers identified a new market for their products: bicycle advertisements constituted 10 per cent of national advertising in the United States in the 1890s.[17] Ellen Gruber Garvey writes:

Manufacturers wanted to sell bicycles to as many people – both men and women – as possible.... So, since the safety, though apparently nongendered, was understood to be masculine, women's riding had to be made socially acceptable to sell safety bicycles to a larger market.[18]

On the other side of the Atlantic, in 1889 a Coventry manufacturer began selling both 'the Psycho Ladies' bicycle, with a drop frame and no shadow of a crossbar of any kind, and a "lady-front" tandem. Shortly afterwards John Kemp Starley brought out his ladies' Rover'.[19] Although the image of a woman on a bicycle is an enduring sign of the optimism of first-wave feminism, it is also an image laced with ambiguity, a symbolic threat to the established social order. As Marilyn Bonnell observes, for the Victorians, 'the bicycle became a terrible reminder of the disruptive power of women, a power which they feared existed and preferred not to witness'.[20] What is evident from a survey of images of women cyclists in cinema is that this figure remains a troubling one. The short Pathé film *La Première Sortie d'une Cycliste* (1907) captures this anxiety in its comic account of a bourgeois woman learning to ride. After taking delivery of a new bike, the woman rides straight out of her house, colliding with a top-hatted gentleman on the pavement, and then races off at furious speed, crashing into a series of obstacles including a pram, a cart, a drilling soldier, a group of picnickers, a landscape painter and a herd of sheep before, finally, riding head-on into a car. After each crash she is chased or attacked, receiving punches and kicks, and the film ends as she returns home and collapses, bruised and bloody, with a black eye, ripped skirt and bicycle in pieces. This is a very fast, violent and funny physical comedy, and the comedy is derived not just from the sequence of slapstick gags but also from its orientation around the disruptive impact of the female cyclist. While *La Première Sortie d'une Cycliste* expresses a prevailing social irritation at the careless 'bicycle cad' or 'scorcher', the film is notable for its sexual politics. As Simpson notes, 'fast riding was also associated with the notion of "fast" women', and so female cyclists were derided not only for being excessively manly and graceless but also for shameless bodily display.[21]

This association of speed with moral laxity had an international register; as Smethurst records, in the same period, for 'the hostesses, dancing partners and prostitutes who were part of the colourful social life of Chinese cities…bicycles were a luxury, but also a convenience and a fitting accoutrement to their alternative lifestyle'.[22] The middle-class woman in *La Première Sortie d'une Cycliste* is a familiar satirical figure, who causes mayhem in presuming to venture out alone, and, in doing so, invites relentless abuse and physical violence. By contrast with the images of decorous, graceful woman cyclists in the films by Paul and Hepworth – symbols of orderly progress – this is an image of social change as unstoppable, chaotic momentum. The fact that the cyclist is apparently played by a man in drag, riding a bike with a crossbar, emphasises the anxiety about women's masculinisation, an anxiety that reflected a broader fear of the feminisation of men during a period of mechanisation: 'Working alongside women, male factory workers clerks and shop assistants felt less "manly" than rural forebears, despite the fact that women had always been equally important to rural labour.'[23]

Occupy All Streets

In venturing out on a bicycle, the female cyclist was undertaking a 'purposeful occupation' of public streets, parks and bridleways, and in the late nineteenth century and early twentieth this involved a transgression of the gendered boundary between the private, domestic sphere and the public sphere.[24] What made this transgression so troubling was the sense that it was 'not simply a matter of extending the range of women's domestic space into the masculine public sphere, but of regendering it altogether.[25] In late nineteenth-century New Zealand 'people believed women were interlopers in public space', and women cyclists often found themselves subject to critical remarks and physical obstruction.[26] As *La Première Sortie d'une Cycliste* suggests, albeit in comically exaggerated fashion, the spectacle of a woman on a bicycle was a disturbing, subversive phenomenon.

Writing about the way that bodily experience is gendered, philosopher Iris Marion Young has argued that one of the principal ways in which men and women are defined in contemporary society is by the different ways that they navigate and occupy space. Whereas, she suggests, men learn to inhabit, and move confidently and expansively through, the space around them, women experience space 'as *enclosed* or confining'.[27] Consequently,

women tend not to open their bodies in their everyday movements, but tend to sit, stand, and walk with their limbs close to or enclosed around them.... [W]omen tend not to reach, stretch, bend, lean or stride to the full limits of their physical capacities, even when doing so would better accomplish a task or motion.... Feminine existence appears to posit an existential enclosure between herself and the space surrounding her, in such a way that the space which belongs to her and is available to her grasp and manipulation is constricted, and the space beyond is not available to her movement.[28]

Young uses the common insult 'throwing like a girl' to highlight the differences in the way men and women learn to move their bodies, observing that this style of movement – running like a girl, hitting like a girl, and so on – is a consequence of systematic training in physical self-restraint. Throughout her life a girl is told that

she must be careful not to get hurt, not to get dirty, not to tear her clothes, that the things she desires to do are dangerous for her. Thus, she develops a bodily timidity which increases with age. In assuming herself as a girl, she takes herself up as fragile.... The more a girl assumes her status as feminine, the more she takes herself to be fragile and immobile.[29]

It is this physical inhibition that Frances Willard railed against nearly a century earlier, and these accounts help us to understand why the image of the female cyclist remains a transgressive figure. In heading out confidently on her bike, enjoying physical exertion and, perhaps, competition, she takes up space reserved for men, and so, whether it is conscious or not, for a woman to ride a bike on a public road is a political gesture, a defiant claim of ownership over the space and a rejection of conventional norms of feminine fragility. In other words, riding like a girl need not mean what Miss

F. J. Erskine describes in her 1897 etiquette guide as 'lady cycling', in which 'overdoing it' is the principal danger for the fragile woman: 'If once a rider overdoes herself, it means months, even years of care to get right again.'[30] Patricia Marks explains that Victorian concepts of gender were premised on 'the belief that muscle and femininity were in a delicate mathematical balance.'[31] The bicycle was a device that threatened to upset this equilibrium.

'Asking for Trouble': Women and Cycle Touring

The sensational perils faced by the female cyclist are the subject of British thriller *And Soon the Darkness* (Fuest, 1970). The film tells the story of two young British nurses, Cathy and Jane, on a cycling tour of the French countryside. After an argument about whether to continue the holiday, Jane cycles off angrily, abandoning her unenthusiastic friend, whereupon Cathy is abducted by an unseen attacker. Jane eventually returns to look for Cathy, and she is joined in her search by a creepy young man called Paul, who claims to be a detective in the Sureté investigating the unsolved murder of a Dutch female tourist on the same road three years earlier. Distrustful of Paul, she enlists the help of the local gendarme in searching for Cathy, and at the film's climax, now convinced that Paul is the killer, Jane seeks refuge in the policeman's house. Paul arrives and tries to break into the house, angrily demanding to speak to her, and Jane flees into the fields, hiding in a decrepit caravan, where she discovers Cathy's fly-strewn corpse.

Paul gives chase, but she surprises him, beating him unconscious with a rock. When the policeman arrives she throws herself into his arms, but he begins to molest her, revealing himself to be the serial killer as he tries to strangle her. At this point Paul rears up, covered in blood, and knocks out the killer with a tree branch. It begins to rain heavily and the final shot, echoing the opening, shows a police car racing along a wet road past a pair of female cyclists heading in the opposite direction.

With an array of eccentric, sinister characters – including a deaf farmer who was gassed in the Somme – a score that recalls Bernard Herrmann's film music and a serial killer preying on female tourists, there are obvious echoes of Hitchcock's *Psycho* (1960). However, the dominant effect is confusing rather than menacing, since the subsidiary characters are all so emphatically untrustworthy that any of them could be a killer or a killer's accomplice. At points the film is an unintentionally comic reprise of the 'old dark house' horror genre, and this is underlined by a xenophobic anxiety about foreignness. Moreover, the film's televisual qualities – high-key lighting, theatrical dialogue, reliance on close-ups and little sense of the affective power of space and landscape – diminish the mood of genuine threat that it reaches for. In fact, its depiction of the curious occupants of a small village in *la France profonde* is not far removed from the comic caricatures of Jacques Tati's *Jour de Fête*.

An unlikely 2010 remake transports the narrative to the more exotic location of Argentina, emphasising the touristic spectacle of the surroundings and the displacement of the protagonists: two young American women on mountain bikes, who have lost contact with the cycling tour they were travelling with, find themselves stranded in a tiny rural village. This stylistically assured film is more effective in establishing a sense of danger, opening with a disjointed sequence that identifies it as a slasher movie: we see a bound woman in a dark room screaming as a man enters, visible only in silhouette, and shocks her unconscious with an electric cable. The remake also goes further than the original film in exploiting the erotic spectacle presented by the two protagonists, Stephanie and Ellie, travelling alone. In a scene in the village bar, recalling the opening of *The Accused* (Kaplan, 1988), Ellie flirts publicly with various men in the bar, dancing suggestively by the jukebox and following one into the toilets, while the following day, as the two bikini-clad women sunbathe by a stream, the camera lingers voyeuristically over their tanned bodies. Although structurally similar, the narrative is resolved differently, since it transpires that the local police chief is running a sex-trafficking operation, kidnapping women and smuggling them across the border to Paraguay. After Ellie is killed, Stephanie is then taken across the river to Paraguay to be sold, but she manages to escape and, after a tense chase following the formula of a slasher film, she shoots the corrupt cop, emerging as 'the final girl'.

As Carol Clover notes, slasher films are 'spectacularly nasty toward women', offering the viewer the pleasure of seeing women tortured and mutilated.[32] However, there is an ambiguity implicit in the narrative formula of the slasher film, which dictates that '[t]he one character of stature who does live to tell the tale is of course female. The Final Girl is introduced at the beginning and is the only character to be developed in any psychological detail'.[33] In this respect, slasher films, directed at male viewers, betray a deep-seated cultural anxiety about the rigidity of gender differences, since 'the categories masculine and feminine, traditionally embodied in male and female, are collapsed into one and the same character': the final girl, the toughest, fastest, smartest and most resourceful of them all.[34] These are not typical examples of the slasher film, in so far as they downplay the visceral spectacle of explicit violence that is a central focus of *Blood Trails* (Krause, 2006), a brutal, low-budget genre iteration in which a cycling serial killer terrorises a couple on a mountain-biking holiday in the mountain range around Whistler in Canada, pursuing the surviving woman through the woods relentlessly until a bloody showdown in which the brutalised, exhausted woman finally cuts his throat. However, this generic frame is the support for a familiar narrative about the female cyclist as an ambiguous figure – both threatening and threatened, wilfully putting herself in harm's way, overdoing it and asking for it. In a melodramatic fashion, the two films explore the dangers of women travelling by bike. Writing about social commentary on women cycling in the 1890s, Kat Jungnickel observes that '[w]hat made many nervous were the possible consequences of new opportunities for interactions with the wrong sort of people', and it is remarkable some 100 years later that this fear remains the preoccupation that motivates these films.[35]

Iris Marion Young observes that one of the mechanisms of physical inhibition to which women are subjected, to 'keep them in their place', is an insistence that women are the object of an ever-present male gaze:

An essential part of the situation of being a woman is that of living the ever-present possibility that one will be gazed upon as a mere body, as shape and flesh that presents itself as the potential object of another subject's intentions and manipulations, rather than as a living mechanism of action and intention.[36]

This helps to explain why women often feel obliged to take up less space, as a defensive response, since to take up space is to make oneself visible. Consequently, to move her body freely and in 'bold outward directedness is for a woman to invite objectification'.[37] The threat of being visible is closely accompanied by the threat of uninvited physical contact, and

[t]he most extreme form of such spatial and bodily invasion is the threat of rape.... The woman lives her space as confined and enclosed round her at least in part as projecting some small area in which she can exist as a free subject.[38]

Whereas films such as *And Soon the Darkness* capture the sinister violence and ever-present threat of bodily invasion, this is reiterated with light-hearted ludicrousness in the transnational romantic comedy *Girl on a Bicycle* (Level, 2013). In this film an Italian tour bus driver in Paris runs over a female cyclist, Cécile, a clumsy but beautiful model with whom he has become obsessed after spotting her riding through the city. Having destroyed her bicycle and hospitalised her with a broken arm and leg, he becomes her full-time carer, neglecting his German flight attendant fiancée, although he ends up falling in love with Cécile's two children, while Cécile falls in love with his English friend. It is an unconvincing premise for a romance, perhaps (in a film riddled

with implausibility and national stereotypes), but it is also deeply hackneyed. Ellen
Gruber Garvey notes that the narrative in which a male cyclist takes a header from his
high-wheel bicycle and is nursed back to health by a woman whom he ends up marrying was such a well-established formula in ten-cent magazines that, as early as the
late 1890s, it was already being parodied as a 'laughable cliché'.[39] Of course, in swap-
ping male and female roles in its recycling of this contrived plot, *Girl on a Bicycle* also
erases any progressive potential, rendering Cécile dependent upon the male character to dress her, bathe her and carry her to the toilet.

If these films dramatise the physical threat faced by women reckless enough to
cycle in public, then the dreadful Italian soft porn film *Monella* (Brass, 1998) epitomises the misogynistic fantasy that, in straddling a bicycle, a woman is signalling her
sexual availability, knowingly making an erotic spectacle of herself. The film opens
with Monella, a young woman in skimpy red vest and tiny skirt hitched up to expose
her knickers, riding a pink bicycle coquettishly around a town square in the 1950s,
chased by a group of children as local men leer at her and women mutter resentful
comments. She then cycles flirtatiously through the countryside, displaying her backside to farmers, a racing cyclist and a couple of priests, who then fall upon Monella's
parked bicycle and smell the leather saddle ecstatically. This fetishistic equation of the
pink bicycle with the female body expresses with crass obviousness the objectification
described by Young. Conversely, the staid British comedy film about the Edwardian
cycling boom, *Isn't Life Wonderful!* (French, 1954), finds humour rather than erotic
excitement in the spectacle of a nervous woman trying to buy a bike, to the amusement of the other customers. 'Go on; take a chance,' sniggers the salesman. 'You've got
nothing to lose – except weight!' Although set in 1902, and reworking a staple gag from
cartoons of the 1890s, it is a scene that could just as plausibly take place in a contemporary cycle shop in Britain.

Incidentally, given that the genitals are a sensitive interface between body and
bike, it is perhaps unsurprising that the auto-erotic pleasure of cycling was a preoccupation of early discourses on women's cycling, with Victorian medical studies warning
that, as well as making women more manly, and hindering their reproductive capacity, '[t]he bicycle teaches masturbation in women and girls'.[40] One response was the
development of women's saddles with a cut-out section to prevent contact with the
vulva, but, as Garvey observes drily, '[t]he issues metaphorized in the medical attacks
on bicycle masturbation are obviously too deep and complex to be addressed by
changing the bicycle saddle'.[41] Instead, what was at issue was that 'both the bicycling
woman and the masturbating woman were out of male control'.[42] Inevitably, there is

a minor narrative tradition of film and literature addressing the fetishisation of the bicycle, extending from Flann O'Brien's absurd fantasy novel *The Third Policeman* – whose protagonist rhapsodises of his bike: 'How desirable her seat was, how charming the invitation of her slim encircling handle-arms, how unaccountably competent and reassuring her pump resting warmly against her rear thigh!'[43] – through Rainer Ganahl's art installation *Étant Donné – Use a Bicycle* (2011) – a reworking of Marcel Duchamp's *Étant Donnés* (1946–1966), which incorporates a 16 mm film of a woman masturbating with a bicycle wheel in droll reference to Duchamp's *Bicycle Wheel* 'readymade' (1913) – to the sex-positive, feminist and queer touring Bike Smut film festival (2006–2018), which specialises in low-budget bicycle-related art films, pornography and performance. The funniest iteration is the music video for Francobollo's 'I Found a Bike Today' (Bailey, 2011). In the video the protagonist finds a bike in a vacant lot, takes it for a stroll in a park and then to a restaurant before having vigorous sex with it. After it is stolen, he steals another bike and has a brief fling with it, before having a furious argument. He then returns home – to find it in his bed with another bike.

In their depiction of vulnerable or harassed women cyclists, the films discussed above demonstrate (and reinforce) the persistence of notions of femininity as fragile and physically incompetent that Frances Willard was already dismissing as 'old fables, myths and follies' in the 1890s. I want to move on to look at two types of film that are far more inspiring and politically interesting in their exploration of different modes of femininity and their explicit, engagement with issues of structural inequality.

Hardihood, Empowerment and Professional Racing

Taking its title from a speech on women's suffrage delivered by American campaigner Susan B. Anthony in 1873,[44] *Hardihood* (Hahn, 2002) is a survey of professional women downhill mountain bike racers in the United States. Stylistically varied, with comic animated sequences and repeated shots of electronic scoreboards with racers' names or fragmented phrases displayed on them, the film outlines the draining routine for professional riders, which involves continual travel, training and racing, and it gives a strong sense of the idiosyncratic and charismatic characters involved in the sport as the cameras follow them on races and when they are at home. These are clearly 'hard' women, who are shown lifting weights, drinking post-race beers and cheerfully discussing the physical hazards of their job, such as broken bones, as well as the effect of menstruation on their racing performance. However, although they are competitors, these women clearly have a sense of belonging to a community of equals. In a comment that is extraordinary in the context of the emphasis on athletic competition in sports films, Elke Brutsaert reflects regretfully that '[s]ometimes winning also means taking the title away from someone else'. Jen Klish, meanwhile, declares that 'that feeling of riding your bike downhill is so fun, but I don't think it's enough to do it basically at the expense of everything else in my life'. As the citation of Susan B. Anthony implies, the riders in the film share and personify a feminist politics, as articulated by tattooed superstar racer Missy 'the Missile' Giove: 'I think achievement and success shouldn't be specific to gender or sexuality or ethnicity. I think it should be available to anybody'.

This inclusive politics is also intrinsic to the organisation of the discipline, since, as Jacquie Phelan, one of the earliest professional riders, notes, men and women used to race together in the early years of the sport in the United States, and men and women continue to compete on the same routes. A fascinating, charismatic figure, who reveals in an interview at the beginning of the film that she has been diagnosed with breast cancer, she founded the Women's Mountain Biking and Tea Society (WOMBATS) in 1987 under the assumed name Alice B. Toeclips, and the film shows her running a WOMBATS workshop for women to learn off-road riding skills. For her – and for some of her contemporaries – cycling remains a means of empowerment, but also, crucially, collectivism and openness.

While *Hardihood* concentrates primarily on American racers, *Half the Road: The Passions, Pitfalls and Power of Women's Professional Cycling* (Bertine, 2014) attacks the misogynistic inequalities of the institutions of international road racing. Directed by professional cyclist and activist Kathryn Bertine, the film highlights the role of sporting organisations – and in particular the UCI, which awards qualification points for the Olympics – in excluding women from competition, usually justifying this segregation on the grounds of women's fragility.[45] 'I don't think that an exact mirror of the Tour de France is appropriate for the physicality of women,' explains Brian Cookson, who was then president of British Cycling (the United Kingdom's governing body for the sport) and the UCI road racing commission, and whose blustering, incoherent attempts to defend UCI policy during the film are, at best, disingenuous.[46] He claims vaguely that commercial 'realities' justify such economic inequalities as the lack of a UCI requirement for a basic minimum wage for professional female riders (although this applies to men) and the huge disparity in prize money. The film recounts the history of female athletes' financial discrimination – and a history of activist responses, from Billie Jean King's 1974 campaign for equal pay onwards – noting the repressive effect this has on female athletes, who are forced to have other full- or part-time jobs in order that they can afford to compete.

Bertine also rubbishes what Nicholas Chare calls 'the myth of male strength and female weakness', noting women's success at ultra-endurance events such as triathlons, in which women and men race alongside one another on the same routes (for the same prize money).[47] A montage of crashes and injuries, including a shot of a car ploughing into a peloton of racers, makes the point about women's bravery dramatically, along with a second montage of cyclists killed in racing or training accidents. Amber Pierce explains that the appeal of road racing is that '[w]e just love the pain.... The pain is a metaphor for the challenge.' And, of course, whether or not this is what Pierce means, the challenge here is also cultural and political as well as personal. Writing about the 'athletic performance of gender', philosopher Judith Butler proposes that

women's sports have the power to rearticulate gender ideals such that those very athletic women's bodies that, at one time, were considered outside the norm (too much, too masculine, too monstrous) can come, over time, to constitute a new ideal of accomplishment and grace, a new standard for women's achievement.[48]

Confronted with a body that combines apparently incompatible elements of masculine and feminine morphologies – hard muscle and smooth contours – 'we enter into precisely the kind of epistemic crisis that allows gender categories to change'.[49]

It is clear that the historical proscriptions on women athletes are a consequence of ignorance and misogyny. As pioneering marathon runner Kathrine Switzer recalls in Bertine's film, in the United States until the late 1960s women were banned from running more than 800 m in case their uteruses prolapsed, while American cyclist Inga Thompson recalls that, as recently as the 1990s, UCI president Hein Verbruggen (1991–2015) was considering excluding women from racing while menstruating. Thus, as *Half the Road* makes clear, the UCI epitomises the social function of sport attacked by Jean-Marie Brohm in the early 1970s in his Marxist counter-blast against sport:

Women are enslaved by the patriarchal structure of capitalist society. As a vector of ruling class ideology, sport reproduces this slavery and provides it with a justification in terms of the 'naturalness' of the individual. Sport aims to get women to be content with their subservient function.[50]

The mechanisms Brohm describes – segregation by sex and the systematisation of 'feminine myths' into certain suitable sports (such as synchronised swimming, gymnastics or ice skating) – are reproduced by the UCI through such policies as a rule that women can race only half the distance of men, or that 60 per cent of women in a race must be under 28.[51] The UCI's unease at the inappropriateness of women's road racing is epitomised by the notorious 'Excessive' memo, in which Verbruggen refused to sanction the Ore-Ida Women's Challenge race in Idaho because of the 'excessive stage distances', 'excessive number of stages', 'excessive climbing' and 'excessive duration' of the race. Verbruggen's is a restatement of the prejudice articulated by Erskine in the Victorian manual *Lady Cycling* that 'women ought not to race, if they have the slightest regard for their own health; and if they do, it is a suicidal policy which is bound to end in disaster'.[52]

However, there is no shortage of evidence of women's success at competitive cycling from the very beginning, as the film makes clear in its overview of the history of women's racing, singling out a Swedish immigrant to the United States, Tillie Anderson, a six-day racer and world record holder over various distances in the 1890s (and who raced until the League of American Wheelmen banned women from competing in 1902). More recently, making a mockery of the UCI's objections to the staging of a women's Tour de France (with Cookson insisting in the film that there aren't enough women cyclists who can compete at that level and that the organisational difficulties would lead to 'devastation'), the film records that between 1984 and 1989 there was indeed a 'Tour de France féminin',[53] which followed the same route as the Tour, taking place a day ahead of the men's race, and simply shortening some of the mountain stages by removing the flat sections while retaining the climbs. Moreover, as the funny but infuriated Emma Pooley, 2010 time trial world champion and winner of the last women's Tour, points out (having suggested archly that the men's race would be improved by shortening it), the spectacle of road racing lies precisely in its difficulty:

I want to ride up mountains and do epic stages in three-week stage races, and it's partly the toughness, the challenge, that's so inspirational and impressive, and that's part of what spectators want to see.... It's not supposed to be easy. [...] It's about racing and winning, and of course people don't finish – in any race.

Like *Hardihood*, Bertine's campaigning film takes inspiration from Susan B. Anthony, citing her comment on cycling's role in promoting equal rights: 'I think [bicycling] has done more to emancipate woman than any one thing in the world. I rejoice every time I see a woman ride by on a wheel. It gives her a feeling of self-reliance and independence the moment she takes her seat; and away she goes, the picture of untrammeled womanhood.'[54] As well as analysing the rotten institutional structure of cycle racing it offers several suggestions about how to combat this, including introducing a minimum base salary, removing age discrimination and distance limits and establishing small nation development funds; Bertine rides for the tiny Caribbean state of Saint Kitts and Nevis, giving her personal experience of the challenges facing athletes from poorer countries who aim to compete on an international stage.

The film concludes by referring to Bertine's campaign to reform cycling, Le Tour Entier,[55] and to grass-roots initiatives such as Little Bellas, an organisation set up by US mountain bike racer Lea Davison and her sister to encourage girls to ride: 'We try to create an environment where these girls, at a crucial point in their lives – coming into the teenage years – they feel comfortable being themselves.' Finally, as Bertine observes, '[a] key factor in establishing equality for women athletes is to get the media on board with the advancement of women's sports', a point made by several of the women interviewed. The comparative invisibility of female athletes on TV and in print media has contributed as much as any other factor to the marginalisation and suppression of women's cycling, and so these films are both a critical comment upon this and an attempt to counter this invisibility by foregrounding scenes from the history of women's sport as well as a large number of sportswomen.

These two documentaries are explicit in linking sport with activism, treating the bicycle as a means of mobilising women literally and socially, expanding and complicating the category of femininity. Nevertheless, the abiding impression of these films is that the tough women featured in them are still engaged in an uphill struggle for control, support, recognition and representation, and the inequalities and obstacles encountered by these women athletes are representative of the frustrations facing women in many areas of everyday life. Indeed, Clare Simpson's examination of the origins of women's cycle racing is a reminder that social change is neither inevitable nor secure. The first documented race in which women competed with men was in 1868 in Rouen, and by 1896 a British journalist reported that 'a troupe of French women employed to give cycling exhibitions of speed and skill during their first visit to England had earned more than their male counterparts.'[56] As Simpson notes of women's velodrome races, this was 'one of the rare times in history when sportswomen have earned more money than sportsmen within the same sporting code', although of course this was partly a consequence of novelty and its commercial exploitability.[57] While '[t]he display of women's bodies was not new, even for bicycle-related events, …what was new in the 1890s was the prolonged exposure of women's bodies to such a mass of spectators'; even so, although women's cycle racing was supported by the dress reform movement, its transformative potential was quickly contained.[58] Simpson observes of these pioneering athletes:

Their foray into the public space of the velodrome or the road race was at a cost: their display brought ridicule and threats, public criticism and, in the interests of their safety, a ban on women's racing that persisted for half a century.[59]

And, as Bertine's film demonstrates, female athletes continue to battle with the same obstacles more than a century later. Simpson writes:

Women's cycle racing can be interpreted as a gendered expression of modernity and thus as quite distinct from men's experiences, whose racing represented speed, freedom novelty, and challenge; whilst this was also true for women, their racing did not necessarily 'free' them in any significant social sense.[60]

Sufferer's Time: The Bicycle and Women's Work

Another theme through which film-makers have explored the relation between cycling and social freedom is that of work – that is, more mundane work than professional racing. Francophone Canadian independent film *2 Seconds* (Briand, 1998) deals with the experiences of a female bicycle messenger in Montreal, suggesting that, even in the context of this romanticised outsider subculture, women remain a troubling presence. *2 Seconds* opens with Laurence (Charlotte Laurier) taking a cable car to the start line of a downhill race. When the gate opens, she freezes momentarily, before taking a breath and heading off (the roar of a rocket engine overlaid on the soundtrack). This unexplained hesitation costs her first place (by two seconds), and as a result she is fired by her male team boss, who castigates her for 'thinking' and tells her she's too old. Permitted to keep one of her bikes, she arrives at her brother's house in Montreal with a newly shaven head, and, after a female cycle courier catches her eye in the street, she gets a job as a bicycle messenger. She is introduced to the competitive, self-aggrandising, insular culture of couriering (familiar from other films and narrative accounts), and finds herself in a job that is as physically hazardous as her previous career, leaving her body bruised and aching, and which also involves riding against the clock. The city is an alienating environment: her ageing mother, suffering from dementia, doesn't recognise her; her geeky brother is an impatient host, as he is pre-occupied with finding a girlfriend; her new boss is perpetually bad-tempered, and her colleagues unfriendly and competitive. If the couriers have a common identity it seems it is due not so much to affinity as to a shared position in the gutters of society; during lunch, one of them explains to Laurie that they urinate in their bidons so they can pour the contents on taxi drivers. However, over time she establishes a friendship with namesake Lorenzo, an irascible Italian bicycle repairman and veteran racer who despises his 'spoiled' hipster customers. The two of them bond over their intimate knowledge of bicycles and their masochistic love of racing. 'Real cyclists enjoy the pain,' he announces one evening as they are drinking shots in his shop. 'Think you're the best sufferer?' she retorts, and they proceed to compare injuries, with flashbacks showing Laurie breaking off from sex with her boyfriend because she was variously too tender or too numb after racing, while Lorenzo recalls being unable to piss after climbing off his bike, and that some fellow riders complained of impotence. Cycling and relationships, they conclude, are mutually exclusive.

Her bike is destroyed when a resentful colleague deliberately rams her with his car and then crushes her bicycle, and the film concludes with her arriving with her new girlfriend, whom she met shortly after throwing her mangled bike into a skip, to watch the messenger race she had been planning to compete in. In the last moments, Lorenzo arrives and gives her his own immaculate Italian racing bike and jersey, and the film ends with Laurie riding through to the front of the peloton, a grin on her face.

2 Seconds is a gentle romantic comedy that emphasises the costs of the passionate commitment to competition and painful bodily modification that are celebrated by most sports films. The reward for abandoning racing, and the destruction of her bicycle, is a fuller life (which also allows Laurie to return joyfully to racing at the film's conclusion). With cropped hair, bruises, scars and bandages, Laurie is the butch fictional counterpart to the tough women of *Hardihood* and *Half the Road*, and the film stands apart from almost all other films about cycling in foregrounding a bisexual character. In cinema, literature, visual art and advertising, the bicycle has functioned as a flexible vehicle with which to represent and explore a wide variety of human experience, but the matter-of-fact treatment of Laurie's sexuality by this casually queer film underlines the fact that sexuality remains a taboo subject for films about cycling, highlighting the conservatism of many aspects of cycling culture.[61]

Becoming Women

The idea of the bicycle as a revolutionary tool for the emancipation of women remains a powerful and engaging notion, its international appeal demonstrated by *The Day I Became a Woman* (2000), the first film by Iranian director Marziyeh Meshkini. Based on a screenplay by Meshkini's partner, Mohsen Makhmalbaf, the film depicts the three ages of woman in three distinct stories of individual struggles for independence. The first is an account of a young girl, Hava, resisting for as long as possible putting on the 'chador' (veil) on the day of her ninth birthday.[62] The second shows a young woman, Ahoo, competing in a women's bicycle race, and the third focuses on Hoora, an elderly widow who goes on a shopping spree in the free trade resort of Kish, using her inheritance 'to buy everything I've never had'. The three sections are loosely linked, with two of the cycle racers and Hava and her mother reappearing towards the end of the third film, but the absurd quality of the three narratives and the surreal aspect of the images of figures isolated in the empty coastal landscapes invite the viewer to understand the film as an allegory about the condition of women in present-day post-revolutionary Iran.

The second section opens *in medias res* with a man riding at full tilt on horseback shouting 'Ahoo!', while antelopes scramble through the bush – *ahoo* is Farsi for 'gazelle' – and he heads over to the shore, where a large group of women, identically dressed in black chadors, are racing along a road next to the sea on mountain bikes, bells ringing. He comes alongside the race leader, Ahoo, demanding: 'Didn't I give you a final warning?' She ignores him, putting her head down and cycling harder, and he then asks the others: 'Why are you cycling? Don't you have husbands?' He warns Ahoo that she'll regret this before he rides off, while the women continue to jockey for position at the head of the race.

Shortly afterwards Ahoo's husband returns with Mullah Osman, who tells her that what she is riding is not a bicycle but 'devil's work', declaring: 'Neither God nor I approve of this. You're at the edge of an abyss.' Ahoo doesn't reply until her husband asks if she will agree to a divorce. She consents – the only time she speaks – and the two men come to a halt, her husband shouting after her: 'Our marriage is annulled!' Some of the women are beginning to slow, but Ahoo continues, racing hard, as four ageing, bearded, toothless relatives ride up alongside her on horseback – all topless, by contrast with the women, who are shrouded in fabric – and they beseech her to return to her husband. A second group of topless riders then comes alongside, among them her father, who tells her she's dishonoured the family. 'Shame on you. I curse you!' he yells, warning her: 'Fear your brothers.' She doesn't respond, and continues riding until she spots two riders ahead of her and draws to a halt. They ride in circles around Ahoo, shouting at her, and one of them picks up her bike and walks away with it, while the other women continue racing and the camera continues along the road, travelling further and further away from Ahoo.

The absence of exposition, the minimal dialogue and the parodic depiction of the archaic community of men as bare-chested hunters means that this section has the tone of a film fable in which narrative events are a coded symbolic representation.

This is compounded in the following section, in which two of the cyclists recount the story of the race to the widow Hoora, disagreeing about whether Ahoo finished. Michelle Langford observes that, in the context of contemporary Iranian cinema, this is 'one of the first films to show women engaged in a highly physical activity such as cycling', and the allegorical register of the film perhaps makes this image of unconventional femininity permissible in the context of the conservative, patriarchal Islamic Republic.[63] As Langford notes, '[a]llegory is a mode of expression that often emerges at times of religious, political, or social upheaval, constraint or censorship', and an emphasis upon the non-realistic symbolic status of the representation mobilises the viewer, inviting her to become an active reader, scrutinising the film for layered meanings.[64] For instance, the camera is tracking throughout the sequence, and thus the 'breathtaking mobility of the camera is paradigmatic of the tale about to unfold: the tale of a woman's desire for social mobility'.[65]

Among the influences folded into Meshkini's film, Yasujiro Ozu's quiet masterpiece *Late Spring* (1949) is particularly significant. *Late Spring* tells the story of Noriko, a young woman who lives with her widowed father but who is under gentle pressure from him and her aunt to marry, despite her devotion to her father and, more importantly, her contentment with being single. Early in the film she cycles to the beach with a male friend, Hattori, who is engaged to another woman, and the two of them ride happily side by side in the sun. Wearing slacks, rather than a kimono or the more feminine clothing she wears elsewhere, she flirts with her friend while they picnic on the beach, and for Noriko it is a brief moment of freedom from other people's expectations, although she eventually succumbs to the pressure to marry. As Noriko and Hattori cycle along the sunny shore road the camera tracks with them, bicycle and camera moving at the same speed. It is the only scene in the film to feature a mobile camera, deviating from Ozu's style, which depends almost exclusively on static shots, and so, by contrast with the visual stasis of the rest of the film, the moving camera (along with the bicycle) articulates the protagonist's ultimately frustrated desire for independence. A prominent shot of a Coca-Cola sign by the road makes it clear that the film is exploring the tensions between cultural tradition and Westernised modernity.

In Meshkini's fable, this race with no beginning or end is a metaphor for escape and individual autonomy, as Ahoo (along with all the other women, perhaps) attempts to ride away from her community, her family and her marriage, but is caught and finally brought to a halt. As a result, Langford suggests, '[r]ather than simply creating a story that offers a utopian vision of female liberation, Meshkini works the notion of struggle into every layer and every image of this episode', Ahoo's silence ensuring that cycling becomes an urgently expressive act.[66] In this sense, it is one of the most sophisticated films discussed in this chapter, since, in its preoccupation with struggles around visibility and concealment, it can be understood as a commentary upon the representational capacity of cinema as well as the situation of women. Produced by the innovative Makhmalbaf Film House, it is informed by Italian neorealist cinema in its reliance largely upon non-professional actors, but also by international art cinema, in its fragmentary, overtly fictitious narratives.

Of course, the veil has an ambiguous political significance in relation to the liberation and exposure of women's bodies when 'some Islamic feminists from Iran and elsewhere have pointed out that the veil can actually help to facilitate women's entry into the public sphere and, by implication, women's entry into Iranian cinema as protagonists with a high degree of narratological agency.'[67] Moreover, in this film, significant male characters are either playful little boys or laughably macho patriarchs. *The Day I Became a Woman* is not a call for a Western model of female empowerment, but instead, as Langford suggests, 'it helps to posit a becoming-woman of a multitude of feminisms, one in which vital, productive, and embodied encounters may take place across both space and time.'[68] The three protagonists in this film negotiate the process of becoming a woman in different, rebellious ways – with childish scepticism in the case of Hava, by taking flight in the case of Ahoo and by realising a longed-for life of consumer luxury in the case of Hoora, who, liberated by widowhood, assembles an army of little boys to help her transport and unpack her purchases. Moreover, the episodic structure implies that, rather than a single transition from one state to another, becoming a woman is an ongoing process of identity formation that persists well into old age.

In Meshkini's film the bicycle is an object charged with contradictory meanings: a device for resisting womanhood, and for expressing a different mode of womanhood. It has similar status in *Wadjda* (al-Mansour, 2012), a Saudi/German co-production that was the first film to be shot entirely in Saudi Arabia, and the first feature by a female Saudi director, Haifaa al-Mansour. Protagonist Wadjda Al Saffan is a cockily confident but unscholarly ten-year-old nonconformist who makes pocket money by selling friendship bracelets to her schoolmates. Walking home from her madrassa one day, she spots a beautiful green bike, an American Electra cruiser, being delivered to a toy shop,[69] and resolves to buy it so that she can settle a score with her friend Abdullah, who teasingly cycled off with her scarf that morning. 'When I get my bike,' she tells him, 'and I win the race, then we'll be even.... Losing to a girl will be a double loss.' Wadjda's family doesn't have a great deal of money (when her teacher orders her to replace her scruffy trainers with leather shoes, she uses a marker pen to colour them black) so she begins to save up funds for the 800 riyal bicycle, instructing the shop owner not to sell the bike and giving him a mix-tape to guarantee their friendship. When a competition to recite the Quran with a 1,000 riyal prize is announced at school, she decides to enter, and, through persistence, and with a little help from her mother, Wadjda eventually triumphs, having transformed herself from a troublesome pupil into a model student. However, when Wadjda explains to the school what she intends to do with the prize money, her furious teacher retorts:

Wouldn't it be better if we donated the money to our brethren in Palestine? You know, a bike isn't a toy for girls. Especially not for well-behaved, devout girls who protect their soul and honour. I'm sure your family won't allow it. We'll donate the money and, God willing, you'll be rewarded for your generosity.

As in Meshkini's film, the chance meeting of a (young) woman and a bicycle disrupts gender categories. The film describes a patriarchal, segregated society in which femininity is surveyed and policed – quite literally; talking to a friend on the phone, Wadjda's mother learns of the scandal that one of Wadjda's schoolmates was caught with a man by the mutawa, the 'religious police' who patrol the streets to ensure conformity with Islamic law. Elsewhere, while playing in the schoolyard, the girls notice some builders on a nearby rooftop, and one announces to the others: 'If you can see them, they can see you. Respectable girls go inside. The rest stay where men can see them.' With typical recalcitrance, Wadjda carries on playing hopscotch, while the others retreat inside. This confinement also extends to a silencing, as is demonstrated when a teacher scolds two girls for laughing as they arrive at school in the morning: 'You forget that women's voices shouldn't be heard by men outside. How often must I repeat this? A woman's voice is her nakedness.'

However, while the film makes the relentless social emphasis on feminine modesty visible, it also makes clear that this does not amount to respect or a recognition of autonomy when, shockingly, female children are treated as sexually available. Walking home from school, Wadjda is harassed by a builder, who yells at her: 'Come up and play with us! Let me touch those little apples.' Later on, at the school's religious club, one of her schoolmates is castigated by the teacher for handing around photographs of her wedding to a 20-year-old husband (because '[p]ictures are forbidden at school'). Thus, when her mother learns that Wadjda has been told to wear the abaya to school (having arrived at school without her headscarf after Abdullah pinched it), and jokes that it might be time to marry Wadjda off, it is far from implausible (even though, as a teacher, her mother is a comparatively progressive figure). At the time, Wadjda is wearing a T-shirt emblazoned with the English phrase 'I AM A GREAT CATCH', a detail that suggests the film also has an ambivalent attitude towards Westernised conceptions of femininity.

These social inequalities are duplicated within Wadjda's own family, as it transpires that her father, who is more or less absent even when he occasionally stays at their house, is considering marrying another woman since her mother can't bear him a son (after a difficult birth with Wadjda). At the film's conclusion, Wadjda returns home after the competition to find her mother smoking on the roof of the house, with newly cropped hair in a gesture of defiance; she told her daughter earlier she longed for short hair like the Egyptian film star Lobna Abdel Aziz, but that Wadjda's father liked it long. Her mother is watching a wedding taking place in the distance at Wadjda's grandmother's house and, realising that it is her father's wedding, Wadjda insists they should 'go over there and get him.' Her mother dismisses the idea, clearly having given up on the humiliating relationship, and then presents her with the bike, explaining: 'The man at the shop had been holding it for weeks for some spunky little girl. I want you to be the happiest person in the world. You're all I have left in this world.'

In the concluding scene, the next morning, Wadjda cycles past the house, where the traces of the wedding party are still visible, and comes upon her friend Abdullah playing football with some boys. He joins her, and they cycle past the smiling shop owner before she challenges Abdullah: 'Catch me if you can!' and races away from him. In the final shot, having come to a junction with a main road, a close-up shows Wadjda joyfully looking back and forth, considering which direction to travel in. Writing about late nineteenth-century caricatures of the 'New Woman', Patricia Marks comments that

the woman on wheels may decide where she wishes to go and what she plans to do when she gets there, regardless of a male companion, or lack of one. Her influence upon the world is more immediate, no longer confined to the home.... [S]he actively seeks new experience and intends to have some impact on the world around her.[70]

The ending of *Wadjda* epitomises perfectly this sense of possibility, as the world opens up before the young cyclist. The bicycle has allowed her to become an independent, mobile and unconventional young woman. The association between sexual maturity and cycling is made explicit in an earlier scene, when Wadjda's mother surprises her when she is practising on Abdullah's bike and Wadjda falls off, grazing her knee. 'Where's the blood coming from?' her mother asks in a panic, hands over her eyes. 'Your virginity?' Dismissing Wadjda's desire for a bike, she warns her (reiterating Victorian medical discourse on the physical harm of cycling): 'You won't be able to have children if you ride a bike.' The bicycle sexes and unsexes the female rider.

The bicycle's empowering potential has a particular force in contemporary Saudi Arabia, where women's independence and mobility are so restricted by the cultural dominance of conservative Islam. In al-Mansour's first film, the guerrilla documentary *Women without Shadows* (2005), one angry anonymous interviewee explains:

Even transportation is difficult. We can't even get into a taxi. A woman getting into a taxi is not allowed. Maybe it is legally allowed, but the society doesn't accept it. And society is so vicious about women's reputations. Everything is prohibited.

Travelling within and outside the country without permission from a guardian or male family member is difficult, and Waad Mohammed, who plays Wadjda, explains with relish that playing with boys, going out on the streets unchaperoned or riding a bicycle by herself are things she would not normally be able to do.[71] These gendered constraints posed problems when film-makers were shooting on the street; the prohibition on men and women working together in public meant that al-Mansour found that 'many times I couldn't go out of the van to be with the actors...; I had to direct them through a "walky-talky" or through the assistant director, and this is sometimes difficult.'[72]

In this respect, even more directly than with *The Day I Became a Woman*, in its preoccupation with the objectification and sexualisation of women, the politics and erotics of visibility and concealment, and issues of representation and the gaze, *Wadjda* is a film about cinema, produced in a country in which Islamic iconoclasm and anxieties about Westernisation mean that there are no cinemas. Thus, it is a film imbued with optimism in the face of oppression. Al-Mansour writes that 'my film is not about complaints or accusations; it is more about what we can do to move ahead, to change our world.'[73] *Wadjda*'s narrative is about an enterprising young woman who is determined to 'move ahead', but the film itself is a product of the director's own resourcefulness and determination to 'move ahead', clearing a path for women film-makers and socially critical cinema. As much as any of the films examined in this chapter, *Wadjda* captures the revolutionary thrill discussed by Frances E. Willard in 1895, of mastering 'the most remarkable, ingenious, and inspiring motor ever yet devised upon this planet.'[74]

6

Kids with Bikes

Figure 6.1
Teenage cycling obsessive Dave Stohler (Dennis Christopher) studies a cycling magazine in his bedroom in *Breaking Away* (Yates, 1979) (© 20th Century Fox/Kobal/REX/Shutterstock)

'Kids love bikes,' Lance Armstrong explains in the documentary *The Armstrong Lie*, 'because it's the first time in their life they're free. It's the first time they're not in mom's car, they're not in mom's living room, they're not in mom's backyard.' He goes on, 'They get on the bike, they go down, they take a right, take a left – nobody sees them; they're completely free.' Cru Jones, the teenage protagonist of *Rad* (Needham, 1986), a coming-of-age feature film about professional BMX racing, corruption and the commercialisation of sport, goes further, reflecting after a difficult week: 'It kinda reminds me of when I was four years old, and the first time my dad let go of that bike. It was like a whole new life. All of a sudden, it was like I was in control. I could go as fast as I wanted. It was scary but it felt good.'

More than any other children's toys, bikes and trikes (and go-carts, scooters, skateboards, baby walkers and various other mobility aids) allow children to move independently of their parents, and to travel beyond the ambit of the family home. As well as the thrills of physical movement, they offer the young rider a pleasurable, if transient, sense of autonomy, and so – as Armstrong suggests – these metal, plastic, leather and rubber objects can become emotionally significant for children. Whether or not we cycle as adults, we probably have detailed memories of learning to ride, while, for parents, teaching a child to ride without stabilisers may be a bittersweet moment of intimate communication and separation.

This emotional ambiguity is captured perfectly in a brief scene from the Oscar-winning melodrama *Kramer vs. Kramer* (Benton, 1979), when Ted Kramer (Dustin Hoffman) is teaching his six-year-old son to cycle in New York's Central Park, while fighting his wife for custody of the boy as the terms of their divorce are thrashed out. Accompanied by a majestic Purcell sonata, he sets his child off, cheering him on and taking a photograph as the boy cycles unsteadily away. A close-up of Kramer's face then shows his expression changing slowly from delight to concern, and he yells after his son: 'Don't go too far!' As the scene implies, the social ritual of teaching a child to ride involves the rehearsal of a series of traumatic separations of parent and child, an Oedipal drama played out on a miniature scale as the son leaves the father behind. Conversely, one of the pleasures of riding a bike as an adult is that it transports us back to childhood, offering a brief, nostalgic sensation of childish freedom, a sensually intense, immediate, carefree, playful and curious relation to the world, even though this is an undoubtedly an idealised misremembering of child-hood experience.

As Karen Lury writes, discussing Iranian and Turkish cinema, for adult view-ers, cinematic children are regarded principally as symbolic devices rather than depictions of individuals. 'The child, the actual body, agency and living-ness that they manifest, disappears and instead the child figure, the child as convenient symbol takes his or her place.'[1] That is to say, typically, 'the child stands in for something else: the ideology of the family and society at large'. However, while children are frequently used in films as semantically flexible figures, the child also remains a potentially troubling textual presence, since, '[l]ike "woman" or women, the child never seems to fit with models conceived with a masculine subject in mind'.[2] The child is not a fixed, emotionally contained, rational individual, but represents an unformed identity that is in the process of becoming someone (else), its appearance, bodily boundaries and sexuality all in fluid motion. In this respect, the figure of the child on a bike epitomises the cultural conception of children as mobile subjects – or subjects that desire mobility.

Boys, Bicycles and Transitional Objects

This is depicted beautifully in *Boy and Bicycle* (1965), a short 16 mm film made by director Ridley Scott while studying photography at the Royal College of Art. Shot around Hartlepool, the film features his 15-year-old brother (and future director) Tony Scott, and follows an unnamed schoolboy over a day as he plays truant and spends the day exploring the industrial seaside town. After waking up to the sound of the radio and his parents squabbling downstairs, he cycles along the high street and arrives at school, lingering on the road outside the schoolyard. On the voice-over – a poetic stream-of-consciousness commentary apparently inspired by James Joyce's *Ulysses* – he observes that the sun is warm and the school's 'like the bloody Kremlin anyway', and so heads off to the docks. He smokes a cigarette, hiding under a concrete causeway and looking out at the sea, investigates the empty seafront amusement park and then heads across the sand and mudflats, entering a fisherman's hut to escape from a rain shower. Hunting through the books and possessions in the shack, he is scared by a broken doll's head and a clap of thunder, and dashes out to find a man standing silently outside. The man stares after him as he runs off, wheeling his bike back across the sand.

For a student film it is a visually sophisticated piece of work, preoccupied with the changing quality of light in rain-dark skies, shadows and reflections in water – visual motifs that run obsessively through all Scott's films.[3] It is also a study of late twentieth-century British industrial and vernacular architecture; as the boy rides through a working seaside town we see railway sidings, concrete jetties, dockside cranes, a steelworks, Victorian shops and houses and vacant beach huts. The spaces the boy moves through are largely empty, leading him to fantasise, as he wanders around and sleeps on the vast beach, 'Here I am, the only one in the world.' The film has a fragmented structure that, along with the voice-over, describes the town through a series of impressions and images. His commentary follows a series of poetic diversions, triggered by the images he encounters on his illicit diversion from school. He is experimenting with language, as he also experiments with the possibility of a different life and other identities: 'I had my groin cut when I was a kid. Double hernia,' he muses while lying on the beach near the groynes buried in the sand. 'Stones build up against groynes. Inland urinous ocean. Fat yellow jello.' Examining the contents of the fisherman's shack a little later, he reflects:

I can remember certain moments very clearly. Little things. Pointless, really. The tiny cut-glass salt cellars at Mrs Smith's in Hartburn. The salt poured very smoothly on the cold white chicken that night. The rubber strip around the French windows rubbed between my fingers. Plaything. Gran sits in faded rust silk from deep chair.

For all their adolescent pretentiousness, the boy's musings capture telling details of a country subject to the petrifying effect of post-war austerity as sharply as a Philip Larkin poem; he imagines that the school lunch he is missing would consist of '[h]otpot and sago, rubberised chocolate custard with flakes of dolly mixtures on top', while that evening's unappetising meal will be '[c]old meat, and potatoes fried up from Sunday on Monday'. It is a moving portrait of an adolescent boy longing for a more exciting, colourful life beyond the confines of the family home, school and a coastal town in northern England suffering from high unemployment (something both brothers would find in Hollywood). Writing about Hartlepool and the region during this period, theatre critic Ronald Bryden observes,

All through the fifties Britain had been heaving with dissatisfaction. In the Autumn of '62 the census figures for the decade began to seep out. What they revealed was a country on the move, voting its discontent with its feet: emigrating (nearly one and a half million in ten years) and fleeing from the waning cities of the North into the South East.[4]

The boy on a bicycle is an effective symbol for this desire for flight in search of a better life; but, more broadly, as an image of joyfully guileless, intuitive and sensory human–machine interaction, the child on a bicycle is also an idealised image of the cinema spectator. As an abstracted film image, its affective power is partly an effect of its semiotic richness, presenting us with a visual condensation of the utopian promise of film to transport us to other places and times.

The bicycle is a means by which children can break away from their parents, but it is also a mediating mechanism, a point of intimate contact between parent and child. This is an idea explored in diverse ways by several films. Polish film *Mój Rower* [*My Bicycle*][5] (Trzaskalski, 2012) is a male melodrama in which a child's bicycle is passed from grandfather to father to son like a baton in a patrilineal relay race. The austere but fairy-tale-like Belgian film *Le Gamin au Vélo* [*The Kid with a Bike*] (Dardenne, Dardenne, 2011) features a motherless 11-year-old boy trying to track down the father who abandoned him in a children's home, roaming the woods and nondescript suburbs on his mountain bike. The teenage protagonist of American TV movie *I Am the Cheese* (Jiras, 1983) cycles across country on a hazardous quest in search of his father, although we gradually learn that his parents have been murdered and he lives in a mental hospital, spending every day cycling in circles around the grounds of the institution.

The bicycle commonly functions as a moving sign of the complex relationship between father and son. The primal scene of the child learning to ride is symbolically powerful both because it marks the irreparable separation of parent and child, which takes place as children age, and because it stages – and thereby reveals – the emotional distance and fear of intimacy that characterise conventional masculinity. In other words, the bicycle often comes to symbolise not so much the close relationship between father and son but its absence – a nostalgic desire for an intimacy that was never available.

As a result, it is an object infused with intense melancholy, the material residue of irretrievable physical and emotional intimacy. We might think of the bicycle on screen as analogous to what psychoanalyst Donald Winnicott has termed a 'transitional object'. In studying the early stages of child development, Winnicott suggests that, by allowing their children to develop an addictive attachment to certain objects – a scrap of fabric, say, or a soft toy – mothers assist their children's recognition of the difference between themselves and the world around them. Whereas a young infant appears to experience the mother's body and the world around it narcissistically as a continuity, as if the infant wills everything into being, the introduction of a '"not-me" possession' allows the infant to begin to recognise a difference between its body and external reality, between what is 'me' and what is 'not me'.[6] This initially happens somewhere from four to 12 months, but this attachment to certain objects develops into broader cultural interests as the child moves into adulthood, and thus Winnicott suggests that there is a connection between the transitional object and 'play, and of artistic creativity and appreciation, and of religious feeling, and of dreaming, and also of fetishism, lying and stealing, the origin and loss of affectionate feeling, drug addiction' – a fairly comprehensive summary of the themes explored by cinema.[7]

In helping the infant to comprehend and accept difference, the transitional object is illusionary, a symbolic substitute for the mother's breast and body, and Winnicott suggests that 'the task of reality-acceptance' that begins with the transitional object

is never completed, that no human being is free from the strain of relating inner and outer reality, and that relief from this strain is provided by an intermediate area of experience (arts, religion, etc.). This intermediate area is in direct connection with the play area of the small child who is lost in play.[8]

Since it is a symbol, the transitional object introduces the possibility of representation – that an object can stand for something that is absent – and so also introduces the infant to a world of signs, language and meaning, to the 'transitional phenomena' of thinking and fantasising.

Although, in clinical terms, the bicycle is not a transitional object, in films about children or adolescents and bikes the bicycle is typically treated as if it were, allowing the child to develop a distinct identity, separating itself from its parents and using the device creatively as the basis for fantasy and play. In other words, Winnicott's term is very helpful for thinking about the meaning of the bicycle, and the cyclist's relationship to her bicycle. As he writes,

the object is affectionately cuddled as well as excitedly loved and mutilated.... [I]t must survive instinctual loving, and also hating and, if it be a feature, pure aggression.... Yet it must seem to the infant to give warmth, or to move, or to have texture, or to do something that seems to show it has vitality or reality of its own.[9]

There are various more or less literal examples of this in cinema, from Wadjda's desire for the green bicycle through Pee Wee Herman's childish, eroticised love of his bicycle to pornographic films in which bicycles are sex toys or fetish objects, and slapstick films in which bicycles, such as that ridden by Jacques Tati's postman, are independent characters with their own agency.[10] Moreover, the metaphor of movement is crucial for Winnicott's analysis; he describes the infant's growth and intellectual development as 'the journey of progress towards experiencing', and it is the transitional object that makes this journey possible.[11] As discussed throughout this book, the bicycle is a transitional object in multiple respects. A key premise of this book is that cinema and the bicycle are closely related technologies or media with parallel functions, and so we might also propose that cinema is a 'transitional object': loved, hated, mobile, a means of escape with a vitality and an illusory reality of its own. A sequence of film showing a bicycle is thus an especially dense illustration of cinema as transitional object, situated at the threshold between subjective fantasy and objective reality.

Good Riders and Battered Bicycles

Perhaps the most well-established genre of films depicting children and bicycles is the public information or public safety film. Produced or commissioned by a wide variety of bodies, including government film units, charities, trade unions and corporations, public information films typically combine scripted action with documentary techniques in the service of propaganda, promotion and education. Designed for TV broadcast or for screening in schools, workplaces or other public spaces, as well as cinemas, these 'non-commercial' films circulate in quite a different way from most of the films discussed in the book. Public information films are designed to direct the attitudes or behaviours of viewers, and one of the rhetorical devices used most frequently is threat. The narrative worlds depicted in these films are often harsh, featuring environments in which injury and death wait just around the corner for the careless and self-absorbed. However, what is at stake in the public information film, beyond individual safety, is the interpellation of the viewer as a dutiful citizen, and the construction of a secure social order and national identity. Public information films tend to impress upon the viewer that she is part of a community, and that she should be guided primarily by social responsibility rather than self-interest or gratification.

A good example is *Riding Abreast* (Jones, 1940), a short silent film produced for the campaigning charity Royal Society for the Prevention of Accidents (RoSPA, established during the First World War in response to the proliferation of road accidents during air raid blackouts). The film warns children to stay close to the edge of the road while cycling, cautioning: 'Riding abreast is selfish and unfair, as well as dangerous.' Intertitles instruct the viewer to '[r]ide in single file whenever road or traffic conditions require it, and never more than two abreast'. *Riding Abreast* opens with three girls, Jill, Mary and Brenda, heading out into the countryside on their bikes at the beginning of the summer holidays. Like a polite motorcycle gang, the trio insist on riding across the full width of the road, ignoring the angry or concerned responses of other cyclists and drivers. Inevitably, Mary, whose red cardigan foreshadowed danger, is hit by a car and thrown into a ditch. Although she survives, her injuries leave her bed-ridden for most of the summer, bored and frustrated, while her friends go horse riding and picnicking in the countryside. It is a pedantic, condescending film that labours its central message; after she is taken home by the driver who ran her over, another driver shows Mary's friends the Highway Code, and later, when she is reading in her sickbed, Mary's mother gives her a copy to study.

Despite the crudity of its central message, it is also rather beautiful. Shot on low-resolution Kodachrome stock, it has the visual quality of old home movie footage, the fading colours and blurred images resembling a cinematic memory image. The film depicts a deeply nostalgic image of Britain as a spacious, pastoral and non-industrial country, a celebratory portrait of a country of small villages, and simple pleasures, heathland, hedgerows and almost traffic-free roads on which children are free to roam and ramble. Given that it was produced during the Second World War, it is tempting to read the film as an allegorical account of a nation at war wherein a traditional, ordered society is threatened by irresponsible individuals who ignore the clearly spelt-out rules. Whether or not that was intentional, the broad ideological function of most public information films is to ensure the integrity of a national body by emphasising the dangers faced by an individual's constituent body, reinforcing a sense of national or social identity, or belonging, in the spectator.

The collection of British public information films released between 1945 and 2006 held in the National Archives addresses such topics as the introduction of decimal currency, the TV licence, the Berlin airlift and the formation of the Commonwealth, as well as the dangers of outdoor swimming, rabies, drugs, smoking, highly polished floors, nuclear war and, notoriously, AIDS. Films about cycling and road safety are consistent with these in their blend of education, dark humour and aggressive threat. *The Ballad of the Battered Bicycle* (Petroleum Films Bureau, 1947), narrated in rhyming couplets by well-known screen actor and monologuist Stanley Holloway, is typically grim. Holloway tells the story of Henry, who rides his new bike recklessly around town, crashing it repeatedly until it is held together with string. Eventually, ignoring a 'Halt' sign, he collides with a bus and finds himself on trial as Holloway reprimands him for his selfishness:

> You might be dead, young Henry Brown, but what occurs to us
> Is how much graver it would have been had you upset the bus.
> The moral of this yarn is clear. To stress it I should like:
> You have a duty to the world when you ride your bike.

Children are both the target audience and the typical protagonists of cycling safety films, and their tone ranges from condescension and sarcasm – as in *Good*

Cycles Deserve Good Riders (RoSPA, 1950), which warns: 'It is stupid and dangerous to misuse your cycle and the road by showing off. Sooner or later it is bound to lead to disaster' – to horror – as in *No Short Cut* (Simmons, 1964) and *Cyclist Turning Right* (Central Office of Information, 1983), films in which the image of a child's bicycle being crushed under the wheels of a vehicle is a chilling motif.

This is a formally and stylistically varied category of films, made on small budgets, sometimes by feature directors. Some were devised as documentaries, some as illustrated lectures, while others incorporate narrative sequences, poems, songs and even – in the cautionary tale of bicycle theft *It's a Bike* (Prendergast, 1983) – a cockney rap commentary. However, whether they are directed at adults or children, the rhetorical emphasis on the dangers of cycling and the culpability of the kid with a bike (rather than the driver) is an insistent theme. It is stressed repeatedly that ignorance, technical incompetence and moments of playful overconfidence have fatal consequences. In fact, the child cyclist's greatest misjudgement often appears to be that of being a child, and a number of these films might well have been designed to deter children from mounting a bicycle at all. Indeed, an underlying assumption of these films – some funded by car companies or energy industry lobby groups – is that cycling is a transitional activity whose principal value is that it prepares the cyclist to drive.[12] It is an extraordinarily sadistic subgenre, whose most consistent feature is the depiction of children under threat of robbery, injury or death, but, rather than constituting an expression of despair, outrage or bewilderment at the senseless brutality of a car culture that treats children as obstacles or targets, these films instruct us to accommodate ourselves to what J. G. Ballard has termed 'a pandemic cataclysm institutionalized in all industrial societies that kills hundreds of thousands of people each year and injures millions'.[13]

Public information films crystallise a set of anxieties about children's mobility as effectively as the disturbing scenes in *The Shining* (Kubrick, 1980) in which little Danny Torrance rides his tricycle around the haunted corridors of an empty hotel, encountering traumatising apparitions. Whether or not they are directed at children, most of these films address the spectator with disdain or weary disapproval. The voice-over commentary on traditional documentaries is often described as 'voice-of-God' narration: a reliable explanation of the images delivered with masculine gravitas by an off-screen performer. In a similar way, regardless of whether there is a spoken voice-over, the public information film addresses us with the paternalistic voice of authority – the voice of the 'daddy state' – situating us in a position of relative ignorance and incompetence. Just as riding a bicycle makes a child of us all, so these films infantilise us, adult and child alike, returning us to the restricted status of child or adolescent.

Making the Break

While the relationship between children and their bicycles is viewed with sceptical concern in public information films, mainstream cinema depicts the image of the child (and the adolescent) on a bicycle in much more romantic terms. Notably, the teenage protagonist of the American feature film *Breaking Away* (Yates, 1979) is driven by a desire for independence and secure self-identity. Set in the college town of Bloomington, the film centres on four friends, Dave, Mike, Cyril and Moocher, at a loose end in the long hot summer; having graduated from high school the previous year, they are reluctant to take on the low-paid menial work that is all that is available to them in a town that was once home to a quarrying industry, but is now overshadowed by Indiana University and its affluent, stylish and entitled students. Dave Stohler is a cycling obsessive; his bedroom is plastered with posters and magazine clippings, and his enthusiasm for cycle racing (after winning an Italian Masi road bike in a race) extends to speaking with an Italian accent (to his xenophobic father's despair), listening to Rossini, renaming the family cat Fellini and pretending to be an Italian exchange student exotically named 'Enrico Gimondi' (after legendary Italian rider Felice Gimondi) when he begins dating a university student, Kathy (or 'Caterina', as he insists on calling her). Against a background of class tensions between the privileged students and working-class locals, Dave strikes up a transgressive relationship with Kathy, secretly enlisting his friend Cyril to accompany him on guitar while he serenades her with an aria on the lawn of her sorority house. Cyril is then beaten up by Kathy's obnoxious boyfriend Rod and his fraternity brothers, and, after Mike, Moocher and Cyril track them down to exact revenge, trashing a restaurant in the ensuing brawl, the university's principal instructs the students: 'If you feel compelled to compete with the kids from the town, you'll do it in a different arena. We've decided to expand the field of this year's Little 500 bicycle race to include a team from the town.'

From the film's opening, Dave's father, Ray, has been relentlessly disparaging about his son's lack of interest in working, complaining to his wife: 'He couldn't find a job to save his life. He's worthless, that one. I tell you, I die of shame every time I see him. Goddamn lazy freeloader.' However, Ray hates his own job as a used car salesman, and is nostalgic for his old profession as a stone cutter in the quarries. He is eventually persuaded by his wife to hire Dave, and works him hard, refusing to let him have Saturday off to ride in the Cinzano 100-mile road race, a race that Dave has been training for since reading that the Italian Cinzano team was competing. As it transpires, Dave is able to race when his father falls ill, and he joins the Italian team in the breakaway at the head of the race, practising the Italian phrases he has learnt. They drop him on a climb, and then, when Dave catches up with them, one of the Italians jams his pump into Dave's front wheel, pitching him into the ditch, out of the race, and bringing him back down to earth. Mike observes to him affectionately afterwards, 'Well, I guess you're just a cutter again, huh? Like the rest of us.'

This act of sabotage shatters Dave's fantasy of assuming a new identity. 'Everybody cheats,' he observes disconsolately to his parents. 'I just didn't know.' He subsequently confesses to Kathy that he is not, in fact, from a long line of Neapolitan fishermen, prompting a slap in the face, and begins to move closer to his father. He agrees reluctantly to race with his friends in the Little 500, and his mother, Evelyn, presents the four of them with T-shirts emblazoned with the team name, CUTTERS. Unsurprisingly, for a film by the director of *Bullitt* (1968), this final race in the university stadium is one of the most dynamic race sequences among feature films about cycle racing, resembling a documentary, with fast, disjointed editing and telephoto shots of the riders and crowd generating a sense of speed, authenticity and physical danger. Dave refuses to hand over the bike to his team-mates for the first half of the 50-mile race, pulling their team into first place, and only when he crashes are the others forced to take a turn. They begin to fall behind until, with 15 laps to go, a bloodied Dave calls Moocher into the pits, has his feet taped to the pedals and sets off, making up ground and just managing to take the race from Kathy's boyfriend, Rod, on the line (accompanied by an aria from Rossini's *The Barber of Seville*).

Whereas the Cinzano race prompted a crisis, the second race enables a resolution. The four friends whose close friendship has been tested over the course of the film are reconciled by their success in the race. The coda reveals that Ray has changed the name of his car lot from Campus Cars to Cutter Cars, embracing his class identity and personal history, and has also taken up cycling, acknowledging his son's passion. Evelyn is pregnant, displacing Dave from the privileged position of only child, and Dave is now a student, having taken the entrance exam secretly. As in the relay race, a handover has taken place between father and son, an exchange of roles, with Dave breaking away from home, and from a class position that was in some respects as much an imaginary identity as was 'Enrico Gimondi'. 'You're not a cutter. I'm a cutter,' his dad explains to his son early in the film, when Dave insists resentfully that he doesn't want to go to college and that he is 'proud of being a cutter.'

Like Ridley Scott's *Boy and Bicycle*, *Breaking Away* is a film about a working-class adolescent boy stranded in a post-industrial town, suspended between school and the adult world of work and family responsibilities, and dreaming of escape. In both films the bicycle is a means of physical and imaginative escape, and, for Dave, this assumption of a new persona involves crossing a class boundary as well as a spatial boundary. Earlier in the film, as Dave walks with his dad through the campus at night, Ray explains proudly that he cut the stones for the building they are passing. 'I'd like to able to stroll through the campus and look at the limestone,' he says, 'but I just feel out of place. So, the only thing you got to show for my 20 years of work is the holes we left behind.'

As a family melodrama, the film is comparatively subtle in its treatment of the themes of inequality, class antagonism and the emotional violence to which the characters are subject. A comparison with the emotionally overwrought *American Flyers* (Badham, 1985), also written by Steve Tesich (who won an Oscar for *Breaking Away*), is instructive in this regard. *American Flyers* uses the Hell of the West three-day cycle race as the stage for the tearful reconciliation of two estranged brothers, Dave and Marcus, the latter a former professional racer, suffering from an inoperable cerebral aneurysm, the condition that killed their father. Marcus has returned home to make friends with his younger brother, knowing that he is likely to die soon, and to motivate Dave to realise his potential by persuading him to compete in the race with him. From the title onwards, which indicates this is a mythic story about the United States, a national allegory, the film stresses the symbolic significance of the drama, with future Hollywood star Kevin Costner delivering his lines with a ponderous weight: 'There are these decisive moments in bike racing, you know?' he tells Dave, as he reflects on his career. 'When the moment came, I gave up.'

As in *Breaking Away*, the race involves the settling of scores – between Marcus and his old rival 'the Cannibal' (the nickname of Eddy Merckx, who has a cameo as the race starter) – and, while to some extent the dialogue is interchangeable, and both films are unusually careful to detail the strategies involved in professional racing, the style of the two films is very different. *Breaking Away* carries its symbolism lightly, and, although the teenage protagonists sometimes slump into self-pity, they respond to their situation with irony and camaraderie rather than morose despair. In place of familiar stereotypes of working-class masculinity, the film shows us young men who are thoughtful, playful and romantic. Similarly, the inevitable rupturing of the family that occurs as Dave grows older and assumes the middle-class identity of a student is treated as humorous rather than traumatic. At the film's conclusion, cycling through the campus, Ray comes across his son, Dave, who is riding in the other direction, talking enthusiastically with a French student about the Tour de France. 'Bonjour, papa!' he yells as he rides past, cycling on to a new identity as a Francophile. As *Breaking Away* makes clear, the bicycle is a visual metaphor for both social mobility and the mobile individual identity of an adolescent that is in dynamic process, taking shape and searching for a stable form. As Ryan Hediger observes, the cycling scenes 'present identity less as fixed or rigid and more as open cosmopolitanism, object-entangled, even musicalized; identity is *performed*, amid a large cast, both human and inhuman.'[14]

'Class' Conflicts

While *Breaking Away* is an examination of a precise time and place – the American Midwest of the 1970s – the film's scenario of class conflict is a flexible narrative template that is recycled in the Hindi film adaptation *Jo Jeeta Wohi Sikandar* (Khan, 1992).[15] Set in the beautiful rural area around Dehradun in northern India, the film focuses on the rivalry between the children of India's wealthiest families, studying at elite boarding schools such as Rajput College, Queen's College and St Xavier's, and the poor local children, studying at Model College.[16] This competition comes to a head in the annual inter-school sports meet, which is dominated by the wealthy schools, and it is personified in the antagonism between Shekhar Malhotra, the obnoxious son of a steel magnate, and two siblings at Model College, the athletic Ratan and his younger brother Sanju (played by future mega-star Aamir Khan). In the opening scenes the contest is won by Rajput when Shekhar beats Ratan by a whisker in the final event, the 50-kilometre marathon cycle race, and a desire to avenge this defeat propels the narrative.

As is typical in Bollywood cinema, the film is punctuated with spectacular musical 'item numbers', and is tonally varied, shifting between slapstick comedy, dramatic action sequences, family melodrama and romance – a commercially refined popular aesthetic that Lalitha Gopalan terms 'the cinema of interruptions.'[17] The theme of class or caste incompatibility is redoubled through a romance between Sanju and snobbish Queen's College pupil Devika, as Sanju pretends to be the aristocratic son of a local landowner (echoing the theme of adolescent fantasy explored in *Breaking Away*). His ruse is exposed at an inter-school dance contest, when Devika sees him dancing with the performers from Model College, but after he is snubbed by Devika, who is disgusted by his poverty and upset by his deception, Sanju comes to realise his real love is his oldest friend, Anjali, who works after school as a car mechanic.

Sanju's older brother Ratan is favourite to win the subsequent cycle race, and their father, who won the race for Model in 1965, saves up to buy him an Italian road bike. However, Ratan is left in a coma after Shekhar and fellow Rajput pupils ambush him during a training ride in the hills, beating him up and accidentally pitching him over a cliff. Following a song about his love for his brother, Sanju resolves to take Ratan's place in the race. After a sweaty training montage sequence, intercut with shots of Ratan's physiotherapy, the tournament arrives, and, as at the beginning of the film, the overall result rests on the final cycle race. The race itself is rough, and at one point Shekhar and Sanju go off the edge of the road as they grapple on their bikes; Shekhar then pins Sanju against a tree, pummelling him, before Shekhar's three friends pile into the brawl. However, they rejoin the race, while a fight breaks out in the stadium between students from Rajput and Model. When they reach the velodrome, pupils are spilling out of the stands onto the track, and some cyclists are sent sprawling in the furious sprint to the finish, but of course Sanju drops down from the bank on the last bend to win the race by a hair's breadth.

The account of the stubborn persistence of caste division offered by *Jo Jeeta Wohi Sikandar* is less nuanced and cynical than that of *Breaking Away*; Sanju's transformation from non-academic truant to heroic athlete, motivated by brotherly love and class resentment, is a meritocratic celebration of hard work and the will to triumph. Moreover, although the bicycle race remains a key plot device and an Italian bicycle an object of desire, cycling culture is less significant, none of the characters sharing Dave's Europhilia or fetishistic love of cycle racing. The bicycle is a marker of class and caste in a more conventional way, since the rich kids drive cars and ride motorbikes, while Sanju and his friends must resort to bicycles or 'borrowing' cars from the garage where Anjali works. This is also an indication of the varied cultural histories of the bicycle in different regions of the world. Smethurst observes, 'Where the bicycle crossed from a microcosm of European society into wider colonial society, it entered a milieu constituted in different social hierarchies, work patterns and cultural practices.'[18] While the 'colonial bicycle boom' constituted '20% of the UK's share of world exports in 1900, rising to nearly 50% in 1912...the majority of these bicycles were still destined for Westerners and colonial administrators.'[19] In this context, the bicycle in India is the vehicle for a complex blend of meanings around nationhood, gender and social status. As John Roselli relates, middle-class Indian men took up cycling in the early twentieth century as a defiant expression of national pride and a rejection of Orientalist stereotypes; in Bengal, cycling was a 'matter of patriotic importance, a means of countering...European representations of Bengali babus as "effeminate", "effete" and physically inept.[20] The intersection of sport and politics is less pronounced in *Jo Jeeta Wohi Sikandar* than it is in *Lagaan* (Gowariker, 2001), Aamir Khan's epic film about a cricket match between British colonists and locals in the British Raj of the 1890s in which sport becomes a means of resisting imperial rule. Nevertheless, the theme of social inequality, caste tensions and the milieu of British-styled boarding schools located in a former colonial hill station mean that the dramatic rivalries of *Jo Jeeta Wohi Sikandar* take place on a post-colonial stage.

Fantasia and Suburban Dreamworlds

While *Breaking Away* uses an Italian road bike as a vehicle to examine working-class American adolescence at the end of the crisis-ridden 1970s, Steven Spielberg's science fiction blockbuster *E.T.: The Extra-Terrestrial* (1982) uses a Japanese Kuwahara BMX bike as the vehicle for its spectacular fantasy of middle-class, suburban adolescence in President Reagan's newly isolationist, neoliberal America. The idea for the film arose when Spielberg was shooting *Close Encounters of the Third Kind* (1977) and wondered what would happen if one of the aliens from that film stayed behind as 'a foreign exchange student'. He had also been wanting to make a film about 'how divorce hits kids', and with *E.T.* he found a way to fuse these into a single narrative. He has said a number of times that this was his first 'personal movie', reflecting upon his own childhood, but notes that the setting is 'almost like my dream of suburbia...a Norman Rockwell fantasy of suburbia'. The sprawling American suburb romanticised in Spielberg's film was the product in the 1950s of cheap energy, growing GDP and an expanded consumer economy 'that locked Western industrialized nations into an automotive existence.'[21] The topographic embodiment of waste in their unrestrained consumption of energy and space, the rapidly expanding suburbs were also the destination for the post-war 'white flight' as the newly affluent white middle classes migrated from racially mixed cities and desegregated areas into more ethnically homogeneous communities. In this context, the film's nostalgic depiction of the imaginative adventures of childhood in the person of Elliott Thomas takes on a more reactionary tone, which helps to explain why it became 'one of the Reagan era's signature narratives.'[22] In the process, it marked a shift into a new phase of Hollywood film production dominated by director/producer Spielberg, by aesthetic and ideological conservatism and by phenomenally expensive fantasy and science fiction blockbusters. As with the first Lumière screenings or the release of *The Bicycle Thieves*, the intersection of the bicycle with cinema once again marks a significant shift in the composition and social significance of cinema.

The scale of suburban estates and their distance from city centres created a dependence upon cars for commuting, shopping and socialising, but, if America's car culture was consolidated by suburbanisation, the bicycle was an important component of suburban infrastructure; as James Longhurst writes, 'suburban children needed bikes; it was in these postwar American suburbs that the strong cultural association between childhood and chainrings was set for marketers and the general public alike'.[23] In *E.T.*, this association takes on an emotionally powerful resonance, captured in the shots of the child taking flight on a bicycle, an image accentuated by John Williams' affecting symphonic music, similarly nostalgic in its citation of classic Hollywood scores of the 1940s and '50s. Although Elliott's bike is a Japanese import,[24] in other respects the BMX bike, which resembles a miniature motorbike, epitomises a particularly American concept of the bicycle as an ambiguous object, and in this sense it is a material expression of his shifting identity. The cinematic child is an ambiguous sign in so far as 'the child becomes the *signifier* of the "future." But the child also simultaneously becomes the *signified* of the "past"'.[25] In a similar way, the bicycle is an indeterminate symbol infused with nostalgia, signifying both the future – since it once represented the cutting edge of industrial technology, and still points towards a post-oil world – and also a pre-automotive past.

From at least the 1950s adulthood was associated in the United States with driving, and consequently, as Longhurst puts it, '[l]ike adolescents, the bicycle occupied a liminal state: not fully an adult, though no longer a child; not fully a vehicle but not really a pedestrian'.[26] For example, the children's public safety film *Bicycle Today, Automobile Tomorrow* (1969) cautions: 'Remember, the bicycle rider of today is the automobile driver of tomorrow', while, in *Bicycles Are Beautiful* (1974), presenter Bill Cosby insists on calling cyclists 'bicycle drivers', emphasising their status as future car owners. This sense that adulthood and cycling are antithetical is reinforced by Hollywood films that convey the message that, if you ride a bike as an adult man, 'you will be seen as a queer, virginal, childish loser'.[27] This assumption that the bicycle propels riders towards driving (echoing the shift many manufacturers underwent in the early 1900s from producing bicycles to producing cars, after the boom of the 1890s died away) is evident in the design features of several popular American bikes for adults and children from the 1930s onwards, which suggest the machines were morphing into motor vehicles; these include the fake petrol tank of the Schwinn Motorbike, or the automobile-style gearshift, and the low-slung frame, banana seat and 'ape-hanger' handlebars of the Schwinn Stingray ('the bicycle with the sports-car look'). Indeed, according to the exhaustive documentary *Joe Kid on a Stingray: The History of BMX* (Eaton, Swarr, 2005), the fashion for BMX bikes was inspired by the cult 1971 documentary *On Any Sunday* by surf film specialist Bruce Brown. A celebration of various forms of amateur and professional motorcycle racing (including speedway, drag racing and motocross), the film's title sequence showed a group of tanned young boys racing Stingrays chaotically around a dirt track.

E.T. tells the story of Elliott, a boy who happens across an alien in his back garden. The child-sized alien, which he later names E.T., was stranded when his/her spaceship left abruptly, and Elliott brings it into the house. Taking care to hide it from his mother, who is too distracted by work and coping as a single parent to notice, he introduces it to his older brother, Michael, and little sister, Gertie, and they begin to communicate with it, teaching it English and feeding it. A telepathic bond is formed between Elliott and E.T. so that they share one another's emotions and subjective experience, culminating in a comic scene in which Elliott gets drunk at school when the alien starts drinking cans of beer from the fridge at home. After some time E.T. begins to build a transmitter, in order, as he explains to the children with the limited vocabulary he has acquired, to 'phone home'.

Using Halloween as an opportunity to take E.T. out of the house unobtrusively, since the streets are packed with children dressed as monsters, Elliott places E.T. in the basket of his BMX bike and cycles to the woods. In the film's most famous sequence – perhaps the most widely viewed cycling sequence in cinema[28] – as Elliott struggles to ride through the forest, the bike begins moving by itself, powered by the alien (who has the magical ability to levitate objects), flies off the edge of a cliff and soars above the trees, passing in front of the Moon before descending again. E.T. assembles his transmitter, while a tearful Elliott tries to persuade it to stay: 'We could be happy here. I could take care of you. I wouldn't let anybody hurt you. We could grow up together, E.T.'

Elliott returns home alone in the morning, and his brother Michael sets out on his bike to search for E.T., finding it lying pale and unconscious on the bank of a stream. He brings it home, and the children finally reveal it to their mother, a sickly Elliott telling her: 'I think we're dying.' At this point the house is suddenly surrounded by the federal agents who have been tracking the alien since the beginning of the film. Dressed in spacesuits, they enter the house through the doors and windows, and seal the house with polythene. Elliott and E.T., both ill, are placed side by side on beds inside another polythene bubble, wired to various instruments and surrounded by scientists. Elliott asks E.T. to stay with him, and E.T. replies: 'I'll be right here', but dies shortly afterwards, whereupon Elliott suddenly recovers.

Elliott is allowed to spend a few moments alone with the body, and realises that the alien has come back to life. Using Gertie to distract the agents, Michael and Elliott steal the van in which E.T.'s coffin has been placed, and rendezvous in a nearby park with their friends, who've brought bikes. Elliott explains quickly, 'He's a man from outer space and we're taking him up to his spaceship.' 'Well, can't he just – beam up?' one of them asks, and Elliott replies impatiently, 'This is reality, Greg.' In the climactic scenes, the five children race through the suburbs on their bikes, pursued by the police and agents lumbering around in their cars and on foot. The children speed past half-built houses and empty areas of levelled earth like a giant BMX track, jumping down hills and over a police car. After splitting up, they reassemble to find their route obstructed by armed police at a roadblock. As they approach it, Elliott closes his eyes and the bikes take flight, gliding over houses and swimming pools towards the setting sun. They touch down in the forest, and E.T.'s spaceship descends through the trees. Elliott's mother arrives in the car with Gertie, and in a moving scene the family says goodbye to the alien. E.T. invites Elliott to come with him, but he refuses, to which E.T. replies: 'Ouch', pointing to his heart. They embrace; E.T. touches Elliott's head, assuring him: 'I'll be right here', and then waddles up the ramp into the spaceship, as John Williams' score strives furiously for new ecstasies of emotion. The ship departs, leaving a rainbow in the night sky, a final allusion to classic Hollywood cinema overlaid with the sound of timpani, recalling the opening of Richard Strauss's symphonic poem *Also Sprach Zarathustra*, as used in *2001: A Space Odyssey* (Kubrick, 1968).

The film's excessive allusiveness invites us to understand it as a fable that is open to interpretation. The scene in which Gertie's mother reads *Peter Pan* to her, while E.T. listens from its hiding place in the wardrobe, is the most direct signpost that we should look for similar themes in the film: family romance, fantasy, nostalgia and sentimental conceptions of boyhood. Vivian Sobchack has observed that the 'privileged figure of the child' in late twentieth-century US cinema is a key device through which American films replay and attempt to resolve the crisis of bourgeois patriarchy and the 'disintegration and transfiguration of the "traditional" American bourgeois family'.[29] This familial crisis is particularly evident in science fiction and horror cinema, through the intrusive presence of alien figures and monsters in the family home:

Figures from the past and future get into the house, make their homes in the closet, become part of the family, open the kitchen and family room up to the horrific and wondrous world outside this private and safe domain. A man's home in bourgeois patriarchal culture is no longer his castle. In the age of television, the drawbridge is always down; the world intrudes. It is no longer possible to avoid the invasive presence of Others – whether poltergeists,[30] extraterrestrials, or one's own alien kids.[31]

With *E.T.*, the wonder and terror of science fiction is relocated to a mundane sub-urban house. *E.T.* depicts the closed world experienced by a child, its limited boundaries encompassing home, school, housing estate and the nearby woods. Thus, the crisis of bourgeois patriarchy is articulated principally in localised terms as the absence of a father, now with another woman. For Elliott and his siblings, the alien is an ideal substitute parent, a hybrid of adult and child. On the one hand, the wrinkled creature is well travelled, wise and knowledgeable, technically skilful and magically powerful, but, at the same time, it is small, relatively immobile with its tiny legs (carried around, like a baby, in a bicycle basket), curious but timid and, initially, unable to speak, write or feed itself. The alien is the means through which the narrative resolves the crisis of patriarchy, a super-father who 'physically escapes traditional patriarchal form without yielding patriarchal power, and thus is able to reside in (terrestrial) domestic space and serve as Elliott's surrogate father'.[32] E.T.'s gender is uncertain – only Gertie asks: 'Is he a boy or a girl?' – but, structurally and symbolically, there is little question that it represents an idealised, emotionally accessible masculinity:

[P]hysically androgynous and sexually unthreatening – all problematic patriarchal, paternal, and male power displaced, condensed and conserved in the sensuously warm glow at the tip of an innocently elongated (and phallic) finger.[33]

'I never thought of *E.T.* as a science fiction film,' Spielberg has said. 'I saw this as a story about a family, just a regular family in disrepair after suffering the tragedy of divorce.' It has a great deal in common with the classic Hollywood melodrama in which the middle-class home is the claustrophobic stage for emotional violence, derangement and inarticulate despair. In a broader sense, much science fiction is melodramatic in its preoccupation with the symbolic significance of physical space and its focus upon the experience of a small range of characters who are driven to emotional extremes, but *E.T.* is a more conventional film melodrama, in terms both of its mise en scène and its central concern with the fragility of the nuclear family and the damage done by masculine irresponsibility and indifference. Whereas the melodramas made by Douglas Sirk and Nicholas Ray in the 1950s were vehicles for a subtle ideological critique of a post-war social order that rested on misogyny, racism and anachronistic concepts of masculinity, and resulted in the crushingly unhappy lives of the desperate protagonists, Spielberg's film is far more conservative. While the fractious, fragile middle-class family itself is the problem for the teenage protagonist of *Rebel without a Cause* (Ray, 1955), in Spielberg's film it is the *disintegration* of the nuclear family that is the problem, manifested in the chaotically untidy and over-stuffed house.

If the film articulates a paternal fantasy, it is also relatively uncritical of patriarchal institutions, as the mysterious government agency tracking the alien is also revealed ultimately to be a benevolent organisation that has been observing events from a distance. E.T. is stranded at the opening when its ship makes a hasty exit to escape the approaching agents. As the film progresses, agents are seen sweeping the surrounding areas in search of the alien, sinister presences shown only in silhouette or from the waist down. Homing in on Elliott's house, they place it under surveillance, listening surreptitiously to conversations, following Elliott's brother Michael and eventually occupying the home, sealing it and cordoning it off from the rest of the estate. Although this depiction of invasive state surveillance recalls the paranoid conspiracy thrillers of the 1970s, we eventually learn that the lead agent is a compassionate figure rather than a vicious, small-minded bureaucrat.

The film is systematic and highly original in its narrative and spatial presentation of a restricted, child's-eye view of the world, using low angles, frequently placing the camera at the height of a child's head and ensuring that, apart from Elliott's mother's, the agent's is the only other adult face to be shown in close-up. For most of the film the unnamed agent has been shown only with a close-up of the jingling bunch of keys attached to his belt, a symbol of institutional authority that is as unmistakably phallic as E.T.'s bulbous finger. His face is finally revealed to us when Elliott and E.T. have been strapped to stretchers, and he explains to Elliott: 'He came to me too. I've been wishing for this since I was ten years old. I don't want him to die.' He tells Elliott that the alien's arrival is 'a miracle, and you did the best that anybody could do. I'm glad he met you first.' Even more than the alien, he is an ideal substitute father, appearing just as E.T. is dying, and then again at the film's conclusion as E.T.'s ship departs. Although it is a convention of American science fiction films that aliens are met with fear and excessive violence by the military and federal agencies, in this film the government shares Elliott's wonder and concern.

A principal criticism of the film is that it epitomises the supposedly simplistic register of popular culture. Ilsa Bick proposes that, '[i]nstead of simply invoking the memories and associations of childhood, Spielberg consistently aims to infantilize the viewer,'[34] while Frank Tomasulo concludes that the combination of nostalgia, product placement and intricate layering of references to fairy tales, children's literature and family films results in 'the infantilization of the audience, making us all children of multinational corporate capitalism.'[35] Of course, for Spielberg, a return to the Neverland of childhood is a measure of cinema's capacity to transport the spectator, reproducing in the viewer the emotionally overwhelming and intellectually disarming experience of awe, love, resentment, desire and sorrow that Elliott cycles through during the film. The final image of Elliott and his family and friends gazing up at the spaceship as it departs is an idealised image of cinematic spectatorship, a reflection of the viewer staring tearfully up at the screen, and, indeed, Spielberg has recalled that, when he was invited to screen the film at the White House, sitting next to Ronald Reagan, he saw the president become a ten-year-old boy as he watched it. The film's extraordinary power is its insistence that 'adult viewers of *E.T.* are Elliott, as well as knowing that they are *no longer* Elliott, and at the same time they want to protect the weeping Elliott'.[36]

Angus McFadzean suggests that *E.T.* is one of the first of a cycle of films he terms the 'suburban fantastic', which are concerned primarily with the experience of teenage and pre-teen boys. This cycle, produced during the 1980s and 1990s, has, ironically, become the focus of a new wave of cultural nostalgia, or meta-nostalgia, with the film *Super 8* (Abrams, 2011) and the TV series *Stranger Things* (Duffer Brothers, 2016) lovingly recreating the milieu of *E.T.*, while the fannish Canadian film *Turbo Kid* (Simard, Whissell, Whissell, 2015), which depicts an apocalyptic post-oil future in which the heroes and villains travel by BMX bike, is an encyclopaedic montage of comics, toys, TV programmes and the science fiction, fantasy and horror films found on the shelves of video rental stores in the 1980s. For these film-makers, Spielberg's suburban fantasia has the affective resonance that Norman Rockwell's *Saturday Evening Post* covers had for Spielberg's generation. For their protagonists, 'suburbia is a self-contained, autonomous world, designed – with its schools, parks, skate parks and so on – with the experience of childhood at its centre, a space in which children experience a degree of freedom and security'.[37] At the same time, for some of these cinematic children, 'suburbia also manifests an uncanny aspect that is the product of their developmental stage and topographical situation'.[38] Their growing frustrations with the physical and cultural constraints of their constructed environment, as well as the physical and emotional challenges of puberty and adolescence, are manifested through disruptive intrusions from worlds beyond the suburban microcosm. The cinematic suburbs are crawling with bullies, criminals, psychopaths and serial killers, ghosts and monsters, but this 'melodrama of growing up is inflected towards a gendered identity crisis'.[39] As Phyllis Deutsch wrote scathingly on the film's release, for all the film's textual richness and dynamic storytelling, Spielberg 'is hampered by his passion for mythologies that separate human beings according to sex and perpetuate unequal power (and hence, love) relations among them'. Most of the film's largely positive reviews 'overlooked the sexist backbone of Spielberg's superficially engaging fairytale', and she concludes: 'We should all stop believing in fairies until someone makes a film in which little girls have adventures on bicycles, too.'[40]

Miracles and Magic Carpets

The global success of Spielberg's film can be explained partly by the skill with which Spielberg and screenwriter Melissa Mathison assembled this allusive narrative and partly by the technical skill with which Spielberg and crew directed the child actors, staged and shot the film and integrated the special effects into the depiction of suburban normality. However, for younger audiences, I suspect that a great deal of the film's appeal was the novel spectacle of kids on BMX bikes, and this was exploited in several films for children and teenagers, including *Rad* and the Australian film *BMX Bandits* (1983), directed by Brian Trenchard-Smith, a specialist in low-budget exploitation and straight-to-video films, and made-for-TV movies, whose fans include Quentin Tarantino. Although brief, the cycling sequences in *E.T.* are one of the principal sources of pleasure, producing a heady sense of free, transgressive movement as the children take their bikes off-road and along short cuts and run rings around the adults – the police and federal agents – outpacing them and riding across a police car as if it were a ramp. The sweeping topography of suburbia (which, as if it is a projection of them, is still under construction) is transformed into a racetrack. As they navigate the territory by improvised routes that betray a different knowledge and experience of their spatial environment from that of the car-bound grown-ups, their cycling expresses a radically different understanding of the space around them. This is epitomised by the two sequences in which the bicycles take flight. Invoking a well-established fantasy of cycling as flight (captured in Ferdinand Zecca's 1901 film of a flying bicycle/dirigible hybrid, his trick film *Slippery Jim* [1909] about a pickpocket who evades the police with impossible leaps back and forth over a canal on his bike, or fin-de-siècle French adverts showing bicycles flying through space), as well as the genealogical link between bicycles and aircraft, personified by bicycle manufacturers-cum-aeronauts Orville and Wilbur Wright, these scenes also express a wistful adult fantasy of childhood as a temporary space of freedom and play, fantasy and innocence that has the familiarity of cliché. In the documentary *Battle Mountain: Graeme Obree's Story*, the world champion cyclist (nicknamed 'the Flying Scotsman') explains that, as a child who was bullied at school, 'I discovered bikes as an escape mechanism, as this magic carpet that just sails through the atmosphere and over the hills and far away'.

Writing about *Breaking Away*, Ryan Hediger observes that the scenes showing Dave riding through the countryside evoke the fluid, embodied experience of cycling, offering 'a kind of cycling dreamworld, a strange space apart, an alternative picture of selfhood'.[41] However, this description captures much more directly the sense and sensation of cycling evoked by *E.T.*, the presence of the alien confirming the strangeness of the experience. What makes these sequences so arresting for adult viewers is the way that they evoke the thrilling experience of learning to ride. The children in both scenes are simultaneously elated but terrified; 'Not so high!' Elliott breathlessly pleads with E.T. in the first scene, while, in the second, one of his friends yells: 'Tell me when it's over', as the group of policemen and agents watch them ride away. 'The bike always starts with a miracle', writes Paul Fournel, reflecting on the moment at which he rode away from a parent:

And then one morning I no longer heard the sound of someone running behind me, the sound of rhythmic breathing at my back. The miracle had taken place. I was riding. I never wanted to put my feet back down for fear that the miracle wouldn't happen again.[42]

For the writer, Fournel, 'it was only really learning to read that equaled the intensity of learning to ride';[43] the related practices of riding and reading shaped his life.

Exploitation and Banditry

Like *E.T*, *BMX Bandits* is a film about the adventures of suburban teenagers flying freely around town on BMX bikes. However, rather than a magical surrogate father, their more mundane desire is for a local BMX track, and, whereas the cycling sequences in *E.T.* are brief, they are a central feature of the Australian film. It follows a template familiar from children's film and literature, in which a group of children, who roam unsupervised through a lawless interzone that is largely empty of adults except for incompetent police and thieves, foil the plans of a criminal gang. For example, *Skid Kids* (Chaffey, 1953), a matinee film by the British Children's Film Foundation, tells the story of a group of children who organise amateur cycle speedway races on empty bomb sites in London and are suspected by the police of being behind a rash of bicycle thefts. In order to ensure they can continue to race, Swanky and his friends track down the gang stealing the bikes and help the police to catch them. At the film's end

Swanky wins the final race, and his team, the Burton Bullets, are rewarded with a slap-up meal.

The self-styled BMX bandits are teenage boys Goose and P.J., and the young woman Judy (Nicole Kidman, in one of her first films), whom they meet when they crash into shopping trolleys outside the supermarket where she works. The three of them ride brightly coloured bikes and wear colourful protective gear and T-shirts with the logo BMX Bandits, as if they were a factory team. While searching for mussels in the bay, to raise money to repair Goose's broken bike, they find a submerged cache of two-way radios a gang had hidden for use in a raid on a payroll truck. The thieves begin to hunt the trio down, and Judy is later caught by the robbers, but P.J. and Goose rescue her from the comically inept thieves, and the three teenagers then set off on their bikes, pursued by the crooks in an American muscle car. A spectacular chase sequence follows them across a water park, a rugby pitch, a shopping precinct and a quarry, and, as in *E.T.*, the streets, gardens, parks and public spaces of the Australian suburbs are reconfigured by the cyclists as a racetrack or playground. After being upbraided by the police chief, the three of them set about trapping the crooks, by allowing Judy to be kidnapped, then cornering them with scores of children on BMX bikes. The children attack the gang with flour in a slapstick battle, and, when the boss escapes in a truck with Judy, P.J. and Goose force it to crash into a fertiliser truck, which then sprays foam everywhere as the police arrive to arrest the crooks. The film finishes with the opening of the Manly BMX track,[44] donated by the Police Department, and (as in *Skid Kids*) Goose, P.J. and Judy all win trophies in the inaugural races.

Although it veers uncertainly between seriousness and slapstick silliness, *BMX Bandits* offers a subtle account of adolescent experience that is entirely free of sentiment. P.J. and Goose are both smart, ironic teenagers who find themselves rivals for Judy's attention. While Judy flirts briefly with P.J. and brushes off Goose's attempt to kiss her, she isn't especially interested in them, and, if Goose is jealous, it doesn't damage his friendship with P.J. The film is casually frank in its acknowledgement of sexual desire as a textural component of their relationships – echoing the cycling love triangle in François Truffaut's *Jules et Jim* (1962) – but what is most remarkable is the depiction of Judy as a desiring subject, rather than just the object of desire. After she buys a BMX bike, a montage sequence shows her expertly performing freestyle stunts on the bike, jumping over P.J. and Goose as they lie on the promenade. These tricks are set to the song 'I See Boys', a celebration of the female gaze and the pleasures – as opposed to the traumas – of adolescence: 'I never listened to my mother when she was telling me to hide away. I never noticed my body changing, I still dance in the same old way.' The US poster features a painting showing the three teenagers jumping out of the picture on their bikes with Nicole Kidman in the centre, flanked by the two boys. As it suggests, *BMX Bandits* is a rare example of a film in which girls have adventures on bicycles, too, and, like a number of the films discussed in this chapter, *BMX Bandits* also demonstrates precisely why, as Lance Armstrong puts it, 'kids love bikes': 'They get on the bike, they go down, they take a right, take a left – nobody sees them; they're completely free.'

7

The Digital Bicycle Boom

Figure 7.1

New perspectives on cycling in the experimental digital video work *Bike* (Hill, 2013) (courtesy Tony Hill)

Salvation through the Bicycle

One of the most famous cycling scenes in cinema occurs midway through New Hollywood western *Butch Cassidy and the Sundance Kid*. While the two outlaws, Butch and Sundance (Paul Newman and Robert Redford), are lying low in a farmhouse with Sundance's partner, Etta (Katharine Ross), Butch appears one morning with a bicycle. 'Meet the future,' he announces to Etta, and then takes her for a ride through the sunny fields while she perches on his handlebars. He proceeds to show off his trick cycling skills flirtatiously (to the accompaniment of slapstick circus music) while she watches from a hayloft, before he crashes through a fence into a field containing a bull, which then chases the pair up a track.

Like a number of westerns from the period, the film is infused with nostalgia for the freedoms of a frontier that was vanishing rapidly in the face of capitalist modernity as railways and telegraph systems laced the country together, and, for Butch, the bicycle stands for industrialisation and the coming century. The anachronistic intrusion of this futuristic technology into this pastoral scene is reinforced by the saccharine '60s pop song that accompanies it: 'Raindrops Keep Fallin' on My Head'. Later on, as they flee the farm to hide from the Pinkerton detectives in South America, Butch pushes the bicycle into a stream, muttering angrily: 'The future's all yours, you lousy bicycles.' Whereas the enthusiasm for the safety bicycle boom of the 1890s was motivated partly by the individual freedoms promised to men and women by this technology, for the outlaw Butch, who was already radically free, it signifies the opposite: enclosure, loss of independence and, ultimately, death when he and Sundance are shot down by the army in Bolivia.

At a moment when the bicycle is commonly regarded as a rudimentary technology whose appeal is that it offers an alternative to fossil-fuel-powered transport, and a slower pace of life, it is easy to forget that the bicycle once represented the future. This is captured particularly well in Polish writer Bruno Schulz's surreal short story collection *The Street of Crocodiles* (1934). In a passage recalling the appearance of the first bicycles at the acme of 'the age of electricity and mechanics', Schulz writes:

It was not long before the city filled with velocipedes of various sizes and shapes. An outlook based on philosophy became obligatory. Whoever admitted to a belief in progress had to draw the logical conclusion and ride a velocipede.... Lifting themselves on their moving pedals, as if on stirrups, they addressed the crowd from on high, forecasting a new happy era for mankind – salvation through the bicycle.[1]

Schulz's account is underlined with irony, as he observes that this self-important display of the mastery of physics and engineering rapidly became an abject spectacle when the fad for cycling quickly descended into 'self-parody', as '[t]he cyclist rode on among elemental outbursts of laughter – miserable victors, martyrs to their genius'.[2] The irony of the cyclists' self-importance is accentuated when it is learnt that an approaching comet is on course to annihilate the Earth, and so technical and scientific progress is exposed as mere vanity.

Nevertheless, in the bicycle boom of the early twenty-first century, the bicycle remains the object of utopian hopes and fantasies (as well as spite, contempt and grim dystopian anxieties), the focus of imagined futures that promise a proliferation of new Amsterdams. American journalist Jeff Mapes writes, with imagery that evokes the mise en scène of *Butch Cassidy*:

A growing number of Americans, mounted on their bicycles like some new kind of urban cowboy, are mixing it up with swift, two-ton motor vehicles as they create a new society on the streets. They're finding physical fitness, low-cost transportation, environmental purity – and, still all too often, Wild West risks of sudden death or injury.

These new pioneers are beginning to change the look and feel of many cities, suburbs and small towns.[3]

The current bicycle boom has several characteristics, which are simultaneously catalysts and consequences of the boom. These include activism or advocacy (such as the global emergence of the Critical Mass movement in the early 1990s and World Naked Bike Ride protests in the early 2000s), technological developments in bicycle design (such as the mountain bike and 'hybrid', electric bikes, carbon frames and ultra-lightweight components), town planning and transport policy that is oriented around cycling (such as the marking out of bicycle lanes, the introduction of rental bike and bike share schemes in cities and the phenomenon of politicians being filmed and photographed on bicycles) and the popularity of the sport in the wake of the successes of Lance Armstrong and of Bradley Wiggins.

Moreover, there is growing academic interest in cycling's technical and social history and in issues of public policy and funding. There is also a minor industry devoted to publishing books and magazines on sport and leisure cycling, ranging from literary and philosophical reflections[4] through extensive histories of cycle racing, biographies and athletes' memoirs, style and fashion guides such as Mikael Colville-Andersen's *Cycle Chic* (2012) and on to travel guides and technical manuals. Most pertinently, one of the distinctive features of this new bicycle boom is the emergence of bicycle film festivals, ranging from small-scale events, with audience-operated bicycle generators to power film projectors, to the annual international Bicycle Film Festival, screening a varied mix of independent shorts, promotional films and classic documentaries.

While Mapes describes the latest boom as a 'pedaling revolution', cycling historian Paul Smethurst is more circumspect about the extent of any bicycle-led political transformation. Although annual 'worldwide bicycle production grew six-fold from just over 20 million units in 1970 to 130 million units by 2007',[5] this has not necessarily corrected deep inequalities of mobility. He observes that, '[a]cross much of Asia, standard roadsters built to last several generations have the stigma of poverty,'[6] while the pattern of bicycle sales in the United States 'suggests that rather than being a social leveler, the bicycle today is as likely to be a discriminatory marker of gender and disposable income,'[7] exemplified in the United Kingdom by the stereotypical figure of the 'Lycra lout' or 'MAMIL' (middle-aged man in Lycra).[8] He goes on to suggest that, although 'critical bicycling' events – acts of protest such as Critical Mass rides – deploy the bicycle as 'a symbol for a host of issues', cycling may actually be a minor concern or an irrelevance for the protestors: 'The political significance of the mass occupation of public space is not necessarily directly concerned with the bicycle at all.'[9]

The complex and historically contingent symbolism of the bicycle is precisely the focus of this book. *Cycling and Cinema* examines aspects of the future anticipated by Cassidy, and the various ways that this future has been storied on film. The period it covers begins with the bicycle boom of the mid-1890s, which was catalysed by the development of the safety bicycle and the pneumatic tyre. That boom coincided with widespread enthusiasm for the novel medium of cinema, made possible partly by the Cinématographe apparatus designed by the Lumières. There have been several subsequent bicycle booms, such as that in Britain in the 1930s and again after the Second World War, when cars were relatively scarce, or in the United States in the 1970s, when an energy crisis, environmental movements and the popularisation of lightweight, ten-speed bikes encouraged a turn to cycling. The latest bicycle boom brings this revolutionary history full circle, since it coincides with a radical shift in representational technologies; whereas the boom of the 1890s coincided with the inception of cinema, the latest boom coincides with analogue cinema's much-discussed 'death', as it has been supplanted over the last two decades by digital image production and distribution. Just as the safety bicycle offers a frame through which to examine the cultural and social significance of cinema, so the modern bicycle offers a frame through which to scrutinise the significance of a moment in which the private and public spaces we inhabit are saturated with screens. It is also a moment in which cyclists become directors and actors in their own cycling films.

Writing about the social and sensory effect of the new visual culture of the nineteenth century, Anne Friedberg suggested that 'print media, photography and cinema extended and commodified the field of the visible', so that 'everyday life was transfigured' by this new abundance of images as these new technologies produced 'imaginary mobilities'.[10] Some 20 years later, discussing contemporary visual culture, she proposed that 'as the display screens of movies, television, and the computer begin to grow more similar to each other…we now see the world in spatially and temporally fractured frames, through "virtual windows".'[11] As a result,

the 'postcinematic' 'post-televisual' viewer has new forms of ever-virtual mobility. New speeds of access to deep histories of images and text, newly mobilized screens that travel in airplanes and automobiles, screens that can be hand-held and wireless. As public buildings and domestic spaces boast image-bearing glass skins, as large-screen televisions are big enough and flat enough to substitute for real windows, as 'windows' within our computer screens stream images from multiple sources, as virtual reality technologies expand from the gaming world into entertainment or daily services, the 'virtual window' has become a ubiquitous portal – a 'wormhole' – to pasts and futures.[12]

Meet the Future

This chapter focuses on three ways in which the mobile technology of the bicycle intersects with the 'ever-virtual mobility' of contemporary culture to ask, if Butch Cassidy was indeed correct in predicting that the future belonged to bicycles, what that future comprises. The first of these is the increasingly common use of mobile or locative media by cyclists, as it becomes more and more normal for us to use GPS devices and map applications on mobile phones as navigation tools to help us find our way as we cycle. Flicking our attention back and forth between the screen – an animated map – and the landscape around us, concentrating on the correspondences between the two-dimensional image and three-dimensional space, the experience of cycling is subtly altered. Applications such as Google Maps foster a cartographic visuality that blurs the distinction between representation and referent, encouraging us to see the world around us as a 1:1 scale map. In itself this is nothing new, since maps, technical diagrams and schematics have always worked on the same principle, producing mediated ways of seeing space – and we should always be suspicious of Luddite accusations that new technology necessarily results in sensory impoverishment – but the textural experience of space produced by GPS devices is quite particular. The maps on a GPS device show us an image of the world as a smoothed, abstracted and rationalised space in which accessible roads and significant buildings are signposted with text. It trains us to see the world instrumentally as a navigable space, and so typifies the ever-virtual mobility examined by Friedberg. For the contemporary cyclist carrying a mobile phone, or with a GPS device mounted on her handlebars, the line between screen space and real space starts to blur.

An application such as Strava is a clear example, since it encourages a self-consciousness with regard to virtual movement, the sense for the cyclist that she is always cycling through code space or across the surface of a map. Like a number of applications, Strava allows the user to record her ride (or run or walk), and to upload the details onto a website afterwards, along with data from heart monitors and power meters, and it produces a map of the route taken. This allows her to compare her performance at different times over the same route – or sections of it – and so it is a helpful training aid for serious or casual athletes. The feature that makes Strava particularly popular with cyclists is that it is also a social networking device through which users can make their results, routes (and accompanying photographs and captions) publicly visible. This means that riders can compete virtually with one another over the same routes and distances as league tables for particular 'segments' of a route, such as a particular hill climb, are published online.

One effect of this is that all cycling excursions, no matter how solitary, become in effect public performances for viewing on a screen. This has been exploited playfully by some runners and cyclists, who have taken to producing 'Strava art', following routes that will appear on on-screen maps as sometimes obscene or comic messages or images. As an art practice it falls somewhere between virtual land art and virtual graffiti, but all users of apps such as Strava are drawing on screens whenever they track their rides, and, collectively, the hundreds of thousands of Strava users are engaged with producing a massively complex digital drawing. If drawing, for Paul Klee, was a matter of taking a line for a walk, Strava converts the bicycle into a rideable drawing tool.[13]

Another feature of Strava is that it potentially exposes the cyclist to intense scrutiny. Thus, as well as representing an example of a post-cinematic screen culture in which the distinction between spectator and performer/producer becomes more provisional, it also offers an example of the ways in which the virtual windows that comprise contemporary screen culture make the user herself highly visible. In tracking the routes taken by the cyclist as well as her bodily efforts, Strava produces a visual record of the cyclist's movement. In this respect, we might understand Strava as a cinematic apparatus, but, more precisely, it is a derivation of the protocinematic devices produced by physiologist Étienne-Jules Marey. Preoccupied with the problem of how to study the body in motion, Marey developed several devices to produce a graphic record of bodily movements. Inspired by Eadweard Muybridge's 'locomotion studies', Marey devised a camera to take a sequence of photographs in quick succession that could be printed onto the same plate, producing what he termed a *chronophotographe*.

In order to make bodily movement more clearly visible – and therefore scientifically and diagnostically valuable – he went on to develop a black velvet suit marked with circles and lines that rendered bodily motion as abstract patterns that were easier to analyse, prefiguring the motion capture suits used in digital cinema. In this regard, a mobile app such as Strava is a more technically sophisticated means of representing bodily movement in a graphic and textual form that is analytically useful.

As a means of abstracted self-representation, Strava depicts the individual as the 'quantified self', reducing the user's behaviour to a matrix of measurable, comparable data that can be studied, shared (willingly or inadvertently) and, of course, exploited. Strava is thus one component in a vast surveillance system devoted to monitoring individuals and harvesting information about them.[14] This is not necessarily sinister, since one feature of Strava is that it can share your location with 'safety contacts' in case you are injured while training. However, in relation to the social and cultural history of cycling, it is ironic that, whereas one of the radical freedoms offered by cycling was the possibility of independence – for young Victorian women, to escape the watchful eye of a chaperone or the disapproving gaze of the general public – technological progress makes anonymous, unsupervised movement less and less possible. If one of the emancipatory attractions of cycling is that physical mobility also puts identity in motion, allowing the rider to assume and perform other identities (a key theme of H. G. Wells' 1895 novel *The Wheels of Chance*, and its 1922 film adaptation), this capacity is foreclosed when smartphones, watches, activity trackers and GPS devices, and even the bike itself (as 'smart' bikes are integrated into 'smart' cities), track our every move. In a critique of the social function of sport, Jean-Marie Brohm proposes:

Sport as a technology of the body structurally reproduces capitalist repressive techniques: the division of labour, ultra-specialisation, repetition, training, the abstraction of space and time... the parcelling up of the body, measurement, stop-watch timing.[15]

To a large degree, activity trackers and 'smart' wireless devices are an intensification of these techniques, extending them to greater numbers of people and into a wide variety of activities beyond traditional sports, including working, walking, having sex and, even, sleeping.

Ride the Future

Another example of the intersection of the bicycle with post-cinematic screen culture is the emergence of virtual cycling simulations, stationary exercise bikes linked with monitors or large screens that allow the rider to follow the route displayed on the screen. In the simplest configuration this comprises videos that can be viewed while using an exercise bike, and which offer point-of-view shots of certain routes, such as 'Summer Rides through Colorful Colorado' or 'The Islands of British Columbia', or race routes such as stages of the Tour de France, some of them featuring on-screen displays showing the distance covered, speed and route profile. Sometimes accompanied by music, or instructions from a trainer to encourage you or direct you to adjust the resistance settings or gears on your bike according to the terrain on the screen, and sometimes featuring other riders, these videos are designed to produce the illusion that you are cycling through a real landscape. More sophisticated apparatuses synchronise the video with 'smart' trainers, bikes that can tilt and alter the pedalling resistance to simulate the gradients of the route displayed on the screen, while some bicycles can be linked with live exercise classes streamed over the internet.

More spectacular still is the Immersive Fitness gym system marketed by Les Mills, in which a roomful of exercise bikes face a wall-sized curved cinema screen, and, rather than real locations, digitally animated fantasy landscapes resembling video game environments are displayed on the screen, given such names as Ascension, Aurea and – in a nod to *The Matrix* – the Rabbit Hole. Promoted as the opportunity to 'ride the future', these installations are a disorienting fusion of theme park ride, video game, cinema, gymnasium and psychedelic concert or rave; the manufacturer describes the system as an 'immersive sensory experience', inviting riders to 'take a trip', racing and plunging through these fictional spaces.

Despite the insistence on the promotional website that this is the 'future of fitness', what is striking about this system is the extent to which it conveys us to a past in which early cinema's principal attraction was the non-narrative spectacle of movement.[16] The subjective 'point-of-view' cycling video has its formal and thematic origins in the 'phantom ride' film of the 1890s, in which forward- or backward-facing cameras were mounted on trains, trams and rickshaws to generate the illusion that the seated viewer was travelling through space. This was developed further by the Hale's Tours attractions of the early twentieth century, in which the audience sat inside a replica rocking railway carriage with a screen showing the view from the front of the train, accompanied by whistling wind noise. Writing in the trade journal *Moving Picture World* in 1916, B. S. Brown reports:

The train thundered along in the shadow of towering mountains, roared over high trestles, through long tunnels, and slid smoothly through great fields of waving grain.... There was intense realism every moment. It was difficult to realize, after such a ride, that one had not actually been in Switzerland, the illusion was so perfect.[17]

The 'Virtual Reality Cycling Journeys' produced by Bike-o-Vision, which allow you to 'ride a new destination every week of the year', promise a similar illusion, although the realism is even more potent, presumably, when it appears that the moving image is produced through your effort. The training videos produced by Sufferfest using shots from on-bike cameras to place you inside the peloton of the Tour de France or the Giro d'Italia (recorded during the actual races), encouraging you to '[p]ush yourself harder than you ever thought possible' (while recording your performance with Strava), potentially intensify this impression even further.

The appeal of such apparatuses is obvious: they allow you to cycle without having to confront the hazards and discomfort of bad weather or inhospitable climate, darkness or traffic. They also spare you the embarrassment of sweating and struggling in public, and they provide distraction from the boredom and sometimes painful effort of using exercise equipment. Indeed, the exercise bicycle makes explicit the central principle of the bicycle as a machine, which is that it is dependent upon human labour. While the effort that we expend on an exercise bike may be directed towards particular, individual goals in the future – a fitter, healthier, more attractive body – it also belongs to a penal tradition of intrinsically pointless hard labour, a connection that is revealed by the Pedal Vision system introduced in a women's prison in Arizona in 2010 by Sheriff Joe Arpaio.[18] Pedal Vision allowed inmates to generate electricity on an exercise bike in order to watch television, and was publicised as the solution to an obesity problem among prisoners, since only those who agreed to pedal were granted the privilege of watching TV. If the pedaller slowed down, an alarm sounded warning that the TV was about to switch off, and, Arpaio suggested, 'peer pressure' from the other inmates would encourage the rider to accelerate. Although the concern for the inmates' welfare may have been genuine, it is notable that the publicity-hungry, far right Arpaio, who styles himself 'America's toughest sheriff' and was notorious for his office's illegal policy of 'racial profiling', was also responsible for forming an armed posse against illegal immigrants in 2010, reintroducing chain gangs for convicts in 1995, establishing the 'Tent City' 'concentration camp' extension to the Maricopa County jail in 1993 and installing 'jail cams' in women's toilets, streaming the humiliating video feed on the internet.

The Pedal Vision apparatus belongs to a dehumanising carceral history in which nineteenth-century prisoners were impelled to do exhausting physical work as part of their punishment, such as shot drill, in which prisoners carried cannonballs back and forth around an exercise yard from one pile to another. Pedal Vision is thus a derivation of the sadistic penal machines installed in Victorian prisons, such as the treadmill and the crank. The crank was a handle attached to a wooden paddle inside a drum filled with sand. The crank pushed the paddle through the sand and was attached to a counter, and prisoners had to complete a certain number of revolutions – up to 10,000 per day – to earn their meals. Prison officers could tighten the screw on the crankshaft, making it harder to turn (thereby earning the slang name for prison guards: screws). While there may have been a residual intention to train prisoners for repetitive manual labour upon release – the crank and the treadmill are almost parodic abstractions of industrial and agricultural machinery – the principal goal was to subject convicts to degrading, crushing physical labour. The Pedal Vision system therefore suggests an intriguing relationship between the disciplinary nature of contemporary exercise cultures and this history of mechanised torture; it also indicates the functional relationship between the bicycle and the film camera or projector, since these are all crank-operated machines; Pedal Vision is a more sophisticated version of the Mutoscope.

The infernal character of fitness culture is highlighted in an episode of the cautionary UK science fiction TV series inspired by *The Twilight Zone*, *Black Mirror*. 'Fifteen Million Merits'[19] depicts a future in which everybody must ride exercise bikes to generate power for the subterranean environment they live in, earning 'merits' in the process, the currency of the time. They spend their days on the bikes, which are arranged in rows in front of wall-sized screens, watching pornography and humiliating game shows, playing virtual instruments or simply gazing at Rolling Road, a cartoonish image of their cycling 'doppel' bobbing in front of them as it travels through a childishly animated landscape. The population is divided into two classes, the grey-clad cyclists and overweight cleaners in yellow overalls, who are abused by the cyclists, humiliated in the TV programme *Botherguts* and blown to bits in a shooter video game. When not on their bikes or in the cafeteria, the cyclists spend the rest of their time in cell-like apartments entirely surrounded by floor-to-ceiling screens, unable to avoid lurid pornography or blaring adverts except by forfeiting merits to skip past them; viewing is compulsory, so that, even when the protagonist Bing (who takes his name from an internet search engine) closes his eyes, the programme on the screen is simply paused until he reopens them.

The only way out of this compartmentalised existence is to enter the televised talent show *Hot Shot* in the hope of becoming a celebrity, although, when Bing uses his savings to buy a 15-million-merit entry ticket for his friend, Abi, the judges dismiss her potential as a singer, recruiting her instead as a porn performer. This narrative visualises a grim dystopia in which the future does not resemble the vast industrial factory of *Metropolis* (Lang, 1927) or the irradiated rubble of *The Bed Sitting Room* (Lester, 1969) but, rather, the sleekly corporate environment of the leisure centre: vending machines, exercise equipment, reflective surfaces and screens – the minimalist mise en scène of exquisite boredom. If the Immersive Fitness gym offers the opportunity to 'ride the future', 'Fifteen Million Merits' offers a depressing image of what that future might consist of: an endless, accelerating cycle of physical activity and consumption. It imagines a hell of 'ever-virtual mobility' in which the individual on a stationary exercise bike is the very image of the new modes of slavish productivity demanded by a post-industrial phase of extractive capitalism, in which the distinction between work and non-work – and between production and consumption – vanishes and all leisure activities are commodified and exploited. It describes an extrapolation of the attention economy, in which individuals must pay simply in order *not* to watch television.

Depressed and enraged by the outcome of Abi's audition, Bing saves up the money to enter *Hot Shot* himself, and breaks off midway through his on-screen dance audition, threatening to slash his throat with a shard of glass from one of the broken screens in his apartment unless they let him speak. He then launches into a tirade against a status quo that has left everybody desperate, numbed and unable to deal with reality: 'All we know is fake fodder and buying shit,' he rants. 'We ride day in, day out. Going where? Powering what? All tiny cells and tiny screens, and bigger cells and bigger screens.' Of course, rather than having him thrown off the show or arrested, one of the unctuous judges tells him: 'That was without a doubt the most heartfelt thing I've seen on this stage since *Hot Shot* began,' agreeing with Bing that '[a]uthenticity is in woefully short supply'. In the programme's bleakly ironic conclusion, we learn that Bing is now doing a weekly 30-minute broadcast, ranting to camera with the shard of glass pressed against his neck as a symbol of authentic rage. The final shots reveal that he has joined the invisible elite, and, rather than a windowless cell, he now lives in a penthouse flat with panoramic views across an endless canopy of trees in place of screens.

Blurring the boundary between screen and reality in a more direct way, wearable computer glasses, such as those manufactured by Recon Instruments or Google, present the wearer with a transparent 'heads-up display' that is overlaid on her field of vision and might consist of text, diagrams (such as maps and tables), photographs and video. A tiny screen mounted on the right side of the glasses frame produces the visual illusion that a screen is positioned a couple of metres in front of the wearer, and so a cyclist using such glasses can follow a GPS map and read performance data, such as heart rate or speed of travel, as well as searching the internet for information, making video calls or capturing film and video using the integrated camera. Whereas a cyclist using a GPS device must direct her gaze at the screen in her hand, on her wrist or mounted on her handlebars, with these glasses the screen floats in front of the eye, and so there is no need for her to avert her gaze. What the user sees effectively resembles the screen of a video game (which typically displays health, ammunition or fuel levels, direction finders or progress through a race), and so the question is raised of whether the dematerialisation of the screen is also accompanied by a perceptual dematerialisation of the physical environment around the rider, as it begins to resemble ever more closely virtual game space. For instance, Recon Jet glasses can show a live video feed from a camera, allowing the cyclist to see what is behind her as well as in front of her simultaneously (and, of course, they can relay the wearer's performance data to apps such as Strava).

Films on Bikes, Bikes on Films

A further manifestation of the new screen cultures of cycling that brings the story told by this book full circle, completing the revolution, is the emergence of the cyclist as documentary film-maker. The development in the early twenty-first century of small, lightweight, high-definition digital cameras, such as GoPro's Digital HERO range, that can be mounted on a cyclist's helmet or body has meant that one of the characteristic features of the current bike boom is the ubiquity of video material shot by cyclists with this wearable technology while cycling, circulated through social media or file-sharing sites such as YouTube and often distributed freely rather than for direct commercial gain. The cyclist film-maker personifies the radical democratisation of film-making that has taken place with the popularisation of digital video cameras. The integration of digital cameras into phones, laptops and computer monitors means that many of us have become amateur film-makers, perhaps shooting hundreds of hours per year, while children and young people have become some of the most prolific contemporary auteurs, shooting, editing and sharing video material continually with friends and networks of their peers. In the new screen culture, film-making is a daily practice for millions.

There are several categories or genres of digital bicycle film, the most familiar of which is footage shot by commuters riding through urban traffic, using the camera to document evidence of incompetent or careless driving (and walking and cycling), poorly designed or maintained roads and cycleways, law-breaking or road accidents. The camera here is a forensic tool that positions the cyclist as volunteer police officer, a mobile component of a panoptic surveillance system in a culture in which cyclists have, at best, an uncertain legal status, but in extreme cases are regarded as targets by frustrated drivers. A striking example of the commuter/film-maker is Lewis Dediare, the Traffic Droid.[20] Having been seriously injured by a car driver while cycling in London, upon learning that the driver's punishment was merely attending a driving education course, Dediare began recording all his cycle journeys while commuting. Wearing up to eight cameras and three lights mounted on his bike, body and helmet, Dediare posts videos of close passes and confrontations on YouTube, and also submits them to the road safety charity RoadSafe, or directly to the police. This type of film, which features collisions, fights, conflict and verbal abuse, inadvertently reprises one of the oldest genres of bicycle film from the early twentieth century,[21] the slapstick chase and crash film, and is a depressing reminder of the enduring history of conflict over urban mobility, in which 'competing users of different technologies have spent more than a century ordering each other out of the road, starting even before the advent of film'.[22] Dediare reflects that '[e]very day is a battle' with other road users, but, as James Longhurst observes, these 'bike battles' have resurfaced periodically with changes in technology or the demographic make-up of road users, against a context in which '[t]he last century and a half of urban development have created a situation in which public roads are the battlegrounds of mismatched competitors' for access to this common-pool resource.[23]

A second key genre of the digital bicycle film is sometimes spectacular footage of mountain bike trail riding and downhill racing. These extend from videos of weekend trips and holiday outings in the hills and forests to breathtaking footage of professional downhill racers tearing down dangerous, technically complex courses at impossible speed. This type of film exploits the hyper-mobile potential of new camera technology to the full. Since wearable cameras such as the HERO series are small, light, increasingly cheap and relatively impact-resistant and waterproof, they can be thrown around by the user in a way that wasn't possible with comparatively expensive, delicate film or video cameras containing fragile film or videotape. The resulting point-of-view footage has a quite specific visual and affective quality. Cameras such as the HERO typically have a fixed, ultra-wide-angle lens with extensive depth of field, which keeps much of the space in front of the camera in sharp focus but which also distorts the image, emphasising depth dramatically, so that the slopes negotiated by riders appear steeper, and the jumps higher, than they would if shot with a longer lens (or viewed by the eye). This vertiginous distortion also emphasises the sense of the speed of movement through space, as the landscape ahead seems to rush rapidly towards the camera before sliding away on either side. Since such cameras can be worn on foreheads, bike helmets or chest harnesses, the point of view is that of the rider – her hands, legs, helmet visor, bike and shadow sometimes visible within the frame – and so what we see is an embodied image, one that moves with the body of the cyclist/camera operator, lurching, shaking and bobbing as the rider pedals and coasts, accelerating and decelerating, shifting her weight as she plunges through the environment. The absence of cuts strengthens this illusion of bodily mobility (since a digital video camera can record hours of footage, depending on the camera's storage capacity and the resolution of the image), and the consequence is that watching a helmet camera film shot by an urban downhill racer riding down flights of steps and narrow alleys, or a 'freerider' racing through a heavily wooded forest or down the face of a cliff, can be a heart-stopping, thrilling experience as you are drawn into the illusion, holding your breath as the bike flies off a ramp, ducking, twisting and trying to turn your head as you scan the frame to anticipate the next fast-approaching obstacle.

The helmet camera film of Colombian champion Marcelo Gutierrez's winning ride in the 2013 Valparaiso Cerro Abajo downhill race in Chile, in which the cyclist careers down back alleys and soars off balconies, skimming off vertical walls and narrowly avoiding railings and lamp posts, is far more dynamic than Claude Lelouch's notorious guerrilla film *C'Était un Rendezvous* (1976), a single-shot 35 mm point-of-view film of an early morning, high-speed drive through the centre of Paris. While Lelouch's short film gives a sense of the illegal velocity of the car, it is the dubbed sound of squealing tyres and revving engine that gives the sequence a sense of real danger. The camera, mounted close to the ground on the radiator of his Mercedes, produces a smoothly stable mobile image that gives a disembodied sense of what driving at speed through a largely empty city might *look* like; but Gutierrez's film shows us what it *feels* like when a body propels itself through crowded, obstacle-ridden space, alternately resisting and succumbing to the pull of gravity.[24]

Films such as this circulate through alternative networks, being screened at adventure sports and cycling film festivals and compiled on DVDs sold at bike shops and sporting events, as well as being posted online and disseminated through social media. Their principal function is commercial – the name of the sponsor of the race and of the rider is visible on his helmet visor at the bottom of the screen throughout – but, more broadly, videos such as these function to promote the sport and its various specialised disciplines (slopestyle, freeriding, downhill racing, street trials).[25]

Notably, one of the earliest instances of helmet camera cycling footage was an instructional video, *The Great Mountain Biking Video* (1987), for some passages of which the director, Mark Schulze, mounted a video camera on a motorcycle helmet, which was connected to a VCR in his backpack. Although 'button', 'lipstick' and 'bullet' cameras represent striking technological advances, Gutierrez's helmet cam film is a throwback to some of the earliest instances of cycling on film, films of spectacular trick cycling by the Lumières and Edison, as well as to early travelogues, since, while cycling is ostensibly the subject of mountain biking videos, the landscapes in which these races and trail rides take place constitute an exotic or spectacularly beautiful backdrop. It is thus unsurprising that Schulze and his partner, Patty Mooney, moved on from instructional videos to produce *Full Cycle: A World Odyssey* (Schulze, 1995), a video documenting their cycling tour through picturesque regions of such countries as Greece, Switzerland, Tahiti and India.

As with most films, one of the pleasures of watching point-of-view footage of cycling is that of identifying with the protagonist, imagining that we are steering that bike along that route as we watch. The micro video camera extends this pleasure, as, by filming ourselves riding – even if we are only documenting our trip to work or a leisurely ride along an undulating stretch of country road – we can imagine that we, too, are professional racers, extreme sports athletes or courageous adventurers. To some degree, then, the point of filming ourselves cycling is only partially to shoot video material that can be edited subsequently, and circulated; it also has a performative function, wherein the process of filming ourselves gives our actions greater drama or moment. The distinction between screen space and real space is blurred yet again, since, in riding while wearing a camera, we are director, cinematographer and star of our own films, riding through a film set peopled with extras. It is the fact that we are filming ourselves that renders our activities dramatic, rather than the activities themselves. HERO, the brand name of GoPro cameras, captures this function perfectly, promising, flatteringly, to record our intrepid journeys and epic holidays.

Going to 'Extremes'

This self-dramatising function is demonstrated especially well by the independent film-maker Lucas Brunelle, whose documentary films make extensive use of helmet cam footage and also construct an image of Brunelle as a fearless outsider. *Line of Sight* (Zenga, 2012), for example, compiles video shot by Brunelle while taking part in 'alley cat' races in cities around the world. Wearing a bicycle helmet with forward- and backward-facing video cameras mounted on either side, Brunelle rides alongside the fastest competitors as they race from one checkpoint to the next through city streets. Alley cat races require participants to race to a sequence of checkpoints, getting a manifest signed or checked at each stop, as if delivering documents to a reception desk, and then heading for the finish line. Because they are illegal, taking place on public roads, often at night, competitors must use the local knowledge and skills they have developed working as cycle couriers in order to negotiate pedestrians, road systems and heavy traffic.

Line of Sight includes footage of races over several years, including the annual Cycle Messenger World Championships, and some of the sequences, set to aggressive rock, heavy metal and electronic music, are hair-raising, as Brunelle accompanies the cyclists, often riding brakeless, fixed-gear bikes, as they speed the wrong way up one-way streets, weaving through moving queues of cars, trucks and buses, running red lights and riding straight at crowds of pedestrians filtering across road junctions. It looks extremely dangerous, and is difficult to watch without flinching at the repeated close shaves as riders allow themselves to be towed at high speed by trucks and buses, squeeze themselves through rapidly closing gaps or ride straight across road junctions, often forcing oncoming traffic to screech to a halt. It is a thrillingly assertive style of riding that expresses an equal claim to the congested and contested space of public roads; rather than ride in the gutter, or give way to motor vehicles and pedestrians, these combative riders assume equal or greater rights of mobility.[26] Although this approach to cycling might seem counter-intuitive, Brunelle claims in *Line of Sight* to feel safe riding in New York, where cycling in heavy traffic is a matter of tuning in to the rhythms that underlie the apparent chaos.

It's a place in between cars, and between trucks and buses, and taking a certain line through a curve or a corner that people just don't realize is there. And we use those spaces, we use those openings, those opportunities, those blind spots, and that's the area we exist in.

As displays of cycling technique, these films are as impressive as the point-of-view films of professional racers mentioned above – and, as one contributor observes, Brunelle is a technically skilful cyclist/cinematographer, capable of keeping up with the fastest riders while riding without moving his head too wildly, ensuring that the image remains remarkably stable and legible. As a celebratory account of these fearless cyclists' feats, *Line of Sight* is also a celebration of a conventional mode of masculinity: the alley cat racers featured in the film are the contemporary equivalent of the Victorian scorchers, athletic young men who frightened horses and sent pedestrians running as they raced down high streets on their high-wheeled bicycles; and, indeed, women are virtually absent from the film, reinforcing a sense that the messenger subculture is exclusively macho. With no discernible irony, Brunelle is shown in the opening of the film posing first with a bike held over his head, and then wielding a machine gun.

As *Line of Sight* progresses, the focus of the film shifts away from the races and riders he is filming to Brunelle himself, who is filmed cycling in various locations around the world, including the Great Wall of China. In one of the last sequences, a travelogue-like depiction of Brunelle's journey through the Guatemalan countryside, he explains sombrely to the camera,

You don't get to a place like this by staying on the beaten path, by not taking a risk. These are the most beautiful places, but they're also the most deadly. To be beautiful it's yin and yang; it has to be that deadly. If it wasn't, it'd be a place that everybody calls paradise, and you'd have malls, and high-price condos and shit. Out here you don't have that.

This is followed by a preposterous action scene in which Brunelle is chased through a village by another cyclist who is firing a machine gun at Brunelle, while Brunelle returns fire with a revolver. The chase concludes as Brunelle is cornered and shot in the head. Despite its incongruity in the context of a documentary about messenger racing, this staged scene reveals the thematic core of Brunelle's films: a celebratory, self-aggrandising account of masculine heroism. However, in a bathetic shift, the credits sequence shows Brunelle's parents talking fondly about their son, and footage of Brunelle playing chess with his father. Whether accidental or not, it undermines the machismo of the earlier sequence by suggesting that Brunelle remains an overgrown child, using the film as an excuse to play with toy guns.

Discussing the emergence of first-person ecotourist documentaries in the early 2000s, in which film-makers film themselves undertaking heroic film-making expeditions to spectacular remote locations, cultural anthropologist Adam Fish characterises the cycle as 'the martial art of performative nonfiction,'[27] and it is an apt description of *Line of Sight*. The home-made helmet camera is a pretext for Brunelle to take the stage with the fearless alley cat riders, his status shifting from observer to participant to performer. Despite the ethical and ecological concerns that motivate the self-reflexive mode of documentary discussed by Fish, these films are also accounts of contemporary colonial adventures in which wealthy Westerners test their mettle in dangerously exotic environments, documenting a 'fear-facing extreme trip' on video. It follows, therefore, that Brunelle went on to make *Lucas Brunelle Goes to Chernobyl* (Brunelle,

2015), an account of an illegal expedition into the abandoned city. Prompted partly by his family's Ukrainian heritage, Brunelle meets a group of people in Kiev, and after being dropped in a forest at night they wade across a river into the exclusion zone around Chernobyl and hike across country, carrying their bikes over their shoulders, before reaching the city, where they camp in uninhabited buildings. Once there they cycle around the ruined city in a sequence captioned 'Tour of Chernobyl', before finding the 'infamous claw', a highly radioactive hydraulic grab supposedly used to clear rubble from the destroyed reactor. Brunelle dons rubber gloves and films himself placing a sticker on it bearing his signature logo, before the group return to Kiev, where they have a celebratory house party.

The film inevitably recalls Andrei Tarkovsky's *Stalker* (1979), and, indeed, one shot shows the cyclists passing a concrete bus shelter graffitied with the word 'STALKER', suggesting that Brunelle recognises the parallel, but the contemplative stillness of that mysterious film is replaced here with a constantly mobile camera and choppy editing. It is a frustrating film that offers virtually no information about the place and its history, or even the identity of Brunelle's cycling companions and his relationship to them, while the reliance upon a mobile camera and night vision shots also means that we are unable to see much of the city and its surroundings clearly. Having made his way to the location – without explaining why it was necessary to do it in such an 'extreme' way, when regular organised tours are available – all he needed to do was film the space. Static shots and still photographs of the ruins would be fascinating enough. In a voice-over at the end of the film, Brunelle reflects that, having visited over 60 countries, this was his most moving trip, but the principal impression of the film is that the filmmaker regards the world indiscriminately as a series of more or less exotic, exciting and 'extreme' spaces through which he can ride his bikes. The world is a source of consumable experiences, and the spectacles of poverty in Central America or the aftermath of a nuclear disaster in Ukraine add intensity to the experience of travelling at speed through unfamiliar and dramatic landscapes. *Lucas Brunelle Goes to Chernobyl* demonstrates inadvertently how extreme sports culture and ecotourism are the expression of an extractive colonial worldview that sees the world as its playground, a resource to be exploited, albeit under the alibi of cultural engagement and self-improvement.

Travelling Full Circle

Perhaps the most formally self-conscious exploration of the relationship between cinema and the bicycle is found in the more modestly scaled work of British experimental film-maker Tony Hill. *Bike* (2013) belongs to a singular body of film and video pieces that explore the different ways of seeing the world offered by mobile cameras, often mounted on his custom-built rigs, and using visual effects and unconventional combinations of sound and image. Just over a minute long – approximately the same duration as the first films screened by Auguste and Louis Lumière in 1895 – *Bike* shows a man setting off on a leisurely bicycle ride, and comprises shots from three cameras, one mounted inside a wheel rim facing inwards, one on a pedal and one looking down on the rider from above; the resulting images are so radically disorienting that viewing the film is a dizzying experience. In general, Hill's films show us images of familiar scenes and objects – streets, beaches, swimming pools, gardens, faces – that are made strange through unconventional camera placement and circular movements. Rather than offering us an embodied, gravity-bound and anthropomorphised point of view in which the camera simulates the human eye, what we see is a defamiliarising machine's-eye view, the camera moving through space in ways that are physically impossible for a person. Thus, rather than a brief film of a middle-aged man riding a bicycle, *Bike* is a bewildering, kinetic collision of distorted, shifting perspectives on the world in which the movements of the machines – cameras and bicycle – are the focus, rather than the rider's journey.

Rotation is also the subject of *A Short History of the Wheel* (Hill, 1992), which dissolves from shots of slowly turning cart wheels – the camera rotating at the same speed as the wheels, so that the world appears to spin while the wheels remain still at the centre of the image – to the wheel of a tractor, then a car, then a bicycle. Literally revolutionary, the 60-second six-shot film makes a quietly provocative claim in placing the bicycle at the end of this historical narrative. As Hill remarks, the film starts 'with a primitive hand-drawn cart and [moves] through horsepower and machine age tractor and car to the ultimate wheeled transport, the bicycle.'[28] Challenging the common-sense view that automobiles are an inevitable, 'evolutionary' progression from the bicycle rather than a deviation onto a dead end, Hill's film reiterates Butch Cassidy's view that the future belongs to bicycles. Indeed, in Hill's films, the world literally revolves around the bicycle. These cinematic bicycles set the world in motion.

This Is the Future

Cycling advocates and campaigners often discuss the bicycle in utopian terms, recognising the machine's potential to liberate us from our oil addiction and dependence on combustion engines, freeing up our congested road networks, reducing pollution and making us healthier. Indeed, architectural theorist Steven Fleming titles his speculative book on bicycle-oriented cities *Velotopia*. However, there are relatively few films that attempt to imagine what a post-oil, velomobile future might look like. Perhaps because it is a product of nineteenth-century technology, bicycles feature only rarely in science fiction cinema, a speculative genre that is often defined by the narrative presence of a futuristic, anachronistic or impossible technological object. *Blade Runner* (Scott, 1984), which includes a brief shot of a peloton of children skimming through the dark, rain-drenched streets, is a rare exception. In this context, the bicycle has a dual significance, both as a symbol of a catastrophic future in which roads are choked with traffic and pedestrians, and the environment is wrecked by pollution, and as a symbol of an 'orientalised' future in which the West has been culturally and economically transformed by globalisation into an ethnically mixed interzone. A bicycle also makes a brief appearance in *Soylent Green* (Fleischer, 1973), the apocalyptic account of overpopulation, global warming and social collapse, in which the protagonists have rigged up a bicycle in their cramped apartment so as to generate electricity.

One of the most systematic attempts to visualise a bicycle-dependent future is the low-budget Canadian film *Turbo Kid* (Simard, Whissell, Whissell, 2015). A product of a nostalgic affection for the popular culture of the 1980s, one of the pleasures of watching *Turbo Kid* is identifying the many allusions to the films of John Carpenter, David Cronenberg, Steven Spielberg, Sam Raimi and Troma Studios, as well as later TV series such as *Power Rangers*. The film is set in a contaminated wasteland familiar from such post-apocalyptic films as *Le Dernier Combat* (Besson, 1983) and *Mad Max 2* (Miller, 1981), but, whereas in Miller's film energy scarcity has meant that cars, trucks and motorbikes are prized possessions, the protagonists of *Turbo Kid* rely on BMX bikes for transport through their post-oil world. Thus, the film is an unlikely fusion of low-budget horror, science fiction and fantasy cinema, and teen films such as *BMX Bandits* and *Rad*.

The 'Kid' is a solitary teenage boy who survives by scavenging and whose room is full of the consumer culture detritus he has found or traded, including treasured comic books featuring a superhero called Turbo Rider. Over the course of the film he joins forces with a young woman, whom he later discovers is a robot, and a cheroot-smoking drifter sporting a cowboy hat, and then he stumbles across the remains of the real Turbo Rider, donning his armour before a climactic confrontation with the sadistic one-eyed villain Zeus, who also turns out to be a machine.

An attempt to make a science fiction film that might have been released in the early 1980s, *Turbo Kid* is an assiduous exercise in pastiche, from the post-industrial set design and scavenger punk costumes, through the synth-pop score to the casting of Michael Ironside, star of David Cronenberg's body horror classic, *Scanners* (1981), as Zeus. The disgusting special effects are one of the most striking features, as prosthetic limbs and heads are severed and skewered while the patient actors are showered with blood and pelted with viscera and chunks of meat. The most gleefully revolting sequence is an interrogation scene that begins with the victim, a merchant named Bagu, waking to find himself tied to a chair; when a canvas hood is removed from his head, he looks down with horror to see that his stomach has been sliced open and his intestines, which are spilling out of his abdomen, are attached by a cord to the rear wheel of a stationary bicycle. Of course, he immediately tells his interrogator, Zeus, everything he wants to know and pleads desperately: 'You're gonna help me put these back in – right? Please.' Zeus, clearly disappointed by the speed with which Bagu has spilt the beans, asks, 'Do you have any idea how long it took to set this up?' The bewildered victim just stares at him as Zeus chuckles: 'I'm sure you'll understand', and signals to his sidekick, mounted on the bike, to start pedalling... Among the numerous depictions of bicycles as weapons or instruments of torture, including the gruelling seven-day ride in Mohsen Makhmalbaf's *The Cyclist*, the agonising Tour de France sequence in *Les Triplettes de Belleville* (Chomet, 2003) or the murder of a student by a satanically possessed man wielding a broken bicycle frame in *Prince of Darkness* (Carpenter, 1987), this stands out for its comically absurd excess.

Turbo Kid opens with a montage of images of drifting smoke and devastated landscapes, accompanied by a voice-over that explains grimly:

This is the future. The world as we know it is gone. Acid rain has left the land barren and the water toxic. Scarred by endless wars, humanity struggles to survive in the ruins of the old world, frozen in an everlasting nuclear winter. This is the future.... This is the year 1997.

It's a nice punchline, highlighting something particularly clear in science fiction film and literature, which is that, in attempting to visualise the future, we inevitably imagine it as an extrapolation of the present, an overemphasis of certain tendencies or preoccupations. Visions of the future quickly become dated as a result, and so, ironically, science fiction is as much an archive of fantasies of the past as it is a space for clear-sighted previsions of the future. The dystopian futuristic imagery of *Turbo Kid* is so closely associated with the 1980s that it has a nostalgic appeal. As an intrinsically paradoxical object, the bicycle is the perfect object for the temporal ambiguity of this cinematic future-past, since it represents both past and future simultaneously, as well as the conjunctions childhood/maturity, slowness/speed, femininity/masculinity, clumsiness/grace, pleasure/pain and body/machine.

For all its playfulness, *Turbo Kid* suggests that we are now already well into the future predicted by Butch. This is a future in which bicycles are ubiquitous but also retain a symbolic power. This is evident in the way that the bicycle stands, in *Turbo Kid*, for an entire socio-technological order. The bicycle exemplifies the collapse of petrocracy and a fossil-fuel-powered world. The symbolic power of the bicycle is also evident in one of the most quietly optimistic films about cycling futures that I have encountered. Screened at the three-day Bicycle Film Festival in Brighton in 2016, amid a diverse collection of short films, including *Lucas Brunelle Goes to Chernobyl*, *Mama Agatha* (Fadi Hindash, 2015) is a simple documentary about Agatha Frimpong, a Ghanaian woman living in Amsterdam, who offers cycling lessons to migrant women. Most of these women are middle-aged and older, coming from a variety of countries including China, Pakistan and Suriname, and they have a deep affection for their polyglot teacher, 'Mama Agatha'. Agatha has helped hundreds of women to learn to ride, and the short film follows the progress of some of her pupils over several weeks as they progress from learning to straddle their bicycles precariously in a gym to learning to navigate around vehicles in an underground car park, before, finally, venturing onto the road in groups. At the graduation ceremony, when they tearfully receive their cycling proficiency certificates in front of their proud families, it is clear how profoundly important it is for these women to be mobilised in this way. *Mama Agatha* makes a powerful argument for the bicycle's enduring potential as an empowering machine that offers these women, who are marginalised by age, gender, ethnicity and language, a greater agency and independence.

A modestly utopian film, it is inspiring in its insistence upon the mundanely emancipatory potential of the bicycle – as well as community activism, and women's groups – and it is a reminder that the future anticipated by Butch Cassidy is continually being made and remade by the bicycle. For each of these women, a different future is made possible by her encounter with a bicycle and with Agatha Frimpong. Released 120 years after the publication of Frances Willard's account of the liberating experience of learning to ride a bike in middle age, *Mama Agatha* demonstrates as effectively as any film that the capacity of the bicycle to alter our way of seeing and being in the world remains just as powerful. As Willard writes:

I realized that no matter how one may think himself accomplished. When he sets out to learn a new language, science, or the bicycle he has entered a new realm as truly as if he were a child newly born into the world.[29]

In learning to ride, Willard reflected in 1895 that 'I had made myself master of the most remarkable, ingenious and inspiring motor ever yet devised upon this planet', and the subsequent history of bicycles and cinema is a rich and fascinating testament to this machine.[30]

Ride on Time

'Knowing the future,' writes sociologist John Urry, 'necessitates examining various "pasts" and developing ways of understanding how past, present and future are mutually intertwined.'[31] Studying the various pasts of the bicycle through the lens of cinema helps us to understand the way that these pasts continually resurface in various cycling presents. Indeed, as is clear in this chapter, the cultural and social history of cycling is marked by repetitions and circularity as much as it is by a sense of linear forward movement or progress. In this respect, the bicycle is a metaphorical figure for two contrasting concepts of time; the machine moves forwards, signifying the concept of time as linear and unidirectional, like a strip of film spooling through a projector – what astronomer Thomas Eddington termed 'time's arrow' – while the wheels trace the same circle again and again, like the spinning reels on a projector, as if to illustrate the concept of eternal return, or Roman philosopher Boethius's concept of the whirling Wheel of Fortune. The value of reflecting upon these repetitions and recyclings in relation to the mediated history of cycling is that it draws our attention to seductive, illusory and dangerous myths of progress. The glittering marvels of new media technologies at the beginning of the twenty-first century are not so far removed from the marvellous new media technologies of the late nineteenth century, while the emancipatory, democratising potential of the bicycle celebrated by Frances Willard or Susan B. Anthony has still not been fully realised. Moreover, as Tony Hill's *Short History of the Wheel* suggests, we should be sceptical of the grand narratives of inevitable linear technical and social advancement and consider that film's proposal that cars are no improvement upon the promise of the bicycle.

Indeed, it is important to recall the comments of cycling historian Andrew Ritchie written during the cycling boom of the 1970s:

The bicycle is a humane machine...which achieves its purpose without accidental negative side-effects.... There is a tendency in the world at the moment to believe in complicated, highly sophisticated solutions to every problem. Simple, elegant and suitable solutions also exist.[32]

At a point when 'the fossil fuels of coal, gas and oil account for over four-fifths of current energy use', finding solutions is a matter of urgency, and, while the bicycle will not by itself be the source of our salvation from the catastrophic future visualised in *Turbo Kid*, it remains a good place to start.[33] 'We take the bicycle too much for granted,' Ritchie writes, 'but at the same time, we in England do not use it enough. It is a simple machine. But it *could* have a far-reaching and revolutionary effect on the world in the next century.'[34] The revolutionary efficacy of the bicycle rests partly in its functionality, but also, as this cinematic history of the bicycle demonstrates, in the way that the bicycle allows us to see, to think about and to inhabit the world differently. Over a century after the Lumières screened a film showing workers cycling out of the gates of their photographic factory in the Grand Café in Paris on 28 December 1895, these revolutionary technologies retain their power to turn our world upside down.

Figure 7.2
The final shot from the 16 mm film *A Short History of the Wheel* (Hill, 1992), Tony Hill's account of the development of wheeled transport from ox cart to carriage to car and, finally, to the bicycle (courtesy Tony Hill)

Notes

1 Cycling and Cinema: Revolutionary Technologies

1 While working on his PhD at Cambridge University, 'McLuhan frequently rode on his bicycle through the southern counties of England, memorizing important material for his thesis': Philip Marchand, *Marshall McLuhan: The Medium and the Messenger* (Toronto: Random House of Canada, 1998), 61.

2 Marshall McLuhan, *Understanding Media: The Extensions of Man* (Cambridge, MA: MIT Press, 1994), 179.

3 David Bordwell, Kristin Thompson, *Film History: An Introduction* (New York: McGraw-Hill, 2003), 10.

4 Tom Gunning, 'Pictures of Crowd Splendour: The Mitchell and Kenyon Factory Gate Films', in *The Lost World of Mitchell and Kenyon: Edwardian Britain on Film*, eds. Vanessa Toulmin, Patrick Russell, Simon Popple (London: BFI, 2004), 50.

5 The sequence in which the films were shot is unclear, although in the third film the workers are more lightly dressed, suggesting it may have been filmed in the summer rather than in spring. It is this film that is usually regarded as the one that was shown at the debut screening.

6 Richard deCordova, 'From Lumière to Pathé: The Break-Up of Perspectival Space', in *Early Cinema: Space, Frame, Narrative*, ed. Thomas Elsaesser (London: BFI, 1990), 78.

7 Ibid., emphasis in original.

8 Ibid.

9 See Stephen Bottomore, 'The Panicking Audience? Early Cinema and the "Train Effect"', *Historical Journal of Film, Radio and Television*, vol. 19, no. 2 (1999).

10 DeCordova, "From Lumière to Pathé", 78.

11 Jonathan Crary, *Techniques of the Observer: On Vision and Modernity in the Nineteenth Century* (Cambridge, MA: MIT Press, 1990), 112.

12 Jennifer Barker, *The Tactile Eye: Touch and the Cinematic Experience* (Oakland, CA: University of California Press, 2009), 134.

13 McLuhan, *Understanding Media*, 181–182.

14 Charles Spencer, 'The Modern Bicycle', 1877. Reprinted in *Cycling: The Craze of the Hour* (London: Pushkin Press, 2016), 10–11.

15 Andrew Ritchie, *King of the Road: An Illustrated History of Cycling* (London: Wildwood House, 1975), 15.

16 Ibid., 16.

17 Benjamin Noys, *Malign Velocities: Accelerationism and Capitalism* (Alresford: Zero Books, 2014).

18 Tom Ambrose, *The History of Cycling in Fifty Bikes* (Stroud: History Press, 2013), 21.

19 Ritchie, *King of the Road*, 32.

20 Ambrose, *The History of Cycling*, 34.

21 David Herlihy, *Bicycle: The History* (New Haven, CT: Yale University Press, 2004), 47–48.

22 Ibid., 78.

23 Ibid., 53.

24 Ibid., 58.

25 Ibid., 63.

26 Ibid., 66.

27 Paul Smethurst, *The Bicycle: Towards a Global History* (Basingstoke: Palgrave Macmillan, 2015), 22.

28 Glen Norcliffe, *The Ride to Modernity: The Bicycle in Canada, 1869–1900* (Toronto: University of Toronto Press, 2001), 15.

29 Ambrose, *The History of Cycling*, 31.

30 Benedict Anderson, *Imagined Communities: Reflections on the Origin and Spread of Nationalism* (London: Verso, 2006).

31 Smethurst, *The Bicycle*, 30.

32 Jon Day, *Cyclogeography: Journeys of a London Bicycle Courier* (Honiton: Notting Hill Editions, 2015), 16.

33 Luis A. Vivanco, *Reconsidering the Bicycle: An Anthropological Perspective on a New (Old) Thing* (New York: Routledge, 2013), 34.

34 Ritchie, *King of the Road*, 99.

35 Vivanco, *Reconsidering the Bicycle*, 32.

36 Norcliffe, *The Ride to Modernity*, 106.

37 Ibid., 108.

38 Ibid.

39 Ibid., 90.

40 Ibid.

41 See Katrina Jungnickel's *Bikes and Bloomers: Victorian Women and Their Extraordinary Cycle Wear* (London: Goldsmiths Press, 2018) for an account of the innovative ways in which Victorian women adapted and redesigned their clothing to allow them to cycle high-wheelers and safety bicycles.

42 Significantly, the series of Rover machines that drove the bicycle boom of the 1890s gave their name to the Rover car company (as well as the Polish word for bicycle, *rower*).

43 Ritchie, *King of the Road*, 129.

44 Ibid., 132.

45 Ibid., 136.

46 Ibid., 160.

47 Robert Penn, *It's All About the Bike: The Pursuit of Happiness on Two Wheels* (London: Penguin Books, 2011), 3.

48 Ibid.

49 See Dan Snow, 'DR Congo: Cursed by Its Natural Wealth', BBC News Magazine, 9 October 2013, www.bbc.co.uk/news/magazine-24396390.

50 Ritchie, *King of the Road*, 102.

51 Patricia Marks, *Bicycles, Bangs, and Bloomers: The New Woman in the Popular Press* (Lexington, KY: University of Kentucky Press, 1990), 185.

52 Peter Cox, Frederick Van De Walle, 'Bicycles Don't Evolve: Velomobiles and the modelling of transport technologies', in *Cycling and Society*, eds. Dave Horton, Paul Rosen, Peter Cox (Aldershot: Ashgate, 2007), 119.

53 Ibid., 113.

54 Ibid., 116.

55 Marja Evelyn Mogk, ed., *Different Bodies: Essays on Disability in Film and Television* (Jefferson, NC: McFarland, 2013), 3.

56 Gilles Deleuze, Claire Parnet, *Dialogues* (London: Athlone Press, 1987), 70.

57 Vivanco, *Reconsidering the Bicycle*, 37.

58 Cox, Van De Walle, 'Bicycles Don't Evolve', 115, emphasis in original.

59 Vivanco, *Reconsidering the Bicycle*, 3.

60 Day, *Cyclogeography*, 94.

61 Sam Ashurst, '150 Greatest Robin Williams Jokes', GamesRadar, 12 August 2014, www.gamesradar.com/150-greatest-robin-williams-jokes.

62 See Jim Fitzpatrick, *The Bicycle in Wartime: An Illustrated History*, rev. edn (Kilcoy, Australia: Star Hill Studio, 2011), for an exhaustive history of the bicycle as a war machine.

63 Lynne Kirby, *Parallel Tracks: The Railroad and Silent Cinema* (Exeter: University of Exeter Press, 1997), 2.

64 Bordwell, Thompson, *Film History*, 15.

65 Herlihy, *Bicycle*, 146.

66 Marta Braun, *Picturing Time: The Work of Etienne-Jules Marey* (Chicago: University of Chicago Press, 1992), 40.

67 Ibid., 18.

68 Bordwell, Thompson, *Film History*, 7.

69 Crary, *Techniques of the Observer*, 10.

70 Jonathan Crary, 'Unbinding Vision: Manet and the Attentive Observer in the Late Nineteenth Century', in *Cinema and the Invention of Modern Life*, eds. Leo Charney, Vanessa R. Schwartz (Berkeley, CA: University of California Press, 1995), 47.

71 Anne Friedberg, *Window Shopping: Cinema and the Postmodern* (Berkeley, CA: University of California Press, 1993), 37.

72 Walter Benjamin, *Illuminations*, trans. Harry Zohn (London: Fontana, 1973), 236.

73 McLuhan, *Understanding Media*, 285, emphasis in original.

74 Tim Cresswell, *On the Move: Mobility in the Modern Western World* (New York: Routledge, 2006), 4.

75 Day, *Cyclogeography*, 15.

76 J. D. Taylor, *Island Story: Journeying through Unfamiliar Britain* (London: Repeater, 2016), 111.

77 Smethurst, *The Bicycle*, 6.

78 Ibid., 35.

79 Steve Jones, *The Language of the Genes: Biology, History and the Evolutionary Future* (London: HarperCollins, 1993), 237.

80 Ibid.

81 Smethurst, *The Bicycle*, 67.

82 Jungnickel, *Bikes and Bloomers*.

83 H. G. Wells, *The Wheels of Chance* (London: Dent, 1914), 33–34.

84 Ibid., 118.

85 Smethurst, *The Bicycle*, 78.

86 Rachel Aldred, 'Does More Cycling Mean More Diversity in Cycling?', 27 February 2015, http://rachelaldred.org/writing/does-more-cycling-mean-more-diversity-in-cycling; Beulah Maud Devaney, 'Women Cyclists Are Dying, Why Are We Still Talking about Their Clothes?', openDemocracy, 24 November 2015, www.opendemocracy.net/5050/beulah/women-cyclists-are-dying-why-are-we-still-talking-about-their-clothes#.VlTLxEr3eyw.twitter.

87 Gunning, 'Pictures of Crowd Splendour', 50.

88 Tom Gunning, *D. W. Griffith and the Origins of American Narrative Film: The Early Years at Biograph* (Champaign, IL: University of Illinois Press, 1991), 152.

89 Charles Musser, ed., *The Emergence of Cinema: The American Screen to 1907* (Berkeley, CA: University of California Press, 1994), 432.

90 Smethurst, *The Bicycle*, 82.

91 McLuhan, *Understanding Media*, 90.

92 Ibid., 291.

93 Ibid., 90.

94 Marshall McLuhan, Quentin Fiore, *The Medium Is the Massage: An Inventory of Effects* (San Francisco: Wired, 1996 [1967]), 26.

95 Day, *Cyclogeography*, 15–16, emphasis in original.

96 Ibid., 84.

97 See, for example, the Magnificent Revolution project (www.magnificentrevolution.org), or the Brazilian Suaveciclos art project (http://vjsuave.com/filter/suaveciclo).

98 Cyclingnews.com, '*My Hour* by Bradley Wiggins: Book Extract', 23 November 2015, www.cyclingnews.com/news/my-hour-by-bradley-wiggins-book-extract.

99 Day, *Cyclogeography*, 14–15.

100 William Saroyan, *The Bicycle Rider in Beverly Hills* (New York: Charles Scribner's Sons, 1952), 12.

101 Ibid.

102 Allan Stoekl, 'Translator's Introduction', in Paul Fournel, *Need for the Bike*, trans. Allan Stoekl (Lincoln, NE: University of Nebraska Press, 2003), vii.

103 The fantastic dimension of cycling is captured with characteristic directness in *Knights on Bikes: A Romance* (1956), the first film by prolific director Ken Russell, in which a knight on a velocipede attempts to save a damsel from a villain in a wheelchair. As if coming full circle, his last substantial work was the UK TV biopic *Elgar: Fantasy of a Composer on a Bicycle* (2002).

2 Mischief Machines: Stunts and Slapstick Comedy

1 Fournel, *Need for the Bike*, 41.

2 Tom Gunning, 'The Cinema of Attractions', in *Early Cinema*, ed. Elsaesser, 56.

3 Ibid., 57.

4 Ibid., 58.

5 Ibid., 60.

6 Glenn Mitchell, *A–Z of Silent Film Comedy: An Illustrated Companion* (London: Batsford, 1998), 217.

7 The Glasgow community cycling group Bike Gob shot a very funny rejoinder in a Glasgow park, *Bike Gob at the Playgirl Palace* (Bike Gob, 2014), in which a woman attempts some laughably rudimentary stunts on a child's bike in front of three adoring, flirtatious men.

8 Clara S. Lewis, 'Danny MacAskill and the Visuality of the Extreme', *Sport in Society* (2015), 888.

9 Ibid., 889.

10 Indeed, MacAskill worked as a stunt person on the thriller *Premium Rush* (Koepp, 2012).

11 This reading has some poignancy, given that Ader died in 1975 while trying to cross the Atlantic in a tiny yacht as part of a performance piece entitled *In Search of the Miraculous*.

12 Alan Dale, *Comedy Is a Man in Trouble: Slapstick in American Movies* (Minneapolis: University of Minnesota Press, 2000), 13.

13 Ibid., 3.

14 Ibid., 5.

15 Ibid., 10.

16 Henri Bergson, *Laughter: An Essay on the Meaning of the Comic*, trans. Cloudesley Brereton, Fred Rothwell (New York: Macmillan, 1911), 29.

17 Ibid., 49.

18 This is certainly not the first example of a bicycle crash on film. An 1897 account of a film screening in China records that '[t]he most peculiar film was about bike racing: one cyclist rode in from the east while

another rode from the west and they collided. One was knocked to the ground and the other one fell while trying to hold up the first; soon many bikes appeared and crashed into one another as the spectators roared laughing and clapped hands. Suddenly the riders all got up and rode their bicycles away': Law Kar, Frank Bren, *Hong Kong Cinema: A Cross-Cultural View* (Lanham, MD: Scarecrow Press, 2004), 314.

19 Tom Gunning, 'Crazy Machines in the Garden of Forking Paths: Mischief Gags and the Origins of American Film Comedy', in *Classical Hollywood Comedy*, eds. Kristine Brunovska Karnick, Henry Jenkins (New York: Routledge, 1995), 98.

20 Gerald Mast, *The Comic Mind: Comedy and the Movies* (Chicago: University of Chicago Press, 1979), 7–8.

21 Ibid., 49–50.

22 Fournel, *Need for the Bike*, 8.

23 David Bellos, *Jacques Tati* (London: Harvill Press, 1999), 31.

24 Bergson, *Laughter*, 6.

25 Ibid., 136.

26 Mast, *The Comic Mind*, 21.

27 Ibid., 341.

28 Dale, *Comedy Is a Man in Trouble*, 69.

29 Bellos, *Jacques Tati*, 59.

30 Brent Maddock, *The Films of Jacques Tati* (Metuchen, NJ: Scarecrow Press, 1977), 4.

31 And also in his last feature film, *Parade* (Tati, 1974), and the short film *Cours du Soir* [*Evening Classes*] (Ribowski, 1967).

32 Bellos, *Jacques Tati*, 73.

33 Ibid., 96.

34 Ibid., 138.

35 Clayton, 2010.

36 A colour version struck from the original Thomsoncolor negatives was released in 1995. The film exists in multiple versions; a third, partially coloured version from 1964 featured new footage introducing an artist observing and sketching the goings-on in the village.

37 David Bellos, 'Tati and America: *Jour de Fête*, and the Blum–Byrnes Agreement of 1946', *French Cultural Studies*, vol. 10, no. 29 (1999), 139.

38 Michel Chion, *The Films of Jacques Tati*, trans. Antonio D'Alfonso (Toronto: Guernica Editions, 2003), 111–112.

39 Maddock, *The Films of Jacques Tati*, 38.

40 Ibid.

41 Bellos, *Jacques Tati*, 130.

42 Bellos, 'Tati and America', 154.

43 Bellos, *Jacques Tati*, 137.

44 Maddock, *The Films of Jacques Tati*, 140.

45 André Bazin, *What Is Cinema?*, vol. 2., trans. Hugh Gray (Berkeley, CA: University of California Press, 1971), 28.

3 The Hard Labour of Cycling

1 James Waddington, *Bad to the Bone* (Sawtry: Dedalus, 1999), 115.

2 David Frayne, *The Refusal of Work: The Theory and Practice of Resistance to Work* (London: Zed Books, 2015), 19.

3   James Longhurst, *Bike Battles: A History of Sharing the American Road* (Seattle: University of Washington Press, 2015), 101.

4   Theodor Adorno, *The Culture Industry* (London: Routledge, 1991), 187.

5   A key film for the Iranian New Wave, it is at the hub of Abbas Kiarostami's masterpiece, *Close-Up* (1990), a partially dramatised film about a film fan who masquerades as Makhmalbaf, carrying a copy of the screenplay with him.

6   Appropriately, in 2009 Makhmalbaf was awarded the Cyclo d'or d'honneur (Golden Cyclo) achievement award at the annual International Film Festival of Asian Cinema in France.

7   David Arnold, Erich DeWald, 'Cycles of Empowerment? The Bicycle and Everyday Technology in Colonial India and Vietnam', *Comparative Studies in Society and History*, vol. 53, no. 4 (2011), 988.

8   Bertolt Brecht, 'Sound Film: *Kuhle Wampe or Who Owns the World?*' [1932], trans. E. J. Campfield. *Prism International*, vol. 21, no. 2 (1982), 47.

9   Frayne, *The Refusal of Work*, 38.

10 For instance, UK TV movie *Bike Squad* (Jenkin, 2008), a gentle comedy about a local police department piloting a bicycle unit, follows the steady acceptance of the new initiative by initially sceptical, contemptuous colleagues. Highlighting a culture of institutional misogyny, it co-stars Maxine Peake, who went on to write, direct and perform in the play *Beryl*, a biography of the legendary professional racer Beryl Burton.

11 Arnold, DeWald, 'Cycles of Empowerment?', 981.

12 Lars Kristensen, 'Work in Bicycle Cinema: From Race Rider to City Courier', in *Work in Cinema and the Human Condition*, ed. Ewa Mazierska (New York: Palgrave Macmillan, 2013), 250, emphasis in original.

13 Vivanco, *Reconsidering the Bicycle*, 46.

14 Martin Wainwright, 'On Yer Bike, as Raleigh Shuts Frame Plant', *The Guardian* (11 December 1999), www.theguardian.com/uk/1999/dec/11/martinwainwright.

15 BikeBiz, 'Raleigh to Cease UK Assembly; Move to New Factory Is Shelved' (13 March 2002), www.bikebiz.com/news/read/updated-raleigh-to-cease-uk-assembly-move-to-new-factory-is-shel/04478.

16 Played by former London courier Michael Smiley.

17 Arnold, DeWald, 'Cycles of Empowerment?', 985.

18 Kristensen, 'Work in Bicycle Cinema', 251.

19 Satyajit Ray, *Our Films, Their Films* (New Delhi: Orient Longman, 1976), 9–10.

20 Lewis Smith, 'Woody Allen Admits He Is Too Lazy to Make Great Films', *The Independent* (31 July 2015), www.independent.co.uk/news/people/woody-allen-admits-he-is-too-lazy-to-make-great-films-10431756.html.

21 Bazin, *What Is Cinema?*, 25.

22 Ibid., 60.

23 Ibid., 21.

24 Elena Lombardi, 'Of Bikes and Men: The Intersection of Three Narratives in Vittorio De Sica's *Ladri di biciclette*', *Studies in European Cinema*, vol. 6, nos. 2/3 (2009), 113–114.

25 Ibid., 120.

26 The influence of De Sica's film on Sembène's work extends beyond his first film. As Nwachukwu Frank Ukadike observes of his second feature, '*Mandabi* has been called by one critic no less than an African rendering of *The Bicycle Thief* (1948)': Nwachukwu Frank Ukadike, *Black African Cinema* (Berkeley, CA: University of California Press, 1994), 86.

27 Ibid., 73.

28 Ibid., 71.

29 The film was released within three years of Senegal's independence from French colonial rule and, significantly, the dialogue is French (and Arabic) rather than Wolof, the indigenous language of the region, used in Sembène's later films.

30 Andrea Dahlberg, 'Film as a Catalyst for Social Change: Ousmane Sembène's *Borom Sarret*', *Bright Lights Film Journal*, no. 42 (2003), https://brightlightsfilm.com/wp-content/cache/all/film-as-a-catalyst-for-social-change-ousmane-sembenes-borom-sarret/#.W7Yv5PZFxZU.

31 Sheila Petty, ed., *A Call to Action: The Films of Ousmane Sembène* (Trowbridge: Flicks Books, 1996), 81.

32 This remains a persistent theme of Sembène's cinema through to his final film, *Moolade* (2004), which examines the traditional practice of female genital mutilation in a number of Africa countries.

33 Marsha Kinder, 'Spain after Franco', in *The Oxford History of World Cinema*, ed. Geoffrey Nowell-Smith (Oxford: Oxford University Press, 1999), 597.

34 Jian Xu, 'Representing Rural Migrants in the City: Experimentalism in Wang Xiaoshuai's *So Close to Paradise* and *Beijing Bicycle*', *Screen*, vol. 46, no. 4 (2005), 433.

35 Ibid., 434.

36 Huang Zhong, 'The Bicycle towards the Pantheon: A Comparative Analysis of *Beijing Bicycle* and *Bicycle Thieves*', *Journal of Italian Cinema and Media Studies*, vol. 2, no. 3 (2014), 352.

37 Ibid., 355.

38 Thomas Chen, 'An Italian Bicycle in the People's Republic: Minor Transnationalism and the Chinese Translation of *Ladri di biciclette/Bicycle* Thieves', *Journal of Italian Cinema and Media Studies*, vol. 2, no. 1 (2014), 94.

39 Ibid., 96–97.

40 Ibid.

41 Xu, 'Representing Rural Migrants in the City', 445.

42 Ibid., 448.

43 See Tao Xu, 'Making a Living: Bicycle-Related Professions in Shanghai, 1897–1949', *Transfers*, vol. 7, no. 1 (2013).

44 Edward J. M. Rhoads, 'Cycles of Cathay: A History of the Bicycle in China', *Transfers*, vol. 2, no. 2 (2012), 95.

45 Smethurst, *The Bicycle*, 119–120.

46 Anne Renzenbrink, Laura Zhou, 'Coming Full Cycle in Chain: Beijing Pedallers try to Restore "Kingdom of Bicycles" amid Traffic Pollution Woes', *South China Morning Post* (26 July 2015), www.scmp.com/news/china/money-wealth/article/1843877/coming-full-cycle-china-beijing-pedallers-try-restore.

47 Kristensen, 'Work in Bicycle Cinema', 251.

48 Bernard Vere, 'Pedal-Powered Avant-Gardes: Cycling Paintings in 1912–13', in *The Visual in Sport*, eds. Mike Huggins, Mike O'Mahony (Abingdon: Routledge, 2012), 77.

49 Emily Chappell, *What Goes Around: A London Cycle Courier's Story* (London: Faber & Faber, 2016), 5.

50 See Zoe Nyssa, 'Running Reds and Killing Peds: The Lexicon of Bicycle Messengers', *English Today*, vol. 20, no. 2 (2004).

51 Day, *Cyclogeography*, 30.

52 See Jack Tigh Dennerlein, John D. Meeker, 'Occupational Injuries among Boston Bicycle Messengers', *American Journal of Industrial Medicine*, no. 42 (2002).

53 Day, *Cyclogeography*, 31.

54 Ben Fincham, 'Bicycle Messengers: Image, Identity and Community', in *Cycling and Society*, eds. Horton, Rosen, Cox.

55 Jeffrey L. Kidder, '"It's the Job that I Love": Bike Messengers and Edgework', *Sociological Forum*, vol. 21, no. 1 (2006).

56 Day, *Cyclogeography*, 32.

57 As well as a similar scene in Harry Langdon's *Long Pants* (Capra, 1927).

58 Kathi Weeks, *The Problem with Work: Feminism, Marxism, Antiwork Politics, and Postwork Imaginaries* (Durham, NC: Duke University Press, 2011), 4.

59 Kristensen, 'Work in Bicycle Cinema', 256.

60 Ibid., 258.

61 Adorno, *The Culture Industry*, 188.

4 Sport and Performance Machines

1 Jean-Marie Brohm, *Sport: A Prison of Measured Time* (London: Ink Links, 1978), 5.

2 Ibid., 28–29.

3 Hibai Lopez-Gonzalez, 'Quantifying the Immeasurable: A Reflection on Sport, Time and Media', *Journal of the Philosophy of Sport*, vol. 41, no. 3 (2014), 353.

4 Michael R. Real, 'MediaSport: Technology and the Commodification of Postmodern Sport', in *MediaSport*, ed. Lawrence A. Wenner (London: Routledge, 1998), 15.

5 Herlihy, *Bicycle*, 395.

6 Toby Miller, *Sportsex* (Philadelphia: Temple University Press, 2001), 23.

7 Owen Gibson, 'Victoria Pendleton: Corrosive Culture Forced Me Out of Cycling', *The Guardian* (26 May 2016), www.theguardian.com/sport/2016/may/26/victoria-pendleton-olympics-shane-sutton.

8 Sean Ingle, 'Jess Varnish Hits Out at "Culture of Fear" inside British Cycling', *The Guardian* (26 April 2016), www.theguardian.com/sport/2016/apr/26/jess-varnish-complaint-british-cycling-shane-sutton.

9 Don Sabo, Sue Curry Jansen, 'Prometheus Unbound: Constructions of Masculinity in Sports Media', in *MediaSport*, ed. Wenner, 203.

10 Ibid., 209.

11 Brohm, *Sport*, 28.

12 Sabo, Jansen, 'Prometheus Unbound', 210.

13 Brohm, *Sport*, 27, emphasis in original.

14 Brohm comments, 'In the race after maximum productivity anything goes. The champion's life-style is drastically rationalized: no drink, no sexual relations, special diets.… *The body itself is "Taylorised"*': Brohm, *Sport*, 107, emphasis in original.

15 The film is adapted from the *Nasu* series of manga comics. 'Nasu' is Japanese for 'aubergine', and the vegetable is a motif in the film, since pickled aubergine is introduced as an Andalusian delicacy. The CGI-heavy sequel, *Nasu: A Migratory Bird with a Suitcase* (Kosaka, 2007), relocates the action to Japan. These sit alongside a small category of less distinguished Japanese animations concerned with cycle racing, including *Hill Climb Girl* (Tani, 2014), about a schoolgirl obsessed with Bradley Wiggins, and *Yowamushi Pedal* (2013–15), a manga adaptation about a high school cycle team that has spawned four films and a live-action adaptation, toys, games and even rather creepy adult costume play fandom.

16 The term was popularised by Dave Brailsford, head of British Cycling, as the strategic focus for assembling winning teams.

17 The black rapper takes his punning stage name from the cyclist ('âme' means 'soul'), but, as he complains, '[y]ou ever see a brother on the Tour? It's not credible.'

18 Garry Whannel, 'Winning and Losing Respect: Narratives of Identity in Sport Films', *Sport in Society*, vol. 11, nos. 2/3 (2008), 198.

19 *A Conversation with Jørgen Leth* (2003).

20 Lopez-Gonzalez, 'Quantifying the Immeasurable', 355.

21 Joshua Malitsky, 'Knowing Sports: The Logic of the Contemporary Sports Documentary', *Journal of Sport History*, vol. 4, no. 2 (2014), 211, emphasis in original.

22 Herlihy, *Bicycle*, 383.

23 Day, *Cyclogeography*, 94.

24 Herlihy, *Bicycle*, 38.

25 Luke McKernan, 'Sport and the First Films', in Christopher Williams, ed., *Cinema: The Beginnings and the Future* (London: University of Westminster Press, 1996), 107.

26 Ibid.

27 Ibid., 111.

28 Ibid., 114–115.

29 Their films also record the changing composition of the sport, with footage of the 1901 Manchester Wheelers' annual race meet including shots of competitors in the two-mile motor race, riding motor tricycles.

30 Roland Barthes, *The Eiffel Tower and Other Mythologies*, trans. Richard Howard (Berkeley, CA: University of California Press, 1997), 84.

31 Roland Barthes, *What Is Sport?*, trans. Richard Howard (New Haven, CT: Yale University Press, 2007), 27.

32 Ibid., 29–30.

33 Ibid., 35.

34 Ibid., 37.

35 Ibid., 41–43.

36 Ibid., 43.

37 Barthes, *The Eiffel Tower*, 85, emphases in original.

38 Barthes, *What Is Sport?*, 59.

39 Ibid., 65.

40 Ibid., 60–61.

41 Brohm, *Sport*, 104.

42 See Longhurst, *Bike Battles*, and Andrew Ritchie, *Major Taylor: The Fastest Bicycle Rider in the World* (San Francisco: Van der Plas/Cycle Publishing, 2009), for a historical account of the racialised segregation of leisure and sport cycling cultures in the United States.

43 The film was to be an adaptation of a 1973 British pulp novel, featuring a tiresomely sexist veteran cycling coach (and antiques dealer) who comes out of retirement to ride the Tour. See Feargal McKay, 'The Curse of the Yellow Jersey – the Cycling Film Hollywood Loved but Could Never Make', Podium Café (4 October 2015), www.podiumcafe.com/book-corner/2015/10/4/9448769/the-curse-of-the-yellow-jersey-the-cycling-film-hollywood-loved-but, for a detailed account of the project's history.

44 All that remains is a VHS tape containing a 20-minute trailer intended to persuade investors to bankroll the film.

45 Possibly the first use of this shot is in *60 Cycles* (Labrecque, 1965), a short Canadian documentary about a 12-day race in Quebec. A catalogue of inventive cinematography, it opens with a 90-second telephoto shot of the approaching convoy.

46 Barthes, *The Eiffel Tower*, 89–90.

47 Indeed, '[o]ne of the key legends of the Tour de France is Henri Desgrange's alleged belief that the perfect Tour would see just one rider arriving into Paris': Feargal McKay, *The Complete Book of the Tour de
France* (London: Aurum, 2014), 5.

48 For instance, Jacques Anquetil, whose 'palmarès', or achievements, by then included five Tour wins,
two Giro titles and the Vuelta as well as setting the hour record, wrote an article for the periodical
France Dimanche in 1967 entitled 'Yes, I've Taken Drugs'. 'All you have to do is look at my thighs and my
buttocks – they're veritable pin cushions. You have to be an imbecile or a hypocrite to imagine that a
professional cyclist who races 235 days a year in all weathers can keep going without stimulants': Paul
Howard, *Sex, Lies and Handlebar Tape: The Remarkable Life of Jacques Anquetil, The First Five-Times
Winner of the Tour de France* (Edinburgh: Mainstream Publishing, 2011), 240–241.

49 Roland Barthes, *Mythologies*, trans. Annette Lavers (London: Jonathan Cape, 1972), 13.

50 See Annette Hill, 'Spectacle of Excess: The Passion Work of Professional Wrestlers, Fans and Anti-Fans',
European Journal of Cultural Studies, vol. 18, no. 2 (2015).

51 Brohm, *Sport*, 23.

52 Ibid., emphasis in original.

53 Kristensen, 'Work in Bicycle Cinema', 254.

54 Ibid.

55 *Olympia* represented a new order in which sporting events were staged for the film camera. 'With the
release of Leni Riefenstahl's two-part *Olympia* film…, as well as experimentation with television at the
Berlin games, the intrusion of the moving image into the Olympics began': Real, 'MediaSport', 19.

56 The second part, *Olympia: Festival of Beauty* (1938), features the 100-kilometre road race, deploying a
variety of shots, most of which are now central to the repertoire of film and TV coverage: shots of bikes
being prepared, riders receiving massages, shots of the peloton racing through a forest, tracking shots
of riders jostling for position at the head of the race, close-ups of riders' faces, spinning wheels and
pedalling feet, and a nasty crash at the finish line. The sequence also deviates from strict documentary
objectivity to incorporate staged, low-angle shots of riders silhouetted against the sky.

57 William Fotheringham, *Merckx: Half Man, Half Bike* (London: Yellow Jersey Press, 2013), 147.

58 Miller, *Sportsex*, 26.

59 The personification of professional cycling's gender problem, 'podium girls', or 'tour hostesses', are the
women who present winning riders in European races with flowers, mascots, jerseys and kisses at the
end of stage races.

60 Miller, *Sportsex*, 37.

61 Ibid., 38.

62 Sabo, Jansen, 'Prometheus Unbound', 214.

63 Ibid.

64 The film includes footage of several of the same incidents included in Leth's film, albeit shot from different angles.

65 Andy McGrath, 'Halcyon: La Course en Tête' (interview with Joël Santoni), Rouleur (11 November
2015), https://rouleur.cc/editorial/halcyon-la-course-en-tete.

66 Andy McGrath, ed., *Merckx: The Greatest* (London: Gruppo Media, 2015), 52.

67 Miller, *Sportsex*, 12.

68 McGrath, *Merckx*, 32.

69 The fullest realisation of cinema's contemplative capacity are the documentaries *Football as Never
Before* (Costard, 1971) and *Zidane: A 21st Century Portrait* (Gordon, Pareno, 2006); in an innovative
fusion of television coverage and avant-garde experimentation, both use multiple cameras to follow an

entire football match, restricting their attention to a single player – George Best and Zinedine Zidane respectively.

70 *Muhammad Ali's Greatest Fight* (2013).

71 Fournel, *Need for the Bike*, 124.

72 Ibid., 116.

73 In a rare acknowledgement of the transgressive appeal of doping, Tyler Hamilton, one of Armstrong's team-mates, confesses in *Stop at Nothing: The Lance Armstrong Story* that taking performance-enhancing drugs during the Tour was exciting because it made you a 'deviant'.

74 Fournel, *Need for the Bike*, 24.

75 Brohm, *Sport*, 23.

76 Ibid., 55.

5 Riding like a Girl

1 Frances E. Willard, *A Wheel within a Wheel: How I Learned to Ride the Bicycle* (New York: Fleming H. Revell, 1895), 11.

2 Ibid., 13.

3 Ibid., 18.

4 Ibid., 11.

5 Ibid., 25.

6 Ibid., 26.

7 Ibid., 27–28.

8 Ibid., 44.

9 Ibid., 41.

10 Ibid., 39.

11 Ibid., 73.

12 Clare S. Simpson, 'Capitalising on Curiosity: Women's Professional Cycle Racing in the Late-Nineteenth Century', in *Cycling and Society*, eds. Horton, Rosen, Cox, 56.

13 Beth Muellner, 'The Photographic Enactment of the Early New Woman in 1890s German Women's Bicycling Magazines', in *Women in German Yearbook: Feminist Studies in German Literature and Culture*, vol. 22, eds. Helga Kraft, Maggie McCarthy (Lincoln, NE: University of Nebraska Press, 2006), 168.

14 Wells, *The Wheels of Chance*, 33.

15 Marks, *Bicycles, Bangs, and Bloomers*, 2.

16 Muellner, 'The Photographic Enactment of the Early New Woman', 167.

17 Ellen Gruber Garvey, 'Reframing the Bicycle: Advertising-Supported Magazines and Scorching Women', *American Quarterly*, vol. 47, no. 1 (1995), 82.

18 Ibid., 69.

19 Ritchie, *King of the Road*, 155.

20 Marilyn Bonnell, 'The Power of the Pedal: The Bicycle and the Turn-of-the-Century Woman', *Nineteenth Century Contexts*, vol. 14, no. 2 (1990), 229.

21 Simpson, 'Capitalising on Curiosity', 70.

22 Smethurst, *The Bicycle*, 112.

23 Ibid., 90.

24 Phillip Gordon Mackintosh, Glen Norcliffe, 'Men, Women and the Bicycle: Gender and Social Geography of Cycling in the Late-Nineteenth Century', in *Cycling and Society*, eds. Horton, Rosen, Cox, 153.

25 Smethurst, *The Bicycle*, 93.

26 Simpson, 'Capitalising on Curiosity', 59.

27 Iris Marion Young, 'Throwing like a Girl: A Phenomenology of Feminine Body Comportment, Motility and Spatiality', *Human Studies*, vol. 3, no. 1 (1980), 149, emphasis in original.

28 Ibid., 149–150.

29 Ibid., 153.

30 F. J. Erskine, *Lady Cycling: What to Wear and How to Ride* (London: Walter Scott, 1897), 72.

31 Marks, *Bicycles, Bangs, and Bloomers*, 177.

32 Carol Clover, 'Her Body, Himself: Gender in the Slasher Film', in *Horror: The Film Reader*, ed. Mark Jancovich (London: Routledge, 2002), 86.

33 Ibid., 79.

34 Ibid., 85.

35 Katrina Jungnickel, '"One Needs to Be Very Brave to Stand All That": Cycling, Rational Dress and the Struggle for Citizenship in Late Nineteenth Century Britain', *Geoforum*, no. 64 (2015), 366.

36 Young, 'Throwing like a Girl', 154.

37 Ibid.

38 Ibid.

39 Garvey, 'Reframing the Bicycle', 89.

40 Ibid., 74.

41 Ibid., 78.

42 Ibid.

43 Flann O'Brien, *The Third Policeman* (London: Flamingo, 1993), 178.

44 'The only question left to be settled now is: are women persons? And I hardly believe any of our opponents will have the hardihood to say they are not.'

45 Although, as one interviewee points out, the epidemic levels of doping in men's cycling make any comparison of the performance levels of male and female cyclists virtually meaningless.

46 Ironically, given the increasingly clear picture of British Cycling's endemic institutional sexism outlined recently by top British riders Victoria Pendleton, Jess Varnish and Nicole Cooke, Cookson is described on the UCI's website as a 'huge advocate of women's cycling': see www.uci.ch/womens-cycling/deserved-place-for-women-cycling. See Nicole Cooke, 'Welcome to the World of Elite Cycling where Sexism Is by Design', *The Guardian* (25 April 2016), www.theguardian.com/sport/2016/apr/25/nicole-cooke-cycling-sexism-jess-varnish-shane-sutton, for a damning account of this systematic discrimination.

47 Nicholas Chare, *Sportswomen in Cinema: Film and the Frailty Myth* (London: I. B. Tauris, 2015), 45.

48 Judith Butler, 'Athletic Genders: Hyperbolic Instance and/or the Overcoming of Sexual Binarism', *Stanford Humanities Review*, vol. 6, no. 2 (1998).

49 Ibid.

50 Brohm, *Sport*, 181.

51 As is noted in the film's closing credits, this bizarre age stipulation was dropped in 2013.

52 Erskine, *Lady Cycling*, 2.

53 Between 1992 and 2009 shorter variations of the women's Tour were staged, under several different names after the Tour de France organisers insisted that their trademark was being infringed.

54 Ida Husted Harper, *The Life and Work of Susan B. Anthony: Including Public Addresses, Her Own Letters and Many from Her Contemporaries during Fifty Years*, vol. 2 (Indianapolis: Bowen-Merrill, 1898), 859.

55 See www.letourentier.com.

56 Simpson, 'Capitalising on Curiosity', 47.

57 Ibid., 63.

58 Ibid., 52.

59 Ibid., 62.

60 Ibid.

61 Along with *2 Seconds*, American indie film *The Unknown Cyclist* (Salzmann, 1998) is a rare exception to the heteronormative depictions of cycling cultures that dominate film and literature. The dying wish of a much-loved community activist is for his husband, former wife, close friend and estranged twin brother to participate in the 450-mile, six-day West Coast Cycle for AIDS. Over the course of this road movie the ride takes them through individual personal crises, bringing them closer together; the brother confronts his homophobia, the widowed husband comes out to his mother, and the friend learns he is HIV-positive. It is a funny, bitter depiction of the devastation wrought by the disease at a time when AIDS was a death sentence.

62 This first sequence restages exactly the experience of becoming a woman discussed by Frances Willard, who recalls that she 'ran wild' until her 16th birthday, when she had to begin wearing 'hampering skirts' and corsets and move indoors: Willard, *A Wheel within a Wheel*, 11.

63 Michelle Langford, 'Allegory and the Aesthetics of Becoming-Woman in Marziyeh Meshkini's *The Day I Became a Woman*', *Camera Obscura*, vol. 22, no.1 (2007), 14.

64 Ibid., 3.

65 Ibid., 1.

66 Ibid., 17.

67 Ibid., 14–15.

68 Ibid., 25.

69 The colour, associated with Islam and the Saudi flag, highlights the object's symbolic register.

70 Marks, *Bicycles, Bangs, and Bloomers*, 175.

71 See Haifaa al-Mansour, 'Anatomy: The Making of *Wadjda*', *World Policy Journal*, vol. 31, no. 1 (2014), worldpolicy.org/2014/03/18/anatomy-the-making-of-wadjda/.

72 Ibid.

73 Al-Mansour, 'Anatomy'.

74 Willard, *A Wheel within a Wheel*, 75

6 Kids with Bikes

1 Karen Lury, 'Children in an Open World: Mobility as Ontology in New Iranian and Turkish Cinema', *Feminist Theory*, vol. 11, no. 3 (2010), 286.

2 Ibid.

3 Children on bicycles are also an occasional motif for Scott, including the famous 1973 UK TV ad he made for a flour and bread company, showing a baker's boy pushing his bike up a steep early twentieth-century cobbled street and then free-wheeling back down to the baker's cottage.

4 John Bulmer, *The North* (Liverpool: Bluecoat Press, 2012), 114.

5 On its international release the film was given the English-language title *My Father's Bike*, emphasising the theme of paternity explicitly.

6 D. W. Winnicott, *Playing and Reality* (London: Routledge, 2005 [1971]), 2.

7 Ibid., 7.

8 Ibid., 18.

9 Ibid., 7.

10 And, of course, there are numerous literary examples of animated bicycles, including the sentient machines that are 'half-partaking of humanity', in O'Brien, *The Third Policeman*, 88.

11 Winnicott, *Playing and Reality*, 8.

12 This message is more explicit still in American information films. See Longhurst, *Bike Battles*, 169–171.

13 J. G. Ballard, *Crash* (London: Panther Books, 1985), 9.

14 Ryan Hediger, '*Breaking Away* and Vital Materialism: Embodying Dreams of Social Mobility via the Bicycle Assemblage', in *Culture on Two Wheels: The Bicycle in Literature and Film*, eds. Jeremy Withers, Daniel P. Shea (Lincoln, NE: University of Nebraska Press, 2016), 264, emphasis in original.

15 The title is an Indian saying, 'He who wins is Sikandar'. Sikandar is the Indian name for Alexander the Great, and thus the title means 'He who wins is the greatest'.

16 As with many high school films, the children are played by actors clearly well into their 20s – some with full moustaches – inviting us to understand the film as a playful fable rather than an attempt at realistic authenticity.

17 Lalitha Gopalan, *Cinema of Interruptions: Action Genres in Contemporary Indian Cinema* (London: BFI, 2002).

18 Smethurst, *The Bicycle*, 128.

19 Ibid., 126.

20 Ibid., 129–130.

21 Longhurst, *Bike Battles*, 185.

22 Ilsa J. Bick, 'The Look Back in *E.T.*', *Cinema Journal*, vol. 31, no. 4 (1992), 25.

23 Longhurst, *Bike Battles*, 165.

24 The international adoption of BMX bikes is demonstrated by the inspiring 3D documentary *1 Way Up: The Story of Peckham BMX* (Mathieson, 2014), which recounts the attempt of a small BMX club installed on a tiny reclaimed area of waste ground in Peckham, one of the more deprived areas of London, to train some of its members to compete in the 2012 world championships.

25 Vivian Sobchack, 'Child/Alien/Father: Patriarchal Crisis and Generic Exchange', in *Close Encounters: Film, Feminism and Science Fiction*, eds. Constance Penley, Elisabeth Lyon, Lynn Spigel, Janet Bergstrom (Minneapolis: University of Minnesota Press, 1991), 7, emphases in original.

26 Longhurst, *Bike Battles*, 159.

27 Melody Lynn Hoffmann, '"Swerve! I'm on My Bike" Mediated Images of Bicycling in Youth-Produced Hip-Hop', in *Culture on Two Wheels*, eds. Withers, Shea, 300.

28 *E.T.* is one of the ten highest-grossing films (adjusting for inflation). While box-office earnings are an imprecise guide to the overall number of viewers of a film, it is almost certainly the most well known of all the films discussed in this book.

29 Sobchack, 'Child/Alien/Father', 3–4.

30 Indeed, the horror film *Poltergeist* (Hooper, 1982), co-written and produced by Spielberg while making *E.T.*, is a variation on the themes explored in *E.T.*, recounting the haunting of a family home in a California suburb.

31 Sobchack, 'Child/Alien/Father', 4.

32 Ibid., 20.

33 Ibid., 21.

34 Bick, 'The Look Back in *E.T.*', 26.

35 Frank P. Tomasulo, 'The Gospel According to Spielberg in *E.T.: The Extra-Terrestrial*', *Quarterly Review of Film and Video*, vol. 18, no. 3 (2001), 281.

36 Linda Ruth Williams, 'The Tears of Henry Thomas', *Screen*, vol. 53, no. 4 (2012), 463, emphases in original.

37 Angus McFadzean, 'The Suburban Fantastic: A Semantic and Syntactic Grouping in Contemporary Hollywood Cinema', *Science Fiction Film and Television*, vol. 10, no. 1 (2017), 3.

38 Ibid., 4.

39 Ibid., 7.

40 Phyllis Deutsch, '*E.T.*: The Ultimate Patriarch', *Jump Cut*, no. 28 (1983), 13.

41 Hediger, '*Breaking Away* and Vital Materialism', 265.

42 Fournel, *Need for the Bike*, 26.

43 Ibid., 27.

44 Manly, on the outskirts of Sydney, was named by British colonists after the virility of the indigenous inhabitants, but the context of this film lends it an additional irony.

7 The Digital Bicycle Boom

1 Bruno Schulz, *The Fictions of Bruno Schulz: The Street of Crocodiles, and Sanatorium under the Sign of the Hourglass*, trans. Celina Wieniewska (London: Picador, 1988), 99–100.

2 Ibid., 100.

3 Jeff Mapes, *Pedaling Revolution: How Cyclists Are Changing American Cities* (Corvallis, OR: Oregon State University Press, 2009), 7–8.

4 This is parodied in the novel *Ventoux*, whose pretentious protagonist is working on a volume entitled *Spinoza on a Bike* that includes such chapters as 'Merckx's Tour Victories, Philosophically Analyzed', 'The Bike as a Means of Transport to the Truth' and 'Nietzsche was a Doper': Bert Wagendorp, *Ventoux*, trans. Paul Vincent (London: World Editions, 2015), 50.

5 Smethurst, *The Bicycle*, 142.

6 Indeed, as discussed in activist documentary *Bikes vs Cars* (Gertten, 2015), car ownership is rocketing in Asia.

7 Smethurst, *The Bicycle*, 145

8 According to a recent report, locals in Oakland, California, have been vandalising bicycles belonging to a new bike share scheme, since they are seen by some as the vanguard of gentrification: Sam Levin, '"It's Not for Me": How San Francisco's Bike-Share Scheme Became a Symbol of Gentrification', *The Guardian* (21 August 2017), www.theguardian.com/us-news/2017/aug/21/bike-sharing-scheme-san-francisco-gentrification-vandalism?CMP=Share_iOSApp_Other.

9 Smethurst, *The Bicycle*, 148.

10 Friedberg, *Window Shopping*, 5.

11 Anne Friedberg, *The Virtual Window: From Alberti to Microsoft* (Cambridge, MA: MIT Press, 2006), 243.

12 Ibid., 242.

13 Some cyclists use Strava very intentionally as a drawing tool, following routes that, when displayed on the online app and shared on the web, form words or drawings, such as the 'Big Bike' by David Taylor, who cycled 341 kilometres around Hampshire in 2014 to 'draw' it. Meanwhile, San Francisco runner Claire Wyckoff uses a GPS app for what she calls 'running drawing', and mostly draws erect penises on maps of US cities.

14 It also seems that the recent expansion of investment in dockless bike share schemes in cities is driven not so much by environmental concerns or an idealistic interest in fluid urban mobility as by the opportunity offered to gather information about the users through the smartphone apps that are required to rent the bikes: Carlton Reid, 'Data Mining Is Why Billions Are Being Pumped into Dockless Bikes', BikeBiz (9 August 2017), www.bikebiz.com/news/read/data-mining-is-why-billions-are-being-pumped-into-dockless-bikes/021696?platform=hootsuite.

15 Brohm, *Sport*, 50, emphasis in original.

16 See www.lesmills.com/immersive-fitness.

17 B. S. Brown, 'Hales Tours and Scenes of the World', *Motion Picture World* (15 July 1916), 372.

18 Kealan Oliver, 'Sheriff Joe Arpaio Presents Prison Exercise Plan: Inmates Pedal for TV Privileges', CBS News (7 April 2010), www.cbsnews.com/news/sheriff-joe-arpaio-presents-prison-exercise-plan-inmates-pedal-for-tv-privileges.

19 Transmitted on 11 December 2011.

20 Laura Laker, 'Traffic Droid: I'm No Vigilante', Road.cc (13 December 2015), http://road.cc/content/news/173007-traffic-droid-im-no-vigilante.

21 Of course, as documentary records of his journey to and from work, Dediare's videos also invoke the very first (cycling) film, *La Sortie de l'Usine Lumière à Lyon* (Lumière, 1895).

22 Longhurst, *Bike Battles*, 23.

23 Ibid., 3.

24 For all its celebrated authenticity, it is increasingly clear that Lelouch's film offers a nostalgic fantasy of automobility in which powerful cars can be driven at unregulated speeds through more or less empty city streets. What was an example of *cinéma-vérité* has come to resemble a car advert or a video game sequence.

25 Road racing can be added to this list, since the UCI has begun to experiment with 'on-bike' cameras in order, according to Brian Cookson, 'to embrace innovation and sell our sport': Bicycling, 'UCI President Proposes On-Bike Cameras' (9 April 2014), www.bicycling.com/racing/uci-president-proposes-bike-cameras.

26 In a novel variation on sensational media effects, a British courier who killed a pedestrian in a collision in 2016 was accused by prosecutors of copying Brunelle's videos: Jamie Grierson, 'London Cyclist Accused of Killing Woman Denies Being Thrill-Seeker', *The Guardian* (17 August 2017), www.theguardian.com/uk-news/2017/aug/17/charlie-alliston-london-cyclist-front-brake-collision-kim-briggs-old-bailey.

27 Adam Fish, 'Television, Ecotourism, and the Videocamera: Performative Non-Fiction and Auto-Cinematography', Flow (12 January 2007), www.flowjournal.org/2007/01/television-ecotourism-and-the-videocamera-performative-non-fiction-and-auto-cinematography.

28 See http://tonyhillfilms.com/films.

29 Willard, *A Wheel within a Wheel*, 44.

30 Ibid., 75.

31 John Urry, *What Is the Future?* (Cambridge: Polity Press, 2016), 8.

32 Ritchie, *King of the Road*, 178–179.

33 Urry, *What Is the Future?*, 41.

34 Ritchie, *King of the Road*, 179, emphasis in original.

Bibliography

Adorno, Theodor. *The Culture Industry*. London: Routledge, 1991.

Al-Mansour, Haifaa. 'Anatomy: The Making of *Wadjda*', *World Policy Journal*, vol. 31, no. 1 (2014): 10–15. Available from: www.worldpolicy.org/journal/spring2014/anatomy.

Aldred, Rachel. 'Does More Cycling Mean More Diversity in Cycling?' (27 February 2015). Available from: http://rachelaldred.org/writing/does-more-cycling-mean-more-diversity-in-cycling.

Ambrose, Tom. *The History of Cycling in Fifty Bikes*. Stroud: History Press, 2013.

Armstrong, Lance, with Sally Jenkins. *It's Not About the Bike: My Journey Back to Life*. London: Yellow Jersey Press, 2001.

Anderson, Benedict. *Imagined Communities: Reflections on the Origin and Spread of Nationalism*. London: Verso, 2006.

Arnold, David, DeWald, Erich. 'Cycles of Empowerment? The Bicycle and Everyday Technology in Colonial India and Vietnam', *Comparative Studies in Society and History*, vol. 53, no. 4 (2011): 971–996.

Ashurst, Sam. '150 Greatest Robin Williams Jokes', GamesRadar (12 August 2014). Available from: www.gamesradar.com/150-greatest-robin-williams-jokes.

Ballard, J. G. *Crash*. London: Panther Books, 1985.

Barker, Jennifer. *The Tactile Eye: Touch and the Cinematic Experience*. Oakland, CA: University of California Press, 2009.

Barthes, Roland. *The Eiffel Tower and Other Mythologies*, trans. Richard Howard. Berkeley, CA: University of California Press, 1997.

Barthes, Roland. *Mythologies*, trans. Annette Lavers. London: Jonathan Cape, 1972.

Barthes, Roland. *What Is Sport?*, trans. Richard Howard. New Haven, CT: Yale University Press, 2007.

Baudelaire, Charles. *The Painter of Modern Life and Other Essays*, trans. Jonathan Mayne. London: Phaidon, 1964.

Bazin, André. *What Is Cinema?*, vol. 2, trans. Hugh Gray. Berkeley, CA: University of California Press, 1971.

Bellos, David. *Jacques Tati*. London: Harvill Press, 1999.

Bellos, David. 'Tati and America: *Jour de Fête*, and the Blum–Byrnes Agreement of 1946', *French Cultural Studies*, vol. 10, no. 29 (1999): 145–159.

Benjamin, Walter. *Illuminations*, trans. Harry Zohn. London: Fontana, 1973.

Bergson, Henri. *Laughter: An Essay on the Meaning of the Comic*, trans. Cloudesley Brereton, Fred Rothwell. New York: Macmillan, 1911.

Bick, Ilsa J. 'The Look Back in *E.T.*', *Cinema Journal*, vol. 31, no. 4 (1992): 25–41.

Bicycling. 'UCI President Proposes On-Bike Cameras' (9 April 2014). Available from: www.bicycling.com/racing/uci-president-proposes-bike-cameras.

BikeBiz. 'Raleigh to Cease UK Assembly; Move to New Factory Is Shelved' (13 March 2002). Available from: www.bikebiz.com/news/read/updated-raleigh-to-cease-uk-assembly-move-to-new-factory-is-shel/04478.

Bonnell, Marilyn. 'The Power of the Pedal: The Bicycle and the Turn-of-the-Century Woman'. *Nineteenth Century Contexts*, vol. 14, no. 2 (1990): 215–239.

Bordwell, David, Thompson, Kristin. *Film History: An Introduction*. New York: McGraw-Hill, 2003.

Bottomore, Stephen. 'The Panicking Audience? Early Cinema and the "Train Effect"', *Historical Journal of Film, Radio and Television*, vol. 19, no. 2 (1999): 177–216.

Braun, Marta. *Picturing Time: The Work of Etienne-Jules Marey (1830–1904)*. Chicago: University of Chicago Press, 1992.

Brecht, Bertolt. 'Sound Film: *Kuhle Wampe or Who Owns the World?*' [1932], trans. E. J. Campfield. *Prism International*, vol. 21, no. 2 (1982): 46–48.

Brohm, Jean-Marie. *Sport: A Prison of Measured Time*. London: Ink Links, 1978.

Brown, B. S. 'Hales Tours and Scenes of the World', *Motion Picture World* (15 July 1916): 372–373.

Bulmer, John. *The North*. Liverpool: Bluecoat Press, 2012.

Butler, Judith. 'Athletic Genders: Hyperbolic Instance and/or the Overcoming of Sexual Binarism', *Stanford Humanities Review*, vol. 6, no. 2 (1998): 103–111.

Chappell, Emily. *What Goes Around: A London Cycle Courier's Story*. London: Faber & Faber, 2016.

Chare, Nicholas. *Sportswomen in Cinema: Film and the Frailty Myth*. London: I. B. Tauris, 2015.

Chen, Thomas. 'An Italian Bicycle in the People's Republic: Minor Transnationalism and the Chinese Translation of *Ladri di biciclette/Bicycle Thieves*', *Journal of Italian Cinema and Media Studies*, vol. 2, no. 1 (2014): 91–107.

Chion, Michel. *The Films of Jacques Tati*, trans. Antonio D'Alfonso. Toronto: Guernica Editions, 2003.

Clover, Carol. 'Her Body, Himself: Gender in the Slasher Film', in *Horror: The Film Reader*, ed. Mark Jancovich, 77–89. London: Routledge, 2002.

Colville-Andersen, Mikael. *Cycle Chic*. London: Thames & Hudson. 2012.

Cooke, Nicole. 'Welcome to the World of Elite Cycling where Sexism Is by Design', *The Guardian* (25 April 2016). Available from: www.theguardian.com/sport/2016/apr/25/nicole-cooke-cycling-sexism-jess-varnish-shane-sutton.

Cox, Peter, Van De Walle, Frederick. 'Bicycles Don't Evolve: Velomobiles and the Modelling of Transport Technologies', in *Cycling and Society*, eds. Dave Horton, Paul Rosen, Peter Cox, 113–132. Aldershot: Ashgate, 2007.

Crary, Jonathan. *Techniques of the Observer: On Vision and Modernity in the Nineteenth Century*. Cambridge, MA: MIT Press, 1990.

Crary, Jonathan. 'Unbinding Vision: Manet and the Attentive Observer in the Late Nineteenth Century', in *Cinema and the Invention of Modern Life*, eds. Leo Charney, Vanessa R. Schwartz, 46–71. Berkeley, CA: University of California Press, 1995.

Cresswell, Tim. *On the Move: Mobility in the Modern Western World*. New York: Routledge, 2006.

Cyclingnews.com, '*My Hour* by Bradley Wiggins: Book Extract' (23 November 2015). Available from: www.cyclingnews.com/news/my-hour-by-bradley-wiggins-book-extract.

Dahlberg, Andrea. 'Film as a Catalyst for Social Change: Ousmane Sembène's *Borom Sarret*', *Bright Lights Film Journal*, no. 42 (2003). Available from: https://brightlightsfilm.com/wp-content/cache/all/film-as-a-catalyst-for-social-change-ousmane-sembenes-borom-sarret/#.W7Yv5PZFxZU.

Dale, Alan. *Comedy Is a Man in Trouble: Slapstick in American Movies*. Minneapolis: University of Minnesota Press, 2000.

Day, Jon. *Cyclogeography: Journeys of a London Bicycle Courier*. Honiton: Notting Hill Editions, 2015.

DeCordova, Richard. 'From Lumière to Pathé: The Break-Up of Perspectival Space', in *Early Cinema: Space, Frame, Narrative*, ed. Thomas Elsaesser, 76–85. London: BFI, 1990.

Deleuze, Gilles, Parnet, Claire. *Dialogues*, trans. Hugh Tomlinson, Barbara Habberjam. London: Athlone Press, 1987.

Dennerlein, Jack Tigh, Meeker, John D. 'Occupational Injuries among Boston Bicycle Messengers', *American Journal of Industrial Medicine*, no. 42 (2002): 519–525.

Deutsch, Phyllis. '*E.T.*: The Ultimate Patriarch', *Jump Cut*, no. 28 (1983): 12–13.

Devaney, Beulah Maud. 'Women Cyclists Are Dying, Why Are We Still Talking about Their Clothes?', openDemocracy (24 November 2015). Available from: www.opendemocracy.net/5050/beulah/women-cyclists-are-dying-why-are-we-still-talking-about-their-clothes#.VlTLxEr3eyw.twitter.

Durgnat, Raymond. *The Crazy Mirror: Hollywood Comedy and the American Image*. New York: Delta, 1969.

Erskine, F. J. *Lady Cycling: What to Wear and How to Ride*. London: Walter Scott, 1897. Reprinted by British Library, 2014.

Fincham, Ben. 'Bicycle Messengers: Image, Identity and Community', in *Cycling and Society*, eds. Dave Horton, Paul Rosen, Peter Cox, 179–196. Aldershot: Ashgate, 2007.

Fish, Adam. 'Television, Ecotourism, and the Videocamera: Performative Non-Fiction and Auto-Cinematography', Flow (12 January 2007). Available from: www.flowjournal.org/2007/01/television-ecotourism-and-the-videocamera-performative-non-fiction-and-auto-cinematography.

Fitzpatrick, Jim. *The Bicycle in Wartime: An Illustrated History*, rev. edn. Kilcoy, Australia: Star Hill Studio, 2011.

Fleming, Steven. *Velotopia: The Production of Cyclespace in Our Minds and Our Cities*. Rotterdam: nai010, 2017.

Fotheringham, William. *Merckx: Half Man, Half Bike*. London: Yellow Jersey Press, 2013.

Fournel, Paul. *Need for the Bike*, trans. Allan Stoekl. Lincoln, NE: University of Nebraska Press, 2003.

Frayne, David. *The Refusal of Work: The Theory and Practice of Resistance to Work*. London: Zed Books, 2015.

Friedberg, Anne. *Window Shopping: Cinema and the Postmodern*. Berkeley, CA: University of California Press, 1993.

Friedberg, Anne. *The Virtual Window: From Alberti to Microsoft*. Cambridge, MA: MIT Press, 2006.

Garvey, Ellen Gruber. 'Reframing the Bicycle: Advertising-Supported Magazines and Scorching Women', *American Quarterly*, vol. 47, no. 1 (1995): 66–101.

Gibson, Owen. 'Victoria Pendleton: Corrosive Culture Forced Me Out of Cycling', *The Guardian* (26 May 2016). Available from: www.theguardian.com/sport/2016/may/26/victoria-pendleton-olympics-shane-sutton.

Gopalan, Lalitha. *Cinema of Interruptions: Action Genres in Contemporary Indian Cinema*. London: BFI, 2002.

Grierson, Jamie. 'London Cyclist Accused of Killing Woman Denies Being Thrill-Seeker', *The Guardian* (17 August 2017). Available from: www.theguardian.com/uk-news/2017/aug/17/charlie-alliston-london-cyclist-front-brake-collision-kim-briggs-old-bailey.

Gunning, Tom. 'The Cinema of Attractions', in *Early Cinema: Space, Frame, Narrative*, ed. Thomas Elsaesser, 56–62. London: BFI, 1990.

Gunning, Tom. *D. W. Griffith and the Origins of American Narrative Film: The Early Years at Biograph*. Champaign, IL: University of Illinois Press, 1991.

Gunning, Tom. 'Crazy Machines in the Garden of Forking Paths: Mischief Gags and the Origins of American Film Comedy', in *Classical Hollywood Comedy*, eds. Kristine Brunovska Karnick, Henry Jenkins, 87–105. New York: Routledge, 1995.

Gunning, Tom. 'Pictures of Crowd Splendour: The Mitchell and Kenyon Factory Gate Films', in *The Lost World of Mitchell and Kenyon: Edwardian Britain on Film*, eds. Vanessa Toulmin, Patrick Russell, Simon Popple, 49–58. London: BFI, 2004.

Hediger, Ryan. '*Breaking Away* and Vital Materialism: Embodying Dreams of Social Mobility via the Bicycle Assemblage', in *Culture on Two Wheels: The Bicycle in Literature and Film*, eds. Jeremy Withers, Daniel P. Shea, 265–280. Lincoln, NE: University of Nebraska Press, 2016.

Herlihy, David. *Bicycle: The History*. New Haven, CT: Yale University Press, 2004.

Hill, Annette. 'Spectacle of Excess: The Passion Work of Professional Wrestlers, Fans and Anti-Fans', *European Journal of Cultural Studies*, vol. 18, no. 2 (2015): 174–189.

Hoffmann, Melody Lynn. '"Swerve! I'm on My Bike" Mediated Images of Bicycling in Youth-Produced Hip-Hop', in *Culture on Two Wheels: The Bicycle in Literature and Film*, eds. Jeremy Withers, Daniel P. Shea, 300–317. Lincoln, NE: University of Nebraska Press, 2016.

Howard, Paul. *Sex, Lies, and Handlebar Tape: The Remarkable Life of Jacques Anquetil, The First Five-Times Winner of the Tour de France*. Edinburgh: Mainstream Publishing, 2011.

Husted Harper, Ida. *The Life and Work of Susan B. Anthony: Including Public Addresses, Her Own Letters and Many from Her Contemporaries during Fifty Years*, vol. 2. Indianapolis: Bowen-Merrill, 1898.

Ingle, Sean. 'Jess Varnish Hits Out at "Culture of Fear" Inside British Cycling', *The Guardian* (26 April 2016). Available from: www.theguardian.com/sport/2016/apr/26/jess-varnish-complaint-british-cycling-shane-sutton.

Jhally, Sut. 'Cultural Studies and the Sports/Media Complex', in *Media, Sports, and Society*, ed. Lawrence A. Wenner, 70–97. London: Sage, 1989.

Jones, Steve. *The Language of the Genes: Biology, History and the Evolutionary Future*. London: HarperCollins, 1993.

Jungnickel, Katrina. '"One Needs to Be Very Brave to Stand All That": Cycling, Rational Dress and the Struggle for Citizenship in Late Nineteenth Century Britain', *Geoforum*, no. 64 (2015): 362–371.

Jungnickel, Katrina. *Bikes and Bloomers: Victorian Women and Their Extraordinary Cycle Wear*. London: Goldsmiths Press, 2018.

Kar, Law, Bren, Frank. *Hong Kong Cinema: A Cross-Cultural View*. Lanham, MD: Scarecrow Press, 2004.

Kidder, Jeffrey L. '"It's the Job that I Love": Bike Messengers and Edgework', *Sociological Forum*, vol. 21, no. 1 (2006): 31–54.

Kinder, Marsha. 'Spain after Franco', in *The Oxford History of World Cinema*, ed. Geoffrey Nowell-Smith, 596–603. Oxford: Oxford University Press, 1999.

Kirby, Lynne. *Parallel Tracks: The Railroad and Silent Cinema*. Exeter: University of Exeter Press, 1997.

Kristensen, Lars. 'Work in Bicycle Cinema: From Race Rider to City Courier', in *Work in Cinema and the Human Condition*, ed. Ewa Mazierska, 249–264. New York: Palgrave Macmillan, 2013.

Laker, Laura. 'Traffic Droid: I'm No Vigilante', Road.cc (13 December 2015). Available from: http://road.cc/content/news/173007-traffic-droid-im-no-vigilante.

Langford, Michelle. 'Allegory and the Aesthetics of Becoming-Woman in Marziyeh Meshkini's *The Day I Became a Woman*', *Camera Obscura*, vol. 22, no.1 (2007): 1–41.

Levin, Sam. '"It's Not for Me": How San Francisco's Bike-Share Scheme Became a Symbol of Gentrification', *The Guardian* (21 August 2017). Available from: www.theguardian.com/us-news/2017/aug/21/bike-sharing-scheme-san-francisco-gentrification-vandalism?CMP=Share_iOSApp_Other.

Lewis, Clara S. 'Danny MacAskill and the Visuality of the Extreme', *Sport in Society*, vol. 19, no. 7 (2015): 877–890.

Lombardi, Elena. 'Of Bikes and Men: The Intersection of Three Narratives in Vittorio De Sica's *Ladri di biciclette*', *Studies in European Cinema*, vol. 6, nos. 2/3 (2009): 113–126.

Longhurst, James. *Bike Battles: A History of Sharing the American Road*. Seattle: University of Washington Press, 2015.

Lopez-Gonzalez, Hibai. 'Quantifying the Immeasurable: A Reflection on Sport, Time and Media', *Journal of the Philosophy of Sport*, vol. 41, no. 3 (2014): 347–362.

Lury, Karen. 'Children in an Open World: Mobility as Ontology in New Iranian and Turkish Cinema', *Feminist Theory*, vol. 11, no. 3 (2010): 283–294.

McFadzean, Angus. 'The Suburban Fantastic: A Semantic and Syntactic Grouping in Contemporary Hollywood Cinema', *Science Fiction Film and Television*, vol. 10, no. 1 (2017): 1–25.

McGrath, Andy. 'Halcyon: La Course en Tête' (interview with Joël Santoni), *Rouleur* (11 November 2015). Available from: https://rouleur.cc/editorial/halcyon-la-course-en-tete.

McGrath, Andy, ed. *Merckx: The Greatest*. London: Gruppo Media, 2015.

McKay, Feargal. *The Complete Book of the Tour de France*. London: Aurum, 2014.

McKay, Feargal. 'The Curse of the Yellow Jersey – the Cycling Film Hollywood Loved but Could Never Make', Podium Café (4 October 2015). Available from: www.podiumcafe.com/book-corner/2015/10/4/9448769/the-curse-of-the-yellow-jersey-the-cycling-film-hollywood-loved-but.

McKernan, Luke. 'Sport and the First Films', in *Cinema: The Beginnings and the Future*, ed. Christopher Williams, 107–116. London: University of Westminster Press, 1996.

Mackintosh, Phillip Gordon, Norcliffe, Glen. 'Men, Women and the Bicycle: Gender and Social Geography of Cycling in the Late-Nineteenth Century', in *Cycling and Society*, eds. Dave Horton, Paul Rosen, Peter Cox, 153–177. Aldershot: Ashgate, 2007.

McLuhan, Marshall. *Understanding Media: The Extensions of Man*. Cambridge, MA: MIT Press, 1994.

McLuhan, Marshall, Fiore, Quentin. *The Medium Is the Massage: An Inventory of Effects*. San Francisco: Wired, 1996 [1967].

Maddock, Brent. *The Films of Jacques Tati*. Metuchen, NJ: Scarecrow Press, 1977.

Malitsky, Joshua. 'Knowing Sports: The Logic of the Contemporary Sports Documentary', *Journal of Sport History*, vol. 4, no. 2 (2014): 205–214.

Mapes, Jeff. *Pedaling Revolution: How Cyclists Are Changing American Cities*. Corvallis, OR: Oregon State University Press, 2009.

Marchand, Philip. *Marshall McLuhan: The Medium and the Messenger*. Toronto: Random House of Canada, 1998.

Marks, Patricia. *Bicycles, Bangs, and Bloomers: The New Woman in the Popular Press*. Lexington, KY: University of Kentucky Press, 1990.

Mast, Gerald. *The Comic Mind: Comedy and the Movies*. Chicago: University of Chicago Press, 1979.

Miller, Toby. *Sportsex*. Philadelphia: Temple University Press, 2001.

Mitchell, Glenn. *A–Z of Silent Film Comedy: An Illustrated Companion*. London: Batsford, 1998.

Mogk, Marja Evelyn, ed. *Different Bodies: Essays on Disability in Film and Television*. Jefferson, NC: McFarland, 2013.

Muellner, Beth. 'The Photographic Enactment of the Early New Woman in 1890s German Women's Bicycling Magazines', in *Women in German Yearbook: Feminist Studies in German Literature and Culture*, vol. 22, eds. Helga Kraft, Maggie McCarthy, 167–188. Lincoln, NE: University of Nebraska Press, 2006.

Musser, Charles, ed. *The Emergence of Cinema: The American Screen to 1907*. Berkeley, CA: University of California Press, 1994.

Norcliffe, Glen. *The Ride to Modernity: The Bicycle in Canada, 1869–1900*. Toronto: University of Toronto Press, 2001.

Noys, Benjamin. *Malign Velocities: Accelerationism and Capitalism*. Alresford: Zero Books, 2014.

Nyssa, Zoe. 'Running Reds and Killing Peds: The Lexicon of Bicycle Messengers', *English Today*, vol. 20, no. 2 (2004): 48–53.

O'Brien, Flann. *The Third Policeman*. London: Flamingo Press, 1993.

Oliver, Kealan. 'Sheriff Joe Arpaio Presents Prison Exercise Plan: Inmates Pedal for TV Privileges', CBS News (7 April 2010). Available from: www.cbsnews.com/news/sheriff-joe-arpaio-presents-prison-exercise-plan-inmates-pedal-for-tv-privileges.

Penn, Robert. *It's All About the Bike: The Pursuit of Happiness on Two Wheels*. London: Penguin Books, 2011.

Petty, Sheila, ed. *A Call to Action: The Films of Ousmane Sembène*. Trowbridge: Flicks Books, 1996.

Pratt, Geraldine, San Juan, Rose Marie. *Film and Urban Space: Critical Possibilities*. Edinburgh: Edinburgh University Press, 2014.

Ray, Satyajit. *Our Films, Their Films*. New Delhi: Orient Longman, 1976.

Real, Michael R. 'MediaSport: Technology and the Commodification of Postmodern Sport', in *MediaSport*, ed. Lawrence A. Wenner, 14–26. London: Routledge, 1998.

Reid, Carlton. 'Data Mining Is Why Billions Are Being Pumped into Dockless Bikes', BikeBiz (9 August 2017). Available from: www.bikebiz.com/news/read/data-mining-is-why-billions-are-being-pumped-into-dockless-bikes/021696?platform=hootsuite.

Renzenbrink, Anne, Zhou, Laura. 'Coming Full Cycle in China: Beijing Pedallers Try to Restore "Kingdom of Bicycles" amid Traffic, Pollution Woes', *South China Morning Post* (26 July 2015). Available from: www.scmp.com/news/china/money-wealth/article/1843877/coming-full-cycle-china-beijing-pedallers-try-restore.

Rhoads, Edward J. M. 'Cycles of Cathay: A History of the Bicycle in China', *Transfers*, vol. 2, no. 2 (2012): 95–120.

Ritchie, Andrew. *King of the Road: An Illustrated History of Cycling*. London: Wildwood House, 1975.

Ritchie, Andrew. *Major Taylor: The Fastest Bicycle Rider in the World*. San Francisco: Van der Plas/Cycle Publishing, 2009.

Sabo, Don, Jansen, Sue Curry. 'Prometheus Unbound: Constructions of Masculinity in Sports Media', in *MediaSport*, ed. Lawrence A. Wenner, 202–220. London: Routledge, 1998.

Saroyan, William. *The Bicycle Rider in Beverly Hills*. New York: Charles Scribner's Sons, 1952.

Schulz, Bruno. *The Fictions of Bruno Schulz: The Street of Crocodiles, and Sanatorium under the Sign of the Hourglass*, trans. Celina Wieniewska. London: Picador, 1988.

Simpson, Clare S. 'Capitalising on Curiosity: Women's Professional Cycle Racing in the Late-Nineteenth Century', in *Cycling and Society*, eds. Dave Horton, Paul Rosen, Peter Cox, 47–65. Aldershot: Ashgate, 2007.

Singer, Ben. *Melodrama and Modernity: Early Sensational Cinema and Its Contexts*. New York: Columbia University Press, 2001.

Smethurst, Paul. *The Bicycle: Towards a Global History*. Basingstoke: Palgrave Macmillan, 2015.

Smith, Lewis. 'Woody Allen Admits He Is Too Lazy to Make Great Films', *The Independent* (31 July 2015). Available from: www.independent.co.uk/news/people/woody-allen-admits-he-is-too-lazy-to-make-great-films-10431756.html.

Snow, Dan. 'DR Congo: Cursed by Its Natural Wealth', BBC News Magazine (9 October 2013). Available from: www.bbc.co.uk/news/magazine-24396390.

Sobchack, Vivian. 'Child/Alien/Father: Patriarchal Crisis and Generic Exchange', in *Close Encounters: Film, Feminism and Science Fiction*, eds. Constance Penley, Elisabeth Lyon, Lynn Spigel, Janet Bergstrom, 3–30. Minneapolis: University of Minnesota Press, 1991.

Solnit, Rebecca. *Motion Studies: Eadweard Muybridge and the Technological Wild West*. London: Bloomsbury, 2003.

Spencer, Charles. 'The Modern Bicycle', 1877. Reprinted in *Cycling: The Craze of the Hour*, 1–16. London: Pushkin Press, 2016.

Stoekl, Allan. 'Translator's Introduction', in Paul Fournel, *Need for the Bike*, trans. Allan Stoekl, vii–xi. Lincoln, NE: University of Nebraska Press, 2003.

Taylor, J. D. *Island Story: Journeying through Unfamiliar Britain*. London: Repeater, 2016.

Tomasulo, Frank P. 'The Gospel According to Spielberg in *E.T.: The Extra-Terrestrial*', *Quarterly Review of Film and Video*, vol. 18, no. 3 (2001): 273–282.

Ukadike, Nwachukwu Frank. *Black African Cinema*. Berkeley, CA: University of California Press, 1994.

Urry, John. *What Is the Future?* Cambridge: Polity Press, 2016.

Vere, Bernard. 'Pedal-Powered Avant-Gardes: Cycling Paintings in 1912–13', in *The Visual in Sport*, eds. Mike Huggins, Mike O'Mahony, 70–87. Abingdon: Routledge, 2012.

Vivanco, Luis A. *Reconsidering the Bicycle: An Anthropological Perspective on a New (Old) Thing*. New York: Routledge, 2013.

Waddington, James. *Bad to the Bone*. Sawtry: Dedalus, 1999.

Wagendorp, Bert. *Ventoux*, trans. Paul Vincent. London: World Editions, 2015.

Wainwright, Martin. 'On Yer Bike, as Raleigh Shuts Frame Plant', *The Guardian* (11 December 1999). Available from: www.theguardian.com/uk/1999/dec/11/martinwainwright.

Weeks, Kathi. *The Problem with Work: Feminism, Marxism, Antiwork Politics, and Postwork Imaginaries*. Durham, NC: Duke University Press, 2011.

Wells, H. G. *The Wheels of Chance*. London: Dent, 1914.

Whannel, Garry. 'Winning and Losing Respect: Narratives of Identity in Sport Films', *Sport in Society*, vol. 11, nos. 2/3 (2008): 195–208.

Willard, Frances E. *A Wheel within a Wheel: How I Learned to Ride the Bicycle*. New York: Fleming H. Revell, 1895.

Williams, Linda Ruth. 'The Tears of Henry Thomas', *Screen*, vol. 53, no. 4 (2012): 459–464.

Winnicott, Donald W. *Playing and Reality*. London: Routledge, 2005 [1971].

Xu, Jian. 'Representing Rural Migrants in the City: Experimentalism in Wang Xiaoshuai's *So Close to Paradise* and *Beijing Bicycle*', *Screen*, vol. 46, no. 4 (2005): 433–449.

Xu, Tao. 'Making a Living: Bicycle-Related Professions in Shanghai, 1897–1949', *Transfers*, vol. 7, no. 1 (2013): 6–26.

Young, Iris Marion. 'Throwing like a Girl: A Phenomenology of Feminine Body Comportment, Motility and Spatiality', *Human Studies*, vol. 3, no. 1 (1980): 137–156.

Zhong, Huang. 'The Bicycle towards the Pantheon: A Comparative Analysis of *Beijing Bicycle* and *Bicycle Thieves*', *Journal of Italian Cinema and Media Studies*, vol. 2, no. 3 (2014): 351–362.

Figures

Index